turned on or bef

The Practice of
Operational Research

The Practice of Operational Research

George Mitchell

JOHN WILEY & SONS

Chichester · New York · Brisbane · Toronto · Singapore

Other Wiley Editorial Offices

John Wiley & Sons, Inc., 605 Third Avenue,
New York, NY 10158-0012, USA

Jacaranda Wiley Ltd, G.P.O. Box 859, Brisbane,
Queensland 4001, Australia

John Wiley & Sons (Canada) Ltd, 22 Worcester Road,
Rexdale, Ontario M9W 1L1, Canada

John Wiley & Sons (SEA) Pte Ltd, 37 Jalan Pemimpin #05-04,
Block B, Union Industrial Building, Singapore 2057

Library of Congress Cataloging-in-Publication Data

Mitchell, George
     The practice of operational research / George Mitchell.
        p.   cm.
     Includes bibliographical references and index.
     ISBN 0-471-93982-X
     1. Operations research. I. Title.
     T57.6.M574 1993
     658.4'034—dc20   93–7352
                                                     CIP

British Library Cataloguing in Publication Data

A catalogue record for this book is available from the British Library

ISBN 0-471-93982-X

Typeset in 10/12pt Palatino from author's disks by Text Processing Department,
John Wiley & Sons Ltd, Chichester
Printed and bound in Great Britain by Biddles Ltd, Guildford, Surrey

Contents

Preface

This book is about issues that arise in the practice of operational research (OR). It draws on material developed for various reasons, but mainly for talks and lectures given to MBA courses or to MSc courses in OR or Management Science. When I have been asked to give such talks and lectures, I have usually been asked to speak as a practitioner. The book is written in that same spirit. It might be thought of as a collection, more or less structured, of the things which someone who has engaged in the practice of OR for 30 years or so has found worth thinking about, and feels others might also find worth thinking about. There is, however, no conscious presumption that the reader has himself or herself been engaged in OR. There are occasional references to the techniques associated with OR (such as simulation or mathematical programming) or with mathematical statistics, and I suppose my imagined reader has taken or is taking courses covering such matters. However, the references are so few and usually so tangential that they should not deter a reader unschooled in the techniques.

STANCE OF THE BOOK

The topics covered and the issues raised in the book are not only or mainly the result of my own introspection, but reflect discussions with, and accounts variously rendered by, other OR practitioners. I should like to think that the issues raised, and the relative significances attached to them, are consistent with the views of many reflective experienced OR practitioners; and I have certainly sought to make them so. However, many of the issues are, I shall contend, ones about which the individual practitioner, in his or her particular context, must make up his or her own mind. The book does not, therefore, aim to be narrowly prescriptive. When, as inevitably I shall be tempted to do, I offer views or advice, these will be qualified unless I believe they too are consistent with those of other experienced practitioners.

In spite of this attempt to reflect the views of a wider grouping, it is nonetheless a truism that the book is to a greater or lesser extent a subjective one. I should, therefore, make clear what my background is. To do so, it is perhaps sufficient to say that I have done OR in scarcely any other environment than British Coal (until recently the National Coal Board) and it is from this that all my first-hand experience derives. Moreover, my second-hand experience, that is, the experience I have derived from contact with other OR practitioners, is fairly heavily biased towards the large bureaucracy—government, nationalised industry, large public company—sector of the British economy. In addition, practically all of my first-hand, and most of my second-hand, experience is of so-called in-house OR, that is, doing OR for an organisation of which one is an employee. I have tried to avoid letting this biased experience influence what I say, but, of course, it is impossible to do so.

More generally, I shall try to avoid speaking from any highly particularised value system, as, for example, one which might be called a political stance. This is not to say that I discount the importance of politics in the practice of OR: on the contrary, I believe that political reality—the virtual inevitability of conflict and exploitation of power—is of great importance in the OR process. What I shall not consciously do, however, is to take sides in any sectarian sense, as, for example, by pushing the line that explicit open modelling is good because it gives the workers a chance to participate in company planning. In a rather wider sense I shall inevitably assume an ultimately underpinning value system. The one I shall try to assume is what might be characterised as the value system of liberal Western civilisation. This includes a number of views of which, for our purposes, some important ones are that it prefers rationality to emotion, compromise to conflict, negotiation to the use of physical force, evolution to revolution and freedom to efficiency. I choose this 'middle of the road' viewpoint not because it is necessarily my own, but because I believe it is likely, despite occasional divergences from it, to be the one dominant in the world in which most of us will work, including among our employers. It is also the one which has nurtured OR and has influenced OR's development.

Finally, I have been obliged to make some choice about how deeply philosophical to make the book. By and large, I have chosen not to go too deeply. Thus, I do not intend any lengthy discussion of the nature of reality, the reliance we can put on sense data, the possibility of discovering truth, etc. I intend in short to take a common-sense view of the world, namely that the artefacts we talk about—factories, managers, machinery, trade unions and so on—exist, and that there is at least the potential of their nature, their actions and their beliefs, where relevant, being revealed to us through our senses.

GENERAL STRUCTURE OF THE BOOK

In writing any book such as this, there are two inevitable questions: what material should be covered and in what order. The material to be covered, or rather the criterion for selecting it, is to a large extent discussed above. It is what I think OR practitioners as a whole would say exercised them about OR. This falls under three broad headings. The nature of OR, its aims and the reasons for its existence, offers one heading; a second is the methodological issues which arise in trying to do OR; and a third is the management of OR. These second and third are linked through the notion of the process of OR.

The order in which to arrange the material is more contentious. As between the above three headings, quite good arguments could be made, if not for all six possible orderings, then at least for three or four of them. There are similar difficulties about ordering within a heading, a particularly insidious difficulty here being that an ordering within the methodological issues heading might imply a sequential methodology, an implication I would wish strenuously to avoid.

In the end I have opted for the order foreshadowed above, namely the nature of OR, methodological issues and the management of OR. The book is not, however, written to be read necessarily in order. To a large extent, each chapter stands alone. I would not find reading by dipping offensive. I go on to elaborate what each of the three parts covers.

WHAT IS OR?

Most definitions of operational research are essentially of the form: Operational research is to do with helping to *solve the problems* of some *organised group* by applying the *methods of science*.

(Various alternatives for the italicised phrases occur in different definitions. For example, some phrase about decision making might replace 'to solve the problems'; management commonly occurs instead of 'organised group'; and specific 'methods of science'—quantitative, logical analysis or modelling—are sometimes mentioned. Later I shall point out that some definitions define very closely the type of problem and/or the methods to be used. However, the type of definition I have quoted embraces most of those as special cases. The above is not quite my favoured definition.)

The word 'helping' and each of the italicised phrases seems to me to justify some discussion, not least because the words 'science' and 'problem' have commonly accepted meanings which I believe to be at worst misleading and at best narrow. (To discuss what these words mean might be lightly dismissed as an idle exercise in semantics. I do not believe this to be the case, as in these instances discussion about definitions seems to me to illuminate, in ways which might usefully influence our actions, the kind of activity in which we are engaged.) What I shall try to do is to explore the notion of helping and what help OR might offer; what might be meant by the methods of science by considering what it is that scientists do; what might be meant by an organised group, emphasising the diversity of bodies which might be so called; and then what might be meant by the word 'problem' and the phrase 'to solve problems'. I shall seek to make the points among others that the methods of science are more to do with scientists than with the subject matter of science; that in order to understand an organised group it is necessary to study the group as a particular case (or, in other words, there are few if any fully reliable and relevant general theories about groups); and that problems, while usually plainly prompted by and closely related to objective events in the real world, are nevertheless subjective constructs, as, in consequence, are their solutions. I shall seek beyond that to develop the viewpoint that OR, to be done effectively, entails not merely the use of the methods of science but also a fairly deep understanding of the organised group for which the work is being carried out. In particular, it follows from this that OR is not a science but the methods of science applied purposefully within particular contexts.

METHODOLOGICAL ISSUES

I shall turn next to a discussion of the methodology of carrying out OR projects. I shall do so under four headings—defining problems, data handling, modelling and making choice. I shall seek to emphasise that, in carrying out any particular piece of OR work, methodological issues must be decided in their contexts. I shall also seek to emphasise that defining the problem, data collection and analysis, model building and other parts of the OR process, while useful operational constructs, are continuous, concurrent activities, and not just sequential stages in carrying out a piece of OR work.

MANAGING OR

A good argument can be made that the value of OR to an organisation lies in its continuing involvement, whose value transcends the sum of the values of the individual pieces of work. This added value can be much affected by the way OR is managed. The third part of the book deals with managing OR. In it I shall first try to establish that the view that continued involvement

has a higher value than a series of separate pieces of work is at least plaus
ible. I shall go on to point out that if we wish to secure this higher value
then certain organisational and managerial questions will arise. Among
other things I shall argue that an OR group, anxious to secure this kind of
return, might choose to organise and manage itself in ways which quite
explicitly do not maximise the sum of returns of individual projects.

EXERCISES

It is a commonplace for authors to say that the exercises are part of the text,
and I make no exception of this book. While I do not imagine even the
most enthusiastic reader attempting all the exercises, I hope he will read
them and spend a moment or two thinking about them and why they have
been set.

Some of the exercises are about rather extended case descriptions. These
cases all have some basis in reality, albeit a heavily disguised reality. They
are, however, simplified and to an extent contrived. Short of something
approaching novel length, it is not easy to write cases that capture the full
richness of much OR. The reader is asked to let his imagination elaborate
the cases so as to visualise the usually omitted richness.

BIBLIOGRAPHY

The text nowhere uses direct quotations nor does it otherwise, at least consciously, draw heavily on published work. No references are therefore given
in the text. (In any case, frequent references in the text are, I find, often dis-
ruptive of reading.) A final few pages do, however, give an annotated bibliography, chapter by chapter, which I hope gives acknowledgement where
it is due but which is mainly intended to suggest further reading.

ACKNOWLEDGEMENTS

As earlier noted, the material of the book derives more from the result of
conversation with others than from my own unaided reflections. I am grateful to many friends and colleagues, regrettably too many to list. However,
three deserve special mention: John Ranyard, who read and commented on
the book in draft and suggested numerous improvements, Jenny Grainge,
who helpfully increased the book's readability, and Charu Kamdar, who
showed remarkable tolerance of my penchant for frequent redrafting. I am
grateful also to my former employers, British Coal, in whose time much of

the material in the book was originally developed, for their agreement to the book's publication.

GENDER

A final remark: the book will usually use masculine forms. No chauvinism is here intended. I simply see no literary convention for handling the gender problem which is neither ugly nor inconvenient.

George Mitchell
London
January 1993

Chapter 1

Help

This book is about helping people who face problems. However, it is about giving help of a particular kind and in a particular way. In this chapter the notion of helping and the kind of help with which the book is concerned are explored.

The word 'help' embodies a familiar concept but one which in practice takes many forms. There is much art and skill in human relationships in successfully providing help. It can be difficult to assess what help will actually *be* helpful in any given circumstances. It is easy simply to be mistaken about what those one is helping want to achieve. Aside from simple mistakes there are other dangers. One is that the help may generate a state of dependency on the helper—which may be desirable but which it would probably not be wished should occur unwittingly. Another is that the person helped may simply resent the help, or at least the particular form it takes. A third is that those helped may be so grateful that they do not care to say that the help is useless to them, or they do not understand it, or it could be so much more useful in a different form.

The list could go on. Examples from everyday life of these difficulties are well known. Self-confidence, pride and status are all put at risk if someone is seen to need help, or if the help is offered in an unsuitable way.

What constitutes appropriate help, or an appropriate mode of helping, is to be judged case by case. Consider the following example.

MR BIRD'S DILEMMA

John is a business studies undergraduate. He and a number of other students are working during their vacation in the packing department of Bird's Educational Apparatus Company. The company supplies handmade wooden toys of educational value, mainly for use in special schools for mentally handicapped children. One morning, to the students' surprise, Mr Bird asks John and the others to come up to his office.

They troop into his secretary's room and she takes them straight into Mr Bird's office. It is an untidy room littered with finished toys and part-finished prototypes for new models. Two men are sitting drinking coffee from mugs. The students are introduced first to Mr Bird, who is an elderly man dressed in overalls. Then Mr Johnson is introduced. He was until his retirement a local schools inspector, with special responsibility for schools for the mentally handicapped. He makes his excuses and leaves more or less straightaway.

Mr Bird begins to talk. First he eulogises Mr Johnson, a far-seeing man with the interests of underprivileged children close to his heart. He and Mr Bird are not only professional colleagues but serve on numerous charitable committees together. They have both come a long way since they were at school together as lads.

Next Mr Bird recounts, at some length, his full life history. There is first a tear-jerking account of an impoverished childhood, when his widowed mother struggled to bring up himself and his younger brother, Ernest. Ernest was both mentally and physically handicapped. Unlike today, no state provision was made for such children in Mr Bird's boyhood days. Fortunately Mr Bird had found himself possessed of a rare gift, the ability to make simple wooden toys, which Ernest had enjoyed playing with and which had greatly encouraged his mental development. (Ernest is still alive and, although physically weak, he is mentally normal. He lives with Mr and Mrs Bird.)

Mr Bird goes on. Leaving school at fourteen he had made toys and sold them door to door. It was a struggle, but in those days jobs were hard to find and people were more enterprising than they are now. At twenty, Mr Bird was employing four other men and from then on things had never looked back. Even in recessions he had never laid men off, though the company had sometimes run at a small loss.

Now, Mr Bird explains, he employs over thirty people. He has a design section headed by a qualified educationalist. His workmen are all of crafts-man standard. His products, all hand built, enjoy a national, if not interna-tional, reputation and command a higher price than anyone else's.

But Mr Bird is worried about the future. His only son is a university lec-turer and has no interest in the business. Ernest and Mrs Bird want Mr Bird to retire, but he could go on for years yet. After all, he is only 70 and really fit for his age. Unfortunately, the crunch is coming. A large general toy-manufacturing firm has for several years been on at Mr Bird to sell them his company. Now a schools supply firm has come up with an offer. Mr Bird's accountant has acted for him and negotiated with both firms to see what are the best offers each could make.

Mr Bird received his accountant's report three weeks ago. It advised him to accept one of the offers. He must decide this afternoon what he is going to do as one of the offers expires today. He is worried because he cannot make up his mind. His accountant, the senior partner in a local practice, is an old friend, and they meet a lot through charitable and education work. But Mr Bird is sure the accountant has it all wrong.

After all, if the firm's inventiveness and expertise are worth £2 million today, they are going to be worth as much tomorrow. 'What I want to do,' says Mr Bird, 'is to keep on till I'm 75 and then think about selling.'

Mr Bird stands up and, walking from one to the next of the students, explains his admiration for education. 'Here's the accountant's report. All come up here again for lunch and let me listen to you talk about it. I'm sure that will help me.' (The accountant's report is reproduced in the Appendix at the end of the chapter.)

WAYS OF HELPING

Mr Bird is asking for help, or appears to be. How should John and the others respond to this request?

In practice, and against a tight time scale, they will probably respond intuitively and simply do their best. First aid in an emergency is an important kind of help. Often it is given intuitively. As is well known, the intuitive response is not always helpful and can be positively harmful. If someone expects to be asked to provide first aid, there is a good case for his getting trained to do so.

It is possible that John or others of the students have already learned some of the tricks of the trade for applying first aid in business situations. Thus, John might start by asking himself a few questions.

What is Mr Bird really after? On the face of it, it seems utterly implausible that Mr Bird is going to take what could be the most important decision of the rest of his life on the basis of listening to a few students discussing the analysis of the issue that they have made in a couple of hours or so. There are many other reasons why Mr Bird might have made his curious request. Some verge on the cynical. He might, for example, enjoy showing off, or enjoy young people's company over lunch, or simply have an idle hour which he wants filling in some reasonably intellectually stimulating way. But there are other possible reasons, perhaps corresponding to the view that he is a serious man who values his own time. One possibility is that the superficial reason is valid: he is genuinely undecided and wants advice. Another, closely related to this, is that he is suspicious of the advice he has received or of the analysis supporting it. The suspicions might be about the competence of his accountant, say, or even of his accountant's motivation— the accountant might be getting a secret commission from a potential buyer. Yet another reason is that the whole thing seems a mess to Mr Bird and, in the jargon, he would like the issue structured—that is, set out in a form which is capable of being relatively easily understood by the exposure of key facts and relationships. Finally, and this is a reason that should never be overlooked, it is possible that Mr Bird has firmly decided what to do and wants to justify his decision to himself and others.

John might also ask why Mr Bird has turned to him and his student colleagues. It appears Mr Bird is a man of some consequence and with extensive connections. He could probably command a lengthy interview at short notice with a variety of other potential helpers—an accountant, a lawyer, a management consultant, a business studies lecturer at the local university, say. Or he could discuss the matter with his trusted senior staff, who might be as knowledgeable as anybody about the issues. There are other helping professions, some more relevant than others in this context, to whom Mr Bird might have turned for advice: priests, philosophers, doctors, psychitrists and so on. And, of course, John does not know whether Mr Bird has sought further advice from these or any other sources.

John's answers to the twin questions—what does Mr Bird want and why is he asking me—will clearly influence what John decides to do. Taken together, the two answers provide a view of what Mr Bird is expecting. (It is, of course, not just why he is asking me, so much as why me and not others, that is the searching question.)

In practice, anyone playing an advisory or helping role will have to form some view of what his clients want and what, to that end, he can offer them. Needless to say, simply asking them for the answers may not be good enough. They may be unable to articulate their reasons, or refuse to answer, or even lie. Also, needless to say, if he believes their wants cannot be filled by what he can offer them, he should decline to help.

WHAT KIND OF HELP

This book is about giving help of a particular kind. The kind of help in question can be characterised in two ways, the one negative, the other positive. In the first place, the help is not of a kind for which there is a well-developed providing profession or calling, with which the person seeking help, the client, is familiar, and to which he has access. Thus, this is not a book about helping someone who wants his television repaired, or his water chemically analysed, or his letters typed (unless, of course, the client does not know that the relevant services exist—working with a client to decide what kind of help he needs, which may be from an established profession, is included).

The kind of help with which the book is concerned has a number of features:

(i)   The would-be helper will consciously seek to find out what help is needed;

(ii)   He will suggest how the help can best be provided, including that which he thinks he himself can usefully provide;

(iii) Although he will not scorn helping in ways which use his general skills, he will place an emphasis on structuring the issue of concern to those seeking help;

(iv) He will seek to provide a structuring whose subjective content derives from his client, and whose content is otherwise objective;

(v)   His structuring will be orientated towards action and he will help ensure that the actions are taken; and

(vi) In all this, he will work with his client.

The larger part of this book explores how this kind of help can usefully be given. The kind of help outlined above broadly characterises the helping activity known as operational research (OR). The remainder of this chapter examines briefly some of the issues raised by points (i) to (vi) above. Before that, however, note that all of points (i) to (vi) cannot always be met. In particular, those seeking help will not necessarily be prepared to work with those offering it. (This is not to say that they will sometimes work against them, although they might. Rather it is meant to draw attention to a common enough point, namely that people often expect help to be provided in a detached way—'come back to me when you have the answer'.) It is of some consequence that those intending to help should develop relationships which allow them to work with those they are seeking to help. Plainly, John may find this difficult to do with Mr Bird, for many reasons, not least the apparent shortage of time.

WHAT HELP IS NEEDED?

Most helpers have some preconception of the help they can give. This may predispose them to think people need that help. A religious zealot, for example, might perceive that everyone needs his help to save themselves from damnation. Others, perhaps more modestly, will only presume to offer their particular form of help when it is clearly needed. Thus, a proponent of some form of natural childbirth is unlikely to offer his help to any but pregnant women, or at least to women of a relevant age and social role. In many important circumstances, however, it will be apparent that help is needed but far from apparent what form of help is appropriate.

If time permits, it will be usual in such cases to spend time deciding on a suitable form of help. If a would-be helper is himself the person engaged in deciding the appropriate help, he will doubtless be influenced in his judgement by the help of which he knows himself capable. That said, it is clear that the activity of helping to decide what help is needed is, if usefully and productively carried out, likely to be highly valued. In order to perform the activity well, the helper must possess in some measure at least three qualities: an ability to diagnose the help needed; an awareness of the kinds of help available; and the capacity to synthesise a useful programme of help from the two. It is to be assumed that this skill will be most highly valued if it is seen to be exercised dispassionately and not in the pursuit of self-interest.

The three skills of diagnosis, awareness of kinds of help, and synthesis into a help programme, are recurrent topics in the book.

STRUCTURING ISSUES

A particular form of help is to facilitate the structuring of an issue. Many of life's more pressing problems appear set within some melange of ill-assorted facts and opinions, diverse and contradictory actions, conflict and coalition among relevant parties, and so on. A person charged to act on such a problem, perhaps given responsibility to alleviate it, may be baffled as to what is going on and why. Something he may seek to do is to develop a structured understanding of the situation he finds himself in. He may ask someone to help him do so.

Structure is a verb that has a rich variety of meanings. It is used here and in what follows to mean simplify, but simplify in a way which does not lose the essence of the situation in question while at the same time increasing understanding of it. Thus, it is possible that a collection of apparently haphazard facts and observations might become very largely explicable by a handful of statements which describe the mechanisms giving rise to them. To watch cricket in ignorance of the aims and rules of the game must seem to be watching something curious and inexplicable. A determined observer, thinking there must be something to it, could, however, probably develop some simple statements that increased his understanding of what was going on. He could read about the game, consult others more knowledgeable than he, or make a scholarly study of the published rules. His progressive understanding of the game would be an exercise in structuring. Initially, structuring is gaining some perhaps simple but incomplete understanding, followed by progression towards a fuller understanding. Almost always it involves some degree of abstraction.

A plausible definition of science is that it is the activity of gaining a structured understanding of the natural world. Science has been conspicuously successful in providing useful structures for many natural phenomena. It might reasonably be supposed that the methods scientists use would help structure many kinds of issue.

Some issues of concern do not, however, lend themselves readily to the same kinds of approach as natural phenomena of the kind studied by, say, physicists. The issue could well be a mix of objective fact (an elusive concept, but see below) and subjective opinion. The learner about cricket may progress to the question of deciding the best batsman in the world. Cricket is a game with objective facts and statistics, including the scoring records and so-called averages (the higher the better, in the common view) of batsmen. However, quite other things than mere statistics could influence a competent judge in deciding who was his choice as the best batsman. Many of these things—elegance, range of strokes, character, for want of a better word—would be assessed more or less subjectively by that judge. However, it is quite possible to conceive of structuring these subjective things so that the judge has a clearer perception of the factors he is judging subjectively, the relative weight he is giving to them, and so on.

Note, also, that a structured understanding of an activity involving animate beings, and specifically people, is quite likely to involve gaining some understanding of what is motivating those taking part. A person's understanding of a particular cricket match might be deficient if he did not know whether it was being played for the amusement of the players, to entertain the spectators, by each side to win with perhaps large prizes at stake, or by the individual players differently. Note that a simplistic reading of the rules would suggest the aim is necessarily to win. Note, too, that the choice of the best batsman might be different from that wished if a player were mistakenly judged on his performance when he was not expecting to be so judged. He may perhaps be playing more light-heartedly or carelessly than he would if he knew he were being judged, and doing so for quite acceptable reasons—for example, to entertain the crowd in a match fated otherwise to be a dull draw.

A person choosing or invited to act as someone's helper in achieving a structuring of something might wish to take the line that he will work with that someone and others to develop a structure of the objective facts which is itself objective, together with an objective structuring of the subjective opinions that the person being helped—not the helper, nor anyone else—holds. The whole question of structuring pervades the book. Special attention is given to the scientific method because, pragmatically, it has been so successful in generating useful structures.

CAUSING ACTION

If help is to be orientated towards action, and helping to effect that action, it will be well to reflect on the mechanisms for effecting action. The literal meaning of the word action has a connotation of physical activity, and its result is to have caused a change in the physical world. This meaning can be usefully extended to include mental activity. The action's result would then have been to cause a change in someone's understanding or beliefs. (Either change may simply preserve the status quo ante, but it is to be presumed that this would not have been preserved without the action.) It follows that action and change are intimately related. If someone chooses to take an action, or urges someone else to do so, it will usually be because he thinks the change the action will induce is for the better. How does he know this will be so? Insofar as he does know, it will be through his understanding of the context or, putting it another way, through the structure he has developed relevant to the context. Any structuring might, therefore, well be based round the consequences of actions.

The relationship of action and change also suggests the possibility of two approaches to deciding what action to take. A person might, on the one hand, consider various actions, estimate and weigh up their consequences, and decide which action to take by choosing the one whose consequences he liked best. On the other hand, he might choose the consequence he wished to ensue, or putting it another way, what changes he would like to make. The question then would be: what action or actions would give rise to this consequence or cause these changes?

Whichever way it is viewed, the kind of help here being discussed is about causing change. The helper will seldom be able to cause the changes unaided, and the changes will not usually be those in his own narrow interest but in the interest of whomever he is helping. In both choosing and causing the change he will have to work with others, and specifically the individual or group he is helping.

Much of such work, one way or another, will be set within a more or less organised group of people. The subject of help might indeed be a more or less organised group of some kind—a company, a residents' association, the out-patients at a hospital, a committee charged to organise and run a major spectacle. It is clear helpers are likely to be more effective if they understand something of the way the relevant group works than if they ignore the social setting of the issue on which they are helping. This, again, is something that will recur in the book.

CLIENT/HELPER RELATIONSHIPS

As already noted, the helper needs to develop some mutually understood and acceptable relationship with the person he is seeking to help, namely the client. The general supposition of this book is that the relationship is that which is often described as a client/consultant relationship. In this relationship, the client is supposed to engage the helper, the consultant, to act in the client's interest. In this case, the consultant is engaged to help the client with a problem he, the client, has. The engagement might manifest itself as full-time employment, as payment of a fee for the help, or simply as an understanding between friendly parties. The engagement is likely to be the subject of a contract, or at least a clear understanding, that defines roles and responsibilities in the given context. The roles and responsibilities will usually be negotiated case by case, and possibly renegotiated as the case develops. However, in general, the client can be expected to retain responsibility for ultimate choice of actions to be taken or changes to be made. To that extent, the consultant's role and responsibilities can be described as advisory.

The relationship, to be effective, will need to be close. There will need to be close identity of aims and values, or at least the consultant must act as if there were. If there is not this identity, or even if the client is suspicious about whether there is, the help is likely to be of little use or simply rejected.

One value the client is likely to have is that he will not want his time or money to be wasted. More generally, he will want good value for the resource consumed in providing the help. The consultant, if he identifies with his client, will so provide his help as to give the client the best value, taking account of costs and time, in the sense of when the value is obtained. These matters are also addressed recurrently throughout the book.

RANGE OF APPLICATION

As previously remarked, the kind of help here being discussed is, in essence, operational research (OR). The practice of OR is what this book is about. OR has a wide potential range of application, from the strategic or life problems facing an individual or large organised group, to the tactical problems facing, say, a works manager.

Mr Bird's dilemma is, for him, his family and (if they are aware of it) his staff, a strategic problem. He might have asked John and his colleagues for advice about setting up a lathe or scheduling work through his workshop, problems of a more tactical, technical kind. In detail, the means of offering help might differ, not least because the worthwhile level of resource commitment will vary with the importance of the problem. However, the general stance of this book is that help offered in the spirit described above, that is OR, will be useful to people facing most kinds of problem.

In practice, OR has been found to be widely applicable. The boards of large corporations exploit it to help decide company policy. Community groups (e.g. residents' associations) find OR helpful as a means of deciding their negotiating stance on social matters (e.g. the provision of care services). Those responsible for supplying spare parts to engineering activities use OR to help decide their stocking and service policies. In short, OR is a widely used form of help, with a track record of successful application over almost as wide a spectrum of issues as can be imagined.

In this connection, a word of caution is perhaps desirable. The book contains several cases. These are necessarily simplified and, in the interests of comprehensibility, many are given somewhat homely settings. The reader is asked to imagine for himself extensions of the cases to wider and perhaps more important contexts.

SKILL REQUIREMENTS

In order to give help of the kind discussed successfully, in other words to practise OR successfully, a wide range of skills will need to be brought to bear. The book will, it is hoped, demonstrate and explain something of the range of skills required. It is perhaps sufficient at this stage to draw attention to three broad skills headings.

First, the skill to acquire an understanding of the context in which the problem is set is necessary. The context has many aspects. There will usually be some technical context (making wooden toys), a social context (Mr Bird's responsibilities to other parties, theirs to him and so on), and some kind of cultural context (a point elaborated later).

Second, the skills associated with the ability usefully to structure issues are necessary. (Mr Bird would probably welcome some structuring of the position he is in, perhaps by way of two or three key statements that summarise the issues for him.) These skills, which are analytic in nature for the most part, include also a capacity to think creatively or at least to transfer structuring ideas from one context to another.

Finally, there are those skills associated with developing effective working relationships with the client and other relevant parties, including here skills associated with communicating effectively with people. (Mr Bird would like to be assured that John and his colleagues understand him and his concerns, and himself to understand what they have to tell him.)

Whether the full range of skills is commonly available in a single person is perhaps doubtful. Recourse has often to be made to team working to assemble the necessary skills. However, anyone seeking to work in OR is unlikely to be successful unless he has a modicum of all the skills, or at least an understanding of the need for them.

APPENDIX: MR BIRD'S DILEMMA: THE ACCOUNTANT'S REPORT

The accountant's report, referred to on page 3, is reproduced below. (It is addressed to Mr Bird.)

(1) Acting on your instructions, I have been in contact with Messrs Bentley Toy and Plaything Co. Ltd (BTP) and Messrs Schools Supply Services Ltd (SSS).

I have received from each a draft contract for the purchase of your firm as a going concern.

(2) As your accountant I should recommend you to accept the BTP offer, but may I presume to act as an old friend, in which case I unhesitatingly recommend you to accept the SSS offer. My reasoning is as follows.

(3) First I must urge on you the commercial necessity of accepting one of the offers. It is true you have made good profits in recent years, but there is little hope of this continuing. Your raw material, wood, is rising in price almost daily. Your workmen are ageing and moreover are plainly and seriously underpaid. You must therefore expect labour costs to rise or your men to leave. Against this, there is likely to be no scope for increasing prices as all your trade is with local authorities and their spending is severely constrained. All this is confirmed by the trends shown in the following table (in which all monetary figures are given at current prices i.e. are corrected for inflation).

Year (N = last complete year)	N-9	N-4	N-3	N-2	N-1	N
Sales (£m)	1.280	1.216	1.203	1.240	1.240	1.214
Profit (£m)	0.314	0.328	0.238	0.270	0.292	0.180
Ratio of price of wood to general price level (N-9 = 100)	100	98	114	124	143	269
Ratio of wages in Bird's factory to general price level (N-9 = 100)	100	92	97	95	87	78
Average age of Bird's employees	38.0	39.0	39.3	39.5	39.7	40.0

(4) The BTP offer is financially the more attractive. They are prepared to offer you £2 million cash for your firm. They were at pains to point out that, while they expect to be interested in buying at any time you consider selling, the actual amount of this offer is conditional on acceptance within a month. Obviously, fear of your accepting the SSS offer is pushing up the price they are prepared to pay. They are prepared to enter into a no-redundancy agreement with all your staff and would be prepared also to enter into an agreement with you to act as consultant to them for as long as you wish at £2000 per year.

(5) Now we come to the SSS offer. They will pay you £800 000 cash for a half share in your firm. They insist on taking absolute control of the marketing of your products, but this is no bad thing, as I know you have little interest in market-ing as such and rely on personal contacts. SSS is a large, solid, growing, and most up-to-date firm with efficient business methods. In particular they have a very professional national marketing effort and your products, which up to now have been sold only to our local and neighbouring educational authori-ties, will have much greater sales. Profits will therefore increase while you still retain control of the creative parts of the business and continue to draw a salary and a share of the profits. I think the slightly worse financial terms are more than compensated for by this chance to continue doing the work you so much enjoy.

(6) In order to save you the trouble of excessive calculation, I have had certain figures computed. In the table below you will find estimates of the total income,
net of all taxes, which your household (viz. Mrs Bird, Mr Ernest Bird and yourself) will enjoy under the two schemes. In calculating these figures I have taken
account of my knowledge of your current financial position and have assumed:

   (i)   That, as now, your wife, your brother and yourself will be the owners of
the firm (or half of it in the case of your accepting the SSS offer) and that
you will pay the owners the same directors' fees as now; also that the
ownership and fees will be arranged, as now, in such a way as to min-
imise tax liabilities; and moreover that you will retain in the firm the
same proportion of profits as now;

   (ii)   That you will wish to make the provisions we recently agreed upon for
your wife, brother, son, daughter-in-law and grandchildren in the event
of your death; and that all capital not absorbed by this should be
invested absolutely securely;

   (iii) For the SSS scheme, that real profits (i.e. profits net of inflation) will
increase at one of three annual rates from a base of £200 000 per year.

Offer	Growth rate	Income (£pa)
BTP		33 664 fixed
SSS	0%	23 860 fixed
SSS	5%	24 760 in first year rising by 5% pa to (e.g.) 35 180 in 10th year
SSS	10%	25 160 in first year rising by 10% pa to (e.g.) 52 550 in the 10th year

EXERCISES

(1) What should John tell Mr Bird over lunch?

(2) If you were John, what questions would you ask Mr Bird so as to
improve the help you gave him? (Imagine he agreed to answer just
one question: what would it be?—just two: what would they be?—
and so on).

(3) Suppose Mr Bird said to you: 'I know I need help. What kind of help
should I get?' How would you go about answering him?

(4) What is the underlying structure of Mr Bird's business and of his
decision? Does structuring these things (i.e. expressing what is going
on in some relatively simple form that explains or elucidates the
whole picture) help? Are there alternative structures? If so, why did
you light on one in particular (if you did)? And how would you choose
between alternative structures?

(5) In what way is it meaningful to talk of causing change in the Bird case
as you have approached it?

(6)   What individuals and groups are most relevant to Mr Bird in making his decision? What more would you ideally wish to know about them before helping Mr Bird?

(7)   What, in your view, really is Mr Bird's dilemma?

(8)   Different helpers assume different levels of responsibility towards those they are helping. Some, for example, help by taking all responsibility while others help by advising but are unconcerned whether their advice is accepted. Think of different examples from your own experience.

   Can the examples be usefully classified and any general lessons drawn? (Some possibly fruitful ideas might include expert help, professional help, imposed help, financially charged help, fanatical help, etc.)

(9)   Some helping activities (e.g. medical and legal help) are provided by people who usually belong to a professional body which has a code of good, even ethical, helping practice. Discuss the strengths and weaknesses of this circumstance.

   What does 'professional' mean in relation to providing help? Should all help be provided professionally?

Chapter 2

Science

Science has been singularly successful in structuring understanding of aspects of the world. Phenomena which are superficially almost magical, or at least incomprehensible, take on an almost mundane quality when a handful of statements is shown to account for them.

It is to be supposed that the methods used to develop these structures are powerful and of even wider potential value than has already been secured. A helper will perhaps wish to use these methods in developing his own structures of issues he addresses.

In order to talk sensibly about a process which uses the scientific method, it seems a desirable preliminary to discuss what constitutes the scientific method, and this chapter does so. The relationship of scientists with society at large and some of the limitations of science are also touched on. No attempt is made, however, to give a comprehensive account of these issues. Rather, those aspects of them which are relevant to helping, and specifically to working in OR, are developed.

THE SUBJECT MATTER OF SCIENCE

Scientists deal with theories (that is, statements which are not tautologies) about the real world. These theories summarise, in a more or less general way, the behaviour scientists have experienced of the things in the real world to which the theories refer. The theories might be proposed by almost any process, though doubtless some ways of proposing theories will be more fruitful than others. All these theories are conjectures: they may be right or wrong, true or false. The current scientific theories are those which have not yet been falsified. However, to qualify as a scientific theory, a statement must be falsifiable in principle. That is, it must be possible to conceive of events occurring which contradict the theory. However, this contradiction must be of a special kind.

Consider the two statements (i) at equal temperatures and pressures, iron is denser than water, and (ii) Bach is a better composer than Beethoven. Most people would accept statement (i) as a scientific theory (though care must be exercised with this, and other scientific statements, to avoid tautology: the concept 'iron' used in this statement must be one which does not include a statement about density in its definition). All competent scientists accept that it summarises experience about iron and water, but they also accept the possibility of water being found to be denser than iron in some (admittedly difficult to conceive) circumstances. Moreover, all scientists agree what the concepts iron, water, denser, same, temperature and pressure mean. There would, therefore, be no doubt among scientists about the theory having been falsified if a scientist could construct an experiment in which, at equal temperatures and pressures, water was denser than some substance, in every way except density like iron, and enough other scientists could repeat this experiment. In short, there is subjective consensus among scientists that statement (i) summarises relevant experience and about the way statement (i) would be falsified. This subjective consensus among scientists is scientific objectivity. Any kind of objectivity is, of course, some form of subjective consensus.

Statement (ii) above would not generally be accepted as a scientific theory. Most people are prepared to accept that scientists are the folk who decide among themselves about scientific theories. On the other hand, many might feel that, as far as statement (ii) is concerned, anyone to whom the concepts Bach, Beethoven and music have meaning is as good as anyone else. Nevertheless, (ii) is a statement about the real world, and it summarises relevant experience for some people (while being contrary to the experience of many other people). However, on the whole they would not be defined save as those who preferred Bach to Beethoven, whereas scientists are defined by their attitudes to theories, not by the content of the theory they are addressing. There is thus no elite in whose subjective consensus most people would feel satisfied. (Some would argue there is not for science. Yet others might argue there is for music—say, all graduates or equivalent in musical theory or performance.)

Moreover, even if there were a group of people, judged competent and among whom there was subjective consensus of statement (ii)'s validity as a summariser of experience, it would probably still not be a scientific theory, because they might not agree that it was falsifiable—they might believe it so strongly that no conceivable event could make them change their minds. Indeed, even if they all accepted it was falsifiable—for example, by the discovery of some hitherto unfound work by Beethoven of exceptional brilliance—they might not agree about how whether the new evidence falsified the theory was to be decided. (This difficulty stems in part from there being no consensus about what 'better' in statement (ii) means, compared with the very general agreement among scientists about what 'denser' means in statement (i).)

Such statements as (ii) therefore have to be accepted as being unscientific. Most statements most people make are unscientific: and so are many theories in which they believe. In consequence, it should not be surprising that science has marked limitations in its application to human affairs.

THE NATURE OF SCIENCE

Science, in the everyday sense of the word, is thus about theories of the real world which, among people called scientists, enjoy subjective consensus that they:

(a)   Summarise relevant experience.
(b)   Are falsifiable by events.
(c)   Are clearly falsified or not by a particular event.

(Note that (b) implies that the theories are not tautologies.)

There may be much argument among scientists before a subjective consensus is reached on any or all of (a), (b) and (c) in the case of some particular theory. Even when it is reached the whole ethos of science is to keep challenging it. The process of publication, challenge and criticism is the means by which a consensus is reached or destroyed as the case may be. Only by some such process can one be sure that the consensus is not just a passive, couldn't-care-less, one.

The process of science is thus the search for ever better theories by the deliberate pursuit of events which falsify currently held theories, thereby forcing the conjecture of a more general theory. The value of a scientific theory is that it is to be presumed that if it summarises all previous experience and has not been falsified by severe testing, then it is quite likely to hold tomorrow and anywhere. Actions can, with some certainty, be based upon the likelihood of the theory being true. A collection of scientific theories about linked phenomena, providing as it does an understanding of them and a capacity to make predictions about them, gives in turn confidence to act in relation to those phenomena with a fair idea of the effects any actions will have. (Some refuted theories, it should be noted, persist as useful ones because they are highly accurate approximations to the currently held theories, at least for many practical purposes. Newtonian mechanics has this relationship to general relativity. It is widely and productively used, in spite of its refutation and known invalidity, because it is a good approximation for many practical purposes.)

The phrase 'consensus among people called scientists' begs a question, namely who are scientists? The answer appears to be people whom other scientists call scientists. To elaborate a little, looking over the centuries, there developed an attitude of mind which was distinctive enough for those with it to be given the name scientist. Scientists coalesced in various ways and set up their own rules, some written and many unwritten. By now, advanced societies acknowledge scientific institutions which administer their own rules, including rules of admission. Scientists, therefore, decide who else can become a scientist, though their decision-making power is under licence from society generally. Established scientists might disagree about whether a person is to be allowed as a scientist. Probably the person will be allowed only if there is near-consensus among the established scientists that he or she should be.

It is perhaps appropriate to note at this stage that many people called scientists, or said to be working in science, are engaged in activities which accept certain current scientific theories and nothing could be further from their minds than the thought of falsifying these theories. To that extent, they are not scientists in the sense here used. For example, most meteorologists would accept scientific theories about rainfall being measurable in certain ways and publish figures of rainfall accordingly. This is the distinction between technology, which (broadly speaking) accepts and uses certain scientific theories, and pure science, which is concerned with theory conjecture, falsification and conjecture again. Technology is essentially the practical application of science in ways, and to the extent, that someone thinks of use or value.

Note, too, that scientific theories do not explain things. They merely summarise the facts. Of course, scientists do seek to explain happenings just as men always have done. Newton's theories of gravitation are commonly explained by the notion that matter reaches out across space to attract other matter to it. Indeed, usually, scientific theories are couched in terms that imply, if they do not make explicit, some explanation of the events in question. Probably this implied explanation derives from the thought processes which led the theory proposer to his proposal.

A familiar pattern in science is that a current explanation persists and is fertile of new theories until the explanation as such is falsified. Thus, the explanation that matter consists of small indivisible units called atoms was fertile of many new and useful theories. Then the atom was found not to be indivisible. When an explanation is falsified, as when a theory is falsified, the search is quickly on for a new one. Moreover, many of the theories which were built on the old explanation, and not just the one whose falsifying led to the falsifying of the explanation, will be tested with renewed vigour. (An explanation of a particular class of phenomena usually embodies a way of looking at those phenomena, like matter as a collection of indivisible atoms. Even if the current explanation is not falsified, a new explanation is sometimes offered which is essentially another way of looking at those phenomena and this can often stimulate new understandings and even new theories.)

The question arises whether science has to do with truth. Quite clearly, by definition, no scientific theory of any kind is demonstrably and irrefutably true: a counter-example might always arise. Nevertheless, it is hard to avoid the feeling that some scientific theories are pretty nearly true, meaning valid everywhere and all the time. For many practical purposes it is very convenient to make this assumption. It must, however, be recognised that scientific theories can logically be regarded as only approximations to the truth; that events might be experienced which contradict them; and that such events are not unnatural but are, indeed, the means by which science advances nearer to whatever absolute truth there might be.

MILTON JONES STUDIES HOW SOCKS WEAR OUT

Consider a hypothetical case study, which describes the scientific process and introduces a few other points.

Jane Martin is a chiropodist's assistant. She helps patients prepare for the chiropodist's attention and attends to them after treatment. Often the patient has to remove both socks. One day Jane helps a young girl to replace her socks and is amused when the girl tells her she is putting the socks on the wrong feet. She writes about this to a newspaper column specialising in the humour of everyday life and wins £5.

The letter is read by Milton Jones, a university textile technologist, who does a good deal of consulting for Dilks, a large sock manufacturing firm. He is in despair. Dilks have asked him to look into a long-standing problem, which manifests itself in complaints they receive and also in market research results, namely that for many of their customers one of a pair of socks always seems to wear out long before the other. Market research suggests about an equal proportion of buyers of rival socks have the same complaint. If Dilks could lick this problem they are confident increased sales would result. Milton has, he thinks, exhausted all technical possibilities.

Jane's letter hits him like a bomb. What if people consistently wear each of a pair of socks on the same foot? Would that not explain the differences in rate of wearing out? Surely this is the breakthrough he has been waiting for. A couple of hours' reflection dims Milton's enthusiasm. He is pretty sure that if people did wear each of a pair of socks consistently on one foot, the socks would wear unevenly. Moreover, he can bring himself to believe that if a person takes off his or her socks, leaves them in a changing room, say, and returns to put them on, then the way in which the socks were left might dictate each being returned to the foot it came from. But he cannot believe this identity with feet would persist through washing, and, although Dilks' market research shows that socks are washed less often than Milton's mother has told him they should be, there is little hope of enough socks being laundered infrequently enough to be worn all the time on the same feet by some process of left and right socks remaining identifiable overnight.

The process Milton is going though now is, of course, the creative one. Ideas from a range of sources are milling round in his mind. He is searching for some pattern, consistent with his general experience and such relevant facts as he has, which will forward his problem solving. He is seeking a theory which he can bring himself to believe is plausible enough not to be trivially falsified. Moreover, he is guided by his wish to solve his problem. He has decided not to bother with pursuing one theory which other scientists with other interests might well have pursued, namely that socks taken off and left in a changing room are restored to the feet they left. He is not bothering with this because he believes it is irrelevant to the problem in hand.

A day of such rather disconnected thinking goes by and, next morning, Milton decides to sit down and think systematically. He notes down two hypotheses or possible theories:

(a)   If a pair of socks are not worn evenly between a person's feet they will wear out at different rates.
(b)   For some reason, a pair of socks is not worn evenly between the feet.

Simply writing (b) down and thinking about it for a few minutes clears Milton's mind. He has written 'for some reason'. But need there by any reason? If people put laundered socks on left and right feet at random, would not a large proportion of pairs of socks be worn unevenly as between feet? He does some rough order of magnitude calculations using his half-remembered probability theory. Yes, if a pair of socks is washed 100 times in its life, more than half the pairs will be such that one is worn on one foot 10 times or more than the other. He makes a note to do a more accurate calculation when he has got the relevant market research data from Dilks.

Hypothesis (a) puzzles him for rather longer. He already believes it, but he feels it is not yet precisely enough stated. He knows from his earlier studies that quality control, while tight, is such that if the socks were worn evenly between feet, one would sometimes wear out while the other appeared scarcely worn. He also knows this effect is nothing like enough to explain the level of complaints about uneven wear. After much thought he redrafts it:

(c)   If a pair of socks is worn unevenly between a person's feet, one or other of the socks will wear significantly more quickly than if not.

This hypothesis remains somewhat imprecise. It is sometimes said that precision is a characteristic of science. However, while science can be made to appear precise, as it is in many school textbooks, by people being wise after the event, the creative part of science is often imprecise, using words and concepts in ill-defined ways and expressing theories in a less than general form. This imprecision in theories being postulated for the first time has, of course, usually to be reduced before a subjective consensus emerges, either that the theory summarises previous experience or that it is falsifiable in some generally agreed way.

Note that the redrafted hypothesis offers no explanation of itself. However, it is (if somewhat imprecisely) falsifiable. It is not as clearly falsifiable as many scientific theories because the word 'significantly' occurs in it. There is the implicit admission that the hypothesised theory will not always hold, but that it will hold more often than would arise by chance. Any test of it will have to be a statistical test. Although many scientific theories are cast as statements of certainty, a great many are in fact statements of a statistical nature.

Milton's next step is to check hypotheses (b) and (c) against as much relevant experience as he can find. He checks that (b), together with the ancillary hypothesis that people wear socks on feet at random, is consistent with all the market research data available to Dilks. He also searches in the university library for published work bearing on this question. He roams widely in this search and finds papers relating to other pairs of things people use together, but which are indistinguishable. He finds that this reported experience tends to bear out his own thoughts. He looks also for published material relevant to hypothesis (c). He finds nothing on it as such, but he does find much work recording that a given person is very likely to wear out consistently either the left or right of succeeding pairs of shoes before the other. He feels this goes some way towards justifying his hypothesis (c), if only because it seems to offer some sort of explanation for it.

What Milton has done here is to persuade himself that his hypotheses are not obviously inconsistent with other theories in which he and other scientists believe. Indeed, the hypotheses really follow from adapting and somewhat extending these beliefs. He has also checked, as far as he is easily able, that the hypotheses describe all other scientifically reported experiences of similar things. When a scientist talks about a scientific theory summarising all relevant experience of the real world, he usually has in mind experience codified and endorsed by other scientists. He would be inclined to ignore contradictory experience reported anecdotally by someone with little knowledge of the field. The scientist would also usually consider whether facts not previously codified could be readily obtained by observation, by enquiry or by experiment. If he thought they could, he might decide to gather them by more or less formal means. He would value and use them according to his view of how other scientists would value them. Publication, criticism and challenge would be at the back of his mind and he would at some stage expose the facts to allow challenge. (There is, between scientists on matters of reporting experience, a strong presumption of honesty and good faith. Contrary behaviour, if detected, leads to significant loss of reputation. It is this presumption, and its near-truth, that makes science work.)

Milton starts now to publish his hypotheses as theories, probably relatively informally—over the coffee cups to interested colleagues, speaking from the floor at relevant conferences, and so on. He weighs others' reactions and takes notice of any relevant experience they might have, perhaps being prompted to research the literature again. At the same time he is thinking how his theories might be refuted, and he is hoping to devise as severe a test of them as he can. It is an important feature of science that one of the first things a scientist does about his own conjectures is to try as hard as possible to refute them. Milton has, of course, already done this to an extent by looking over other experiences of similar things. As it happens, his theories were not refuted by this process, though they might easily have been. Note, however, that their rightness was not proved by the process either, nor could it be by any conceivable process. No matter how many confirmatory cases are brought forward, no theory can be proved right, if only because it might not hold tomorrow.

Milton realises that he might as well test the two theories together as a single combined theory. He hits on what he thinks is a good test and carries it out. If the combined theory fails the test, Milton will forget it and start again. He may try to adapt the theory to take account of some narrow weaknesses which caused it to fail the test, or he might just write his time off and admit the need to start afresh. If the theory does not fail the test Milton will want to publish his theory and the results of the test. Many people see it as of the essence of science that he should publish in this way and expose his theory to the intellectual criticism of other scientists and to their attempts to falsify it by ever more searching tests.

The theory does not fail the test, but unfortunately Dilks are not keen on Milton publishing as fully as he wishes. They insist on the results of his work being disguised to such a point as to render it, in Milton's view, unchallengeable by other scientists. Dilks' attitude upsets Milton, but he hears over a drink with one of his friends from the firm that Milton's attitude upsets Dilks. They see themselves as having put a fair amount of money Milton's way, only to find out there is nothing they can do to solve their problem. Milton has, they admit, hit on a plausible reason for grossly uneven wear of each of a pair of socks: but they cannot possibly act on his results to get one up on their competitors.

SCIENCE AND SOCIETY

Much of what has been said so far makes scientists seem very inbred. Science is pictured almost as a creation of scientists' minds rather as if they were members of an exclusive club, agreement among whose members was the ultimate aim of life. True, the things they seek to agree about are real and often tangible, and their agreement criteria are testing: but the process is one of subjective consensus nevertheless.

This picture, while perhaps not completely unfair, omits one important consideration: scientists are human beings as well as scientists. They mix with groups other than just scientists and are part of society as a whole. Moreover, they wish to feed and clothe themselves and their families, and that usually means getting 'someone' other than a scientist to pay the bill. The someone might be a large corporation or, directly or indirectly, a government or an international authority.

In short, scientists are in some measure or other—in the home, in the golf club, in their bank manager's office—answerable to the rest of society. If their processes, and the emphases in their work, become unacceptable to the world at large, they can be brought to heel. Of course, things seldom come to such a pass, because scientists and the rest engage in continual exchange and revision of views to ensure a state acceptable to all.

It seems that society is relatively tolerant of scientists on the grounds that they deliver the goods (or at least enough of them). To many people, the value of science lies in the power its theories provide to understand and thereby exercise control over the world about us. Any process which generates theories of this kind is likely to be appreciated, at least as long as the power so achieved is widely believed to be used for the good.

Note, however, that there are occasional controversies. For example, when a government agency provides funds to research into a topic which many regard as trivial (for example, whether there are more species of insects in Anglesey than in the Isle of Wight) serious complaints might well ensue. Moreover, scientists sometimes propose to investigate topics which some people regard as unsuitable for open study, or as intrinsically so value-laden as to be untreatable scientifically. (Scientists are, of course, continually seeking to extend the domain of science, and such objections would be one of the hurdles they might encounter at the boundaries of the current domain. Teachers of Darwinian evolution theories were prosecuted comparatively recently, and many people nowadays would regard certain human behaviours as too private for scientific study.) Others might object to the means scientists use in their pursuit of theories or their testing, if not to the intended ends. Vivisection is an obvious example.

Another possible source of controversy between scientists and society is that the scientist might provide understanding of the real world which can be used for what a significant section of society regards as evil purposes. Examples are unnecessary. (It is probably superfluous to add that not everyone sees science as at all controversial. The expression 'blinded by science' has widespread application.)

Some of these topics may become such major issues that society acts to inhibit scientists' freedom of action, for example, by national or international regulation or by withholding research funds (which for much scientific work is as effective as prohibition by law and, because it is less likely to generate secondary controversy than law-making, might be preferred by governments).

The utilitarian view of science suggested above can lead to quite different perceptions of the value of various theories and of various research programmes. A scientist might value a theory for its beauty which others deride as useless; a scientist might regard a theory as convincingly refuted, but an engineer still use it because it is so nearly valid as to make no practical difference; an Indian peasant is scarcely likely to take as charitable a view of research into supersonic travel as the wealthy North Atlantic commuter. It is idle to suppose that science is value-free. What the scientist chooses to work on and what he chooses to ignore usually makes the world better for some people and worse for others.

THE SOCIAL SCIENCES

The methods of science have worked most successfully in the 'hard' sciences—physics, chemistry, biology and their derivatives. These sciences have mature languages. Statements made about their subject matter can be made with precision and near-certainty of being understood by other scientists. Experience can, because of this precise language, be codified and made accessible to all. Thus, theories which summarise previous experience can be proposed with some confidence that nothing has yet been experienced which immediately refutes them. Moreover, and perhaps crucially, the subject matter of hard sciences, linked with the precision with which theories can be enunciated, means that experiments can usually be set up whose results falsify the theories or not with relatively little controversy. At the very least, predictions can be made which are uncontroversially fulfilled or not.

In contrast, some sciences, the 'soft' sciences, fail to measure up to these standards. Fields of scientific enquiry can be imagined in which there is no precision of language, either because of the science's immaturity or because of the inherent difficulty of precisely defining concepts; likewise, there will be subject matter where experience is badly codified or not codified at all; and again theories can be imagined which can never be the subject of attempted refutation by experiment or which, if they are, lead to experiments which have results capable of contradictory interpretations. Indeed, some fields of enquiry will have two, or even three, of these difficulties.

There is obviously a spectrum from hard to soft, but it is difficult not to place the social sciences, including economics, well to the soft end of this spectrum.

In broad terms, the social sciences are those which deal in theories whose subject matter is the way people, as individuals or groups, behave in the real world. Most theories of the social sciences attempt to summarise exper ience of the real world and are cast in an apparently falsifiable form. However, many seemingly basic concepts (such as, for example, personality and attitude) appear ill-defined, so that many of the theories are capable of several interpretations. Controlled experimentation is difficult and sometimes ethically if not practically impossible; and where experimentation is possible, there is often difficulty in reaching a consensus about whether the theory under test has been falsified or not. Moreover, theories about people in general can always be refuted, and might very well be, by people's exercise of their free will. It is conceivable, indeed, that a group of people might deliberately act so as to refute a theory whose application they see as harmful to them. Thus, a powerful group of workers might obtain higher wages at a time of high unemployment in order deliberately to refute a theory that high unemployment cures wage inflation, a theory which they believe employers are acting on with results that the workers dislike.

These strictures are somewhat mitigated if statistical theories and statistical refutation are admitted, and, of course, many of the theories of social science are of necessity presented in this form. They are also mitigated if theories which are precise in themselves but whose information content is relatively low are allowed. Such a theory might be, for example, that the population of a certain country is more disposed to high arms expenditure the more threatened it feels by a neighbouring state, the attitudes being measured by opinion polls, say. Note that this theory is essentially qualitative: the opinion polls produce numbers, but the underlying things they are measuring can only be ranked and not given numerical values. However, new theories can sometimes be logically deduced from such relatively imprecise theories: certain branches of mathematics (for example, catastrophe theory) can yield powerful, but again somewhat imprecise, insights from essentially qualitative theories.

However, many theories in the social sciences are not so much scientific theories as allegorical or explanatory statements: for example, they offer analogies from the hard sciences which frequently help understanding (but might sometimes hinder or blinker it). The rational man of economics, who responds perfectly to market forces, is an allegorical figure; while the notion that the daily journeys people make from home to work are predictable by methods analogous to gravitational theory is an appealing analogy from the hard sciences, which might seem so appealing as to prevent the conjecture of theories inconsistent with it, yet more realistic. Yet again other theories, particularly in economics, are mathematical in basis, that is, they are logical deductions from some set of axioms which may or may not be true of the real world (see below).

These remarks are not intended to be critical of the social sciences so much as to draw attention to their relatively immature stage of development and indeed to point out the difficulty if not impossibility of their ever becoming fully 'hard'. This is unfortunate for those engaging in the essentially social process of help, and in seeking to structure issues involving people, as they might hope to place reliance on the social sciences. However, there seems no denying the relative subjectivity of much social science as yet developed. Once there is argument about what a theory means, or about whether a theory when tested has been falsified, subjective consensus (that is, objectivity) plainly stands little chance of prevailing.

THE SUCCESSES AND FAILURES OF SCIENCE: THE SYSTEMS MOVEMENT

The methods of science have, as remarked, worked best in the hard sciences. Even here, however, it is only in some aspects of the subject matter that science has been conspicuously successful. An important component reason is that science depends on reproducibility of conditions. Science advances theories with a high information content but ones which are often heavily qualified, for otherwise the theories could not be rigorously tested or, alternatively, would be easily refuted. For these reasons science often resorts to proposing theories about very simple situations, and builds the larger picture as a combination of these. Thus, Newtonian mechanics proposes theories about point particles and develops theories about large bodies from them. There has been in science a tendency to what is called reductionism, in other words making the object of study the (usually small) component part of a system and deducing system behaviour from that of the parts. (A system is here used in a general sense to mean simply a collection of things.)

Now it is an observable fact that some systems—for example, animals, including human beings—exhibit behaviours which are not readily inferable from those of their parts. At a simple level it could be said that such systems are simply complex and their behaviours simply difficult to infer from those of their parts, and this may well be true. However, it does not lead very far. More progress might be made by trying to understand systems as wholes.

If this is done, a number of important concepts are revealed. Systems do indeed have properties which are meaningless at lower levels than the system as a whole, even though they might ultimately be explicable by lower-level processes. (These properties are 'meaningless at lower levels' in the sense that theories which adequately describe the properties of the lower levels do not need to incorporate them. Thus, there is nothing in the relevant theories of physics, chemistry, molecular biology etc. which refers to the form a complete human body might take, or the behaviours it might exhibit.) The whole and its properties emerge—a phenomenon known as emergence—as a consequence of complicated processes of organisation and of communication and control.

A whole field of endeavour, known broadly as the systems movement, has developed to further understandings of these so-called systemic matters. It might be construed as a response to the weaknesses of the reductionist approach which characterised science in the Newtonian spirit. It is part of science and uses the familiar broad approaches of science. It is its subject matter (systems) and the way it views them (as irreducible, or at least not easily reducible, wholes) which distinguishes it from the more conventional sciences of particle physics and the like. Its main use has been in the life sciences but the approach is spreading to even harder sciences. In simple terms, its message is that systems can be, and often are, more than the sum of their parts, and that an understanding, however complete, of the behaviour of the parts may not fully resolve the behaviour of the whole.

OTHER SHORTCOMINGS OF SCIENCE

There is another sense in which 'hard' science is restrictive. It tends to treat issues which are describable, problems that are solvable, with the current tools or some relatively simple extension of them. Some topics which, on the face of it, would seem to be treatable scientifically may therefore not be so treated because their scientific treatment would not fall readily into current theories, methods or approaches. Occasionally some new tool, theory or insight is developed which opens up a whole new range of topics to scientific treatment. Two such are catastrophe theory and chaos theory. Each is discussed briefly, with no attempt to develop it so much as to pull possibly useful ideas from it.

Catastrophe theory has already been mentioned. Its subject matter is entities or systems which exhibit drastic changes of form or behaviour. Drastic change, as opposed to continuous change at relatively low rates, is quite common. Thus, stock markets tend not to fall slowly after a boom, but to crash dramatically. Orderly demonstrations do not slowly and continuously turn into riots, but suddenly and discontinuously.

The mathematical theory provides some powerful results. Suppose a system's behaviour is characterised by the system's desire, in some sense, to maximise something. It behaves in a way which means it seeks the local maximum of whatever that something is. (Thus, a group of people may be seeking to maximise their joint income. They perceive this is to be achieved, say, by working together.)

However, the world is changing all the time, and it is possible that a new maximum is available elsewhere. Even if this is a better position the system will not necessarily move to it as long as the present position remains a local maximum. But, should this cease to be the case, the system may move abruptly to the new position. (Thus, the group of people may be working in an environment in which some external change leads to another, possibly better, mode of working such as not working together. As soon as it becomes clear—if it ever does—that the present mode of joint working is inferior to even partial non-joint working, they are likely to switch quickly to complete non-joint working.)

It is possible to show that these drastic switches are the natural consequences of quite few underlying behaviours. Qualitative descriptions of these behaviours can provide helpful qualitative descriptions of the changes. Moreover, only a few qualitatively different ways are needed to describe all kinds of drastic change.

Catastrophe theory offers a reminder that change is not necessarily slow and continuous. In many phenomena there is nothing between black and white: a string is either broken or not. The theory also enables the identification of circumstances in which drastic change might occur.

Many everyday phenomena—the formation of clouds, the behaviour of water in a rock-strewn stream, for example—have eluded scientific description. It is tempting to suppose this has something to do with the obvious complexity of certain systems, with their many parts and the many casual relationships at work in them. Their behaviour appears chaotic but might not be so if those studying the systems were equipped with large enough computers, say.

Over the last few decades much work, drawn together under the title 'chaos theory', has led to a rather different view. Some very complex systems, it transpires, can and do exhibit quite simple behaviours if looked into sufficiently deeply. Equally, and in some ways more surprisingly, quite simple systems can exhibit very complex behaviours. Putting the latter point another way, simplicity of description (as, for example, by few mathematical equations) is no guarantee of simple, easily predicted behaviour.

These ideas are important because two kinds of situations are often met with. First, apparently chaotic situations are found which defy attempts to structure them through, say, theories about the way their component parts work. It may pay to look for more general systemic patterns of behaviour. (The earlier remarks on the systems approach are relevant.)

This first possibility might lead to sins of omission, so to speak, in the failure to structure something that is actually structurable. The second possibility is that it is possible convincingly to structure something but to fail to recognise that the structuring does not allow good predictions, a sin of commission. A simple but important example is the case where a handful of mathematically expressed theories completely describe a system but the parameters of the equations can be estimated only inaccurately. In some cases, the future behaviour of the system depends so critically on these parameters that minute errors in their estimation can lead to large errors in predictions of future behaviour.

PRINCIPLES IN SCIENCE

From time to time, science progresses because a general principle is set out which is prolific of theories. In other cases, principles are set out which distinguish between intrinsically sound theories and others which are only contingently valid. Often these principles can lead to useful insights. Two such principles are discussed, again without thought of developing them, so much as drawing possibly useful lessons.

The first is the so-called anthropic principle. It reflects that, in certain important ways, the world is as it is because people are there to observe it. Putting it another way round, if the world were different in certain ways, human beings or, more generally, sufficiently intelligent beings would not exist to build a science about it. A theory which denies the existence of human life must be wrong. Thus, the solar system must be of an age which is big enough to have allowed the evolution of human beings on one planet but not big enough to have destroyed them. Knowledge of the mechanisms and timescales of evolution thus allows inferences about the age of the solar system.

A possible application of this principle to more everyday matters is as follows. If a person finds himself placed in or invited to occupy a role, this mere fact tells him something about the situation into which he is placed. This contrasts with the reasoning that goes from the situation to the need for that role to be occupied. The reasoning is usually reversible, though often with more or less certainty according to which way it is taken.

Consider the employment of students as temporary postmen at Christmas. This suggests that something is going on in the postal services at Christmas. It might be that many of the regular postmen are ill about then, or that there are more letters and cards to deliver, or that the postal authorities are generously disposed to students at Christmas time, or many other things. In contrast, starting from the proposition that the post office has much extra business at Christmas suggests that one or more of a number of things might occur, including that they might take on more labour.

So quite what his presence in a role tells someone is not certain, but it might be worth his asking why he is there and thinking through plausible answers.

In physics, the theory of general relativity embodies a common-sense proposition in another important general principle: the laws of physics must be expressible in a way that makes them independent of the particular framework from which, or within which, the events they describe are being observed. Another way of putting this is that the essential underlying theories relevant to an issue are those which are observed in the same form by all possible observers. Theories which depend on some privileged point of observation are not wrong so much as of limited application.

The likelihood that a theory which depends on the stance from which it has been developed is not of the essence is of wide potential interest. Thus, an accountant who develops theories about a company purely from its financial statistics may not have got to the heart of things, if only because a sociologist might take a different view from his narrow perspective.

Things agreed from different perspectives might also be expected to be more useful. Thus, suppose a number of people have observed an event or sequence of events. By some means—for example, by giving written accounts, by answering questions, or by being invited to reconstruct the event—each describes what he has seen. Assume each, in giving this description, acts honestly. It is a commonplace that the descriptions will differ. It is not unreasonable to suppose that those matters about which there is whole or substantial agreement are somehow more fundamental than those about which there is substantial disagreement. (This is not necessarily to say that they are more true. For example, observers of a crime may have a strong prior conception that such a crime is likely to be committed by, say, a young, black man, and may all report this when the criminal was actually a middle-aged, white man wearing a dark balaclava helmet and black gloves.)

Of course, all this is not to say that the points of agreement are necessarily more interesting than those of disagreement. Often the reverse is the case.

THE ROLE OF MATHEMATICS AND LOGIC

Mathematical methods are much used in science and it is well to be clear on the role of mathematics (and on logic, which is taken to be a part of mathematics). Mathematics deals with idealised worlds created by the assumption that certain theories, called axioms, hold. (These idealised worlds are not the real world, although sometimes an idealised world is created which seeks to approximate the real world.) The axioms define concepts (for example, numbers in arithmetic) and operations (for example, addition and multiplication). New statements, different from the axioms, are deduced as logical consequences from them. These new statements might be conjectured much as scientific theories are and then proved to follow from the axioms. In other cases (Fermat's last theorem that $x^n + y^n = z^n$ cannot be satisfied by non-zero integers for $n > 2$ is the most famous example) the conjecture cannot (at least yet) be proved, and there is a deceptive similarity to science—the conjecture which is inherently falsifiable (by finding integers x,y,z, and $n > 2$ satisfying $x^n + y^n = z^n$) and not provably true. However, the essence of mathematics is that it deals with statements which are the logical and demonstrably proven consequence of the relevant axioms.

The importance of mathematics to science arises because many scientific theories can be cast in a precise mathematical form. If several such theories bearing on related topics are taken as the axioms, it might be possible to deduce other theories which will be true of the real world inasmuch as the axioms are. (This might be called a mathematical structuring of the topics, and the structured drawing of consequences from it.) So used, mathematics can be a very powerful aid to science. New theories can be derived from old ones. The new theories might be valued in themselves. They might also offer a new means, by testing them, of testing the validity of the old theories.

Moreover, mathematics might well provide the means of giving plausibility to a conjectured theory where relevant codified experience is limited and experimentation difficult. For if a theory, however implausible in itself, can be shown to be a logical consequence of other theories which summarise experience admirably and which have defied strenuous attempts at refutation, then credibility in it is greatly enhanced. It is in just this sense that science can be fairly said to explain things. Suppose some curious and previously unobserved event occurs. The event is conventionally said to be explained if it can be shown to be consistent with currently held scientific theories, that is, if a logical chain of reasoning can be set up which reveals the event to be explicable by current theories. If not, some new theory might have to be proposed.

Mathematics can also provide the means by which the mutual consistency of a set of currently held theories can be determined. The inter-relationships between theories can often be displayed most clearly in mathematical form and inconsistencies thereby exposed. This might be very relevant when one of the currently held theories is refuted and rejected, thereby endangering the status of other theories related to it.

Unfortunately, the power of mathematics is seductive and it can be easily abused. It is sometimes tempting to make the real world fit the mathematics. Some economics, as it seems to some people, deduces theories in a powerful and rigorous way from axioms whose validity in the real world is hard to test and in some cases dubious. There is always the temptation, in all sciences, to set down certain 'self-evident truths' as axioms and to proceed purely mathematically from there. A little thought about just how self-evidently true the axioms are will often pay handsome dividends.

TWO QUESTIONS

Two important questions are the following:

(i) What subjects are treatable scientifically? And what might be meant by the science of a subject?
(ii) What methods would command the support of scientists?

Question (i) is important because subjects which are not conventionally thought of as being treated scientifically might be thought worth structuring. The structuring might involve assembling a set of theories about such subjects, theories which are believed to have the nature of scientific theories, and thus building a science of the subject. The chapter goes some way to answering this question, but it is returned to in due course.

Question (ii) is important because the answer to it defines the scientific method. It is clear that scientists in general would accept that theories should be checked against facts—the acid test of a theory is reality and not tradition or authority—and tested vigorously against new facts, including tests specially constructed to ensure a hard passage for the theory. Scientists would be willing to expose their theories to debate, criticism and test by anyone, including particularly their fellow scientists. Scientists would also accept the application of logic and mathematics to infer new theories from old ones, to verify the internal consistency of a set of theories, and to deduce the consequences of actions from relevant theories.

EXERCISES

(1) Suggest some tests which Milton might have carried out. Which would you have chosen and why?

(2) Did Dilks's refusal to let Milton publish his work vitiate it as science?

(3) Discuss how far the process Milton went through could be described as value-free. Consider how
    (i) A person employed full-time by Dilks,
    (ii) A member of the Sock Users' Council,

    (iii)   An academic scientist interested in knowledge for its own sake, might have approached the situation which faced Milton.

(4)   Set out a list of statements which you personally believe to be scientific theories, stipulating by what means you can conceive of them being falsified. Try these statements on a group of your friends. Do they regard them as scientific? Do they square with their experience of the real world? Do your friends accept your criteria of falsifiability?

(5)   Science is often displayed as an inductive process. Facts are observed, hypotheses (tentative theories) are postulated, consequences of the theories deduced, experiments made to test the validity of these deductions, and the theory accepted if the experiment succeeds. Look at some published scientific papers and see if they follow this pattern. If you find a paper that does, do you think the paper is a faithful account of what the author actually did? If so, do you regard what he did as scientific?

(6)   How far is your behaviour, when faced with an important decision, influenced by your belief in certain scientific theories? List some of the theories which guided you in a recently made decision, and reflect on which of them are scientific theories, which are implied in falsifiable explanations, and which are statements having the general form of scientific theories yet which you know to have been falsified in some cases.

(7)   Are explanations of scientific theories (like 'matter acts as if it reached out across space to pull other matter to it') themselves theories? Are they scientific? What about more general explanations—for example, those of the great religious or political creeds?

(8)   Many scientific theories are not quantitative yet measuring and quantification figure very largely in science. Discuss why this should be so.

(9)   On pages 15–16 the theory 'iron is denser than water' is briefly discussed and it is pointed out that tautology can be avoided only with care. Write down a few other scientific theories. State what they mean in a way which clearly avoids tautology. If a scientist could construct an experiment, repeatable by others, to show that under certain conditions water is denser than iron, how might the original theory be adapted?

(10)   How relevant is consensus among scientists as opposed to consensus among scientists of a given specialism? Thus, if an organic chemist proposes a theory, is the relevant consensus other chemists, other organic chemists, or even just those organic chemists actively working in the field which the theory is in? Are there broad scientific

principles which are acknowledged by all scientists and which makes consensus among all scientists relevant to all scientific theories? What might the phrase 'methods that enjoy consensus support among scientists' mean?

(11) Is scientific knowledge the same thing as public knowledge?

(12) How far can the scientist be described as a problem solver? How does he decide what problems to tackle? (It may be necessary to distinguish between different kinds of scientist in answering this question.)

(13) The mature sciences (physics, for example) might be said to have the following characteristics:
(a) A clearly defined set of phenomena which forms their subject matter.
(b) A particular way of describing, explaining and generally viewing these phenomena, including a precise language.
(c) Widely accepted methods for testing rival theories.
(d) The general aim of explaining the phenomena, and especially patterns in them, by developing theories of cause and effect.
Is this a fair characterisation? Does it also characterise economics and the other social sciences and, if not, why not?

Chapter 3
_____ Organised Groups

As earlier remarked, almost everyone can expect to be working in the context of, or in relation to, some more or less organised group. This chapter discusses some features of organised groups that might prove relevant to a helper working in relation to a group, and particularly an OR worker. The chapter does not pretend to be an authoritative or even thorough account of groups in the round.

Groups are, of course, no more than assemblages of individual people. Individuals are first discussed, therefore, as a preliminary to the discussion of groups.

INDIVIDUALS

People as individuals have beliefs, which they hold consciously or subconsciously. It is these beliefs that determine their actions. (Instinct or intuition which determines action is taken to be a subconscious belief.) In deciding how to act, an individual might articulate the process by which his decision follows from his beliefs, but commonly, of course, he will not.

An individual's beliefs include ones about logic and its application, about the courses of action he has available to him, about the likely outcome of pursuing various courses of action, about past, present and future happenings, about states of the world and the values to be attached to different states, and about what is fair and unfair, good and bad, beautiful and ugly. The individual will also have beliefs about other people's beliefs and about his relation to them and theirs to him. Generally speaking, the individual will not have beliefs about everything but he will certainly have beliefs about things which he judges of relevance to him and usually about some other things as well. He might believe that some statements are meaningless.

The individual's beliefs are entirely subjective and there is no reason to expect any one individual to agree with the beliefs of another, or for the beliefs of a single individual to be consistent among themselves. Moreover, an individual's beliefs will be in a continual state of flux, his mind changing all the time, and the things he thinks worth having beliefs about also changing.

A number of sources of beliefs and reasons for holding them can be distinguished. There are those beliefs which are usually called instincts. These are fairly generally held beliefs and lead to similar actions by different people in similar circumstances. It is probably fair to depict the way in which most human beings would withdraw their hand from fire as a consequence of a very widely held instinctive belief that fire is bad for the hand. Many such instincts are not beliefs in the everyday sense of the word, but are probably rather products of the evolutionary design of human beings or of early socialisation.

The second kind of source of, or reason for holding, a belief is what the individual regards as authoritative sources. Thus, an individual holds many beliefs because he has been told or advised to do so by someone he respects, or he knows them to be held by someone he thinks is likely to be right—for example, his parents or other members of his family, his teachers, his work-mates, his superiors at work, the media, including advertising, or simply most people. Note that many of these sources are not authoritarian, that is, they do not force the individual to believe as they wish him to believe, so much as exceedingly persuasive.

Other beliefs are due to reflection, that is, a process by which the individual constructs beliefs in his mind perhaps by logical deduction from other beliefs he has. Yet others are due to experience. The individual might codify his experiences in a more or less rigorous way and base beliefs upon them. So, a person might have observed that every time a heavy lorry passes his house the picture shakes on his television. His belief that this is the case could be said to be deduced from experience. This is to be contrasted with the same belief being held because a television repair man had told him it is the case (authority), or because he has been thinking and concludes that heavy vehicles are quite likely to shake his television aerial and so set the picture fluttering (reflection).

The true source of a belief, that is, what originally led to it, may not be the current reason for holding the belief. An individual might, for example, now hold a belief which, while originally imparted to him by an authority, he has since come to believe by reflection. Thus, the reason for holding a particular belief might differ from the source and might change through time. Experience as a source of belief is probably less common than experience as a current reason for holding a belief derived from some other source, if only because it is rare if not impossible for experience alone to produce a belief: some hint from an authority or some reflection on the relevant experience seems necessary to formulate a belief.

It is remarked above that there will be some things an individual has no beliefs about, perhaps because he sees these things as irrelevant to him.

However, his circumstances might change and he might be obliged to acquire beliefs about the things in question. For example, the chief executive of a firm may have no idea at all about the quality of the washing and changing facilities for workmen at one of the firm's factories. A strike, ostensibly at least about their poor quality, might well force him to acquire beliefs about them. When forced to acquire beliefs in this way, an individual might turn to many sources, but again authority, reflection and the facts of experience are possible sources.

Another feature of a belief is the strength with which it is held. This is perhaps best thought of in terms of what is needed to change the belief. A weakly held belief might be changed by a casual conversation, while a very strongly held belief might not be changed under threat of death. Among possible sources of change are again authoritative statements, reflection and experience. However, what changes the belief need by no means be the same as what planted the belief in the first place, or as the reason it was held immediately before it was changed. Thus, a person might have had the belief that eating apples is good for you implanted by an authoritative source, say, a parent, but he may change this belief as a consequence of experience, when he finds himself allergic to apples. Even if an individual is disposed to change his belief by the evidence of experience, he might nevertheless continue to maintain a strongly held belief despite evidence which many other people would feel should change it. It is how the evidence appears to the individual that changes the individual's mind or not. He might well twist the evidence alarmingly in order to avoid shedding a cherished belief.

What might be meant by the word 'scientific' referred to an individual? If a man were asked which of his beliefs were scientific he would probably quote some which he had derived from authoritative sources—for example, those he had learned from science teachers or those which he believed scientists to believe. These, and others he might quote, he would probably be prepared to change on the basis of acceptable authority. Alternatively, an individual's belief can be regarded as scientific if it is a belief about the real world, if it derives from his personal experience, if he is prepared to publish it for discussion and attempted refutation, and if he regards it as refutable by experience.

However, if someone were charged to help the man by using the scientific method it is probable that he would be prepared to try to change those of the man's beliefs (if that seemed helpful) which the man was prepared to change on the basis of evidence deriving from experience. He would probably be prepared to do this regardless of the subject matter of the belief and of its source. Of course, someone charged to help in any way he thought fit would probably be prepared to try to change any of the man's beliefs, but someone acting as a scientific helper would probably feel restricted to those which were changeable by factual evidence.

ORGANISED GROUPS

A group is a collection of individuals joined in some relationship with each other, such as kinship, pursuit of a common purpose or shared interest, mutual support, and so on. Individuals are usually recognisably members of one or more groups. An individual may be a member of a group by accident. Some accidental groups may be meaningless to group members and indeed have little relevance to other people. For example, the group formed by people who happen to have 174 as their motorcar registration number means little to the individuals in the group and precious little to almost anyone else. It might, however, mean quite a lot to a person who is sampling vehicles on the basis of their registration numbers. (This is an example of a group which is really meaningful only as the construct of an individual's mind, in this case the surveyor's. It is arguable that all groups are subjective constructs which have an objective existence only because of some relevant subjective consensus.) Other groups which people join accidentally are very meaningful to them. Obvious examples are a person's family, his neighbourhood, and his nation. Two other obvious ways in which an individual might join a group are by coercion and by choice. In some cases groups will have restrictive entry rules and/or complex initiation rites.

In very few groups is there only one method of joining. Most inmates of a prison are presumably there by coercion, but there will be others who deliberately acted in ways which they knew would lead to prison and might therefore be said to be there by choice. Most people owe their national allegiance to an accident of birth, but others choose to change their nationality.

Groups display a greater or lesser degree of organisation, that is, some means of regulating the behaviour of the group (indeed perhaps of defining the group) and the individuals in it. The degree of organisation need not depend on the way the group is formed. Thus, a nation state, joined mainly by accident of birth, is usually highly organised; a group of slaves, formed by coercion, may be organised within itself as well as by the slave master; and a social club, joined by choice, may be ill-organised. Rather, the degree, type and efficacy of organisation is likely to depend on a complex historical process together with the group's aims. In the main, the subject matter of this book relates to organised groups, indeed usually highly organised ones. Henceforth, the word 'group' will imply an organised group.

Most groups have a culture, that is, the members of the group share beliefs, probably including the belief that being a member of the group is for some purpose preferable to going it alone as an individual, and probably including also beliefs about the rightness of pursuing certain aims. The shared beliefs may be held for different reasons and with different strength by the various members of the group. For most groups it would be natural to expect some beliefs to be held quite strongly by practically all members of the group. These might be called the core beliefs of the group. There will be general acceptance in the group that some core beliefs are about the real world, are suitable for publication and open discussion in the group, and are capable of change on the basis of experience. These might be called the scientific beliefs of the group. One group might view a belief as scientific which some others do not.

The culture includes rules which members of the group are expected more or less to obey. Where there is a near group consensus that a rule must be obeyed, it might be said that such a rule is a core rule of the group. The rules may be written or unwritten; some will be derived from the rules of larger groups of which the group is a part; other rules will be merely conventions or about rituals; some will be about ethics; and some about authority and roles within the group. Some of the rules may be about beliefs and some of the beliefs in the group may be about rules. Some of the rules may be about how to get the rules changed. If a group is to cohere, most of its members obey most of its core rules most of the time.

A feature of many groups is that rules are set up that ensure a division of labour. Often it will be this which makes group action preferable to individual action. The division of labour will assign particular tasks to particular individuals, formally or informally. The individuals will be expected to perform the assigned tasks on behalf of the group. The tasks will define roles for the different group members. They will often be accompanied by rules about relationships and accountabilities, as when a task is part of some larger task, other parts of which are to be done by others, and when it is to be performed to the satisfaction of others in their roles. It is these things which help give a group organisation. (These considerations might lead to the thought of organisation as a tool to help achieve group aims.)

Quite how the actions taken in the name of the group are decided depends on the culture of the group. Often the division of labour in the group will allow some individuals to act on the group's behalf in defined matters. Sometimes there will be complex ways of generating proposals for action (including action to change beliefs or rules), weighing these proposals and deciding among them, with again a division of labour among these tasks. The associated roles are recognisable in many groups. Named people might be given authority to commit resources owned by the group. Broadly speaking, these are the managers of the group. They might well also have authority to set group beliefs and rules and to decide all group actions. Other named individuals will be assigned the task of advising the managers. A role designated in some groups is that of the expert, that is, an individual whose beliefs about certain specified subjects are more or less accepted as, or even ruled to be, the group's beliefs about these subjects.

Organisation is possible in a group only if communication is possible. The communication might be primitive—the reception of cultural norms by a child watching its parents, for example. In a highly organised group, however, it is likely to be sophisticated with extensive codification of the culture in libraries, means of notifying changes of individuals' or sub-groups' beliefs through television and the press, information channels for ensuring that rules are understood and kept, and so on. The means of communication—the language(s) of the group—might be, indeed usually are, important features of the culture, in some ways reflecting it, in others shaping it.

GROUPS AND THEIR PARTS

An individual is himself in a sense a group. He or she will hold beliefs and have rules which no other person exactly shares. Frequently the individual will find conflict between being himself and being a member of some larger group. In the absence of anarchy, most individuals accept as rules among their personal set of rules something to the effect that in taking certain actions they will subjugate their own beliefs to the rules or beliefs of one or more of the larger groups to which they belong. As a special case of this an individual might act as his group role requires him to do rather than as he as an individual would act. He will engage in role playing. An individual may therefore be several men—Smith the solicitor's clerk, Smith the family man, Smith the member of the Labour Party etc. each different according to which group he is to be referred.

There will often be groups within groups. Each smaller group will have its own beliefs or priorities among the larger group's beliefs, but each will subscribe to some common set of beliefs cohering the containing group. The rules of groups often explicitly allow for the existence of groups within the group. It is quite common, for example, for the management of a group to be exercised in part through the actions of a committee made up of representatives of the smaller groups. The smaller groups will often be competing, usually within rules, to change the beliefs or rules, or to dominate the belief-producing activity of the larger containing group. Political parties provide obvious examples. Groups might be members of several disjointed larger groups.

If a group is of much significance there will either be at least an apparent logical consistency about the group's beliefs and rules, or, if not, the group will probably be unstable. (In fact in many groups the consistency will be more apparent than real.) In a similar way, an individual is not likely (at least voluntarily) to be a member of several different groups which seem to him wildly inconsistent in their beliefs and rules; nor, however, is it at all likely that an individual will never find conflict between membership of different groups. Individuals join and leave groups, groups fragment and re-form and so on, as belief adherence changes and rules allow.

An individual (or a group) will sometimes join a group as a vehicle for the attainment of his own ends—embodied in his personal beliefs and rules— and not because of his adherence to the group's beliefs. For example, a spy does this. Such an individual will, of course, usually conform to a greater or lesser extent with the group's rules for fear of being thrown out.

CONFLICT AND POWER

Different groups have different cultures and, therefore, different aims and values. However, groups are not isolated one from another. The actions one group takes, or indeed its mere culture, might well be undesirable viewed from the culture of another group. When a group acts or proposes to act in ways which another group finds unacceptable, there is said to be conflict. Conflict, though not necessarily overt, is commonplace if not pervasive. It arises within an individual when his conflicting desires cannot all be met, between individuals whose conflicting desires can only be met by joint action and only one set of desires achieved, between individuals and groups, and between groups within a larger group. Conflict is resolved in a variety of ways, ranging from one party giving in, through compromise, to war. Another way is for some relatively uninvolved party to arbitrate.

A common means of conflict resolution is by negotiation. (At a simple level, negotiation can be viewed as the conflicting parties meeting, engaging in conversation, and achieving conflict resolution. However, examination of any significant negotiation usually reveals a much more complicated process of bluff and double bluff, of intended or unintended deception, of sub-conflicts which have to be resolved sequentially and so on. Insofar as someone negotiates with colleagues or with those he is trying to help, he can often anticipate mutual goodwill and therefore simple negotiation. But this will not always be the case and he might do well to be prepared for rough play on occasion.) Many individuals and groups attach a high value to avoiding the more extreme forms of conflict resolution and elect to sub-jugate their beliefs to those of the larger group or to those of their competitor. There is no reason at all to suppose that there is some objectively right way to resolve conflict, either in general or in any particular case. It is perhaps helpful to think of conflict resolution as the search for, and attainment of, a state from which none of the conflicting parties think it worth moving at the expense of prolonged conflict.

An important component in any conflict is the power wielded by the parties to the conflict. Power is the capacity of a group (or an individual) to get its own way. It is not necessarily selfishly used. Power is often exercised on behalf of others. Some individuals value having power, and actively seek it, whilst others do not. Most groups have rules whose effects are to give some members of the group, or groups within the group, power over others. Insofar as power derives from rules, it can be said to derive from the subjective consensus in the group that the rules should be observed, but while breakdown of this consensus endangers power it does not always destroy it. A dictator may lose the support of nearly everyone in the country, but as long as the military group within the country maintains consensus support for him he remains powerful.

The exercise of power takes many forms, from compelling actions on people to punishing those who threaten group cohesiveness. There are some subtle ways of using power which sometimes go unnoticed. Important examples are the control of information flows ('information is power'); the use of resources to influence people's beliefs; and the use of power to prevent issues being debated, beliefs questioned or conflict articulated.

The powerful members of a group will usually fix the rules and often it will be their beliefs which dictate the group's actions. Those individuals or groups within the group, who find themselves in conflict with the powerful members of the group might well be in trouble if those with the power are motivated by self-interest or are otherwise unsympathetic to those in conflict with them, unless they can themselves acquire power by one means or another (for example, by getting the rules changed). To do so might be possible within the rules but might entail breaking them.

The means by which individuals acquire power in a group or the ear of the powerful, and the means by which the powerful secure their ends, is an important feature of many groups and a preoccupation for some group members. The relevant processes are often referred to as group or organisational politics. The rules by which these processes are governed are an important part of the group's culture. The processes are possibly the most common means by which the pattern of power changes in a group, although external forces can also play a big part in forcing the group, perhaps for its continued survival, to redistribute power. The current political state of a group—who has power, who is favoured by the powerful, who among the powerful are aligned with each other about what issues, and so on—is plainly an important determinant of group behaviour.

CONSENSUS

Hitherto and subsequently the word 'consensus' crops up fairly frequently. Consensus is an important concept. It is the basis of objectivity, and it is an important operational indicator of the core beliefs of a group. Whether it exists about an issue determines whether it is sensible to act as if a group were an individual when addressing that issue. (If a group can be treated as an individual, things are much simpler than if explicit account has to be taken of its inner structure.)

In general usage, consensus tends to imply complete agreement among the parties concerned. In this book it will be used rather to mean the state 'as if there were complete agreement'. This usage reflects the fact that the views of the powerful and influential are likely to count for more than those of the ordinary group member, and, in particular, that these views might be forced upon the group. Consensus (in the general usage of the word) among the powerful members of a group will probably lead to group actions indistinguishable from those in which the same consensus existed among the whole group, even though it does not.

RELATING TO A GROUP

All the foregoing represents one way of looking at groups. To summarise, organised groups have a culture, and both through the culture, and influencing it, a power pattern. Certain of the culture, the core culture, will be more strongly adhered to and defended from attack than other parts of it. Groups are assemblages of individuals whose personal cultures are subjective: the culture of the group is some sort of subjective consensus of the individuals making up the group. Conflict is endemic.

The general backcloth against which this picture is being painted is one of uncertainty and instability. The world is peopled by individuals with conflicting beliefs and motivated by conflicting values and conflicting group loyalties, all of which vie for precedence in their minds, which are also receiving endless stimuli of greater or lesser relevance. There is more order than might be feared because most individuals' behaviour is constrained by group cultures, but group cultures are themselves uncertain and group behaviour unpredictable. There is uncertainty in one group about another group's culture, its aims and intentions, and there is not always easy communication within, let alone between, groups. Ignorance, dishonesty, selfishness, ambition, incompetence and folly further confuse the picture.

It is relevant to have some framework in which to think about groups since everyone needs in some way to relate to groups. A person's relationship with a group is not likely to be productive unless he has some awareness of how the group ticks or, in other words, of the culture of the group. To play a role effectively in a group, especially one which seeks to change the group's culture, entails an appreciation of at least the relevant part of the group's culture. It probably also entails a readiness to acknowledge and sometimes participate in the group's political processes.

That there is wide appreciation of this view is obvious. Groups take pains to transmit the teachable part of their culture through education and other means, like social pressure on parents to pass on cultural norms to their children, and the less explicitly teachable parts of the culture are expected to be picked up by exposure to experience, and so on.

THEORIES ABOUT GROUPS

So far, no theories about groups have been advanced. Statements of the form 'all groups of type X exhibit behaviour of type Y' have not been made. It would be nice to be able to do so, and there is a brief discussion of possible theory-building concepts and of broad types of theory below. However, before embarking on this discussion, it is well to be clear that general theory construction can be expected to be difficult. Among numerous difficulties, one worth special mention is that it might be difficult to be sure whether an observed group is or is not of a certain type, and whether it does or does not exhibit certain behaviour. Thus, many theories might be either too general or too imprecise to be useful. The general validity of any theory offered about groups in general or about a particular group is not, therefore, to be taken for granted. It will almost always be necessary to determine, or at least to confirm, the culture and behaviour of a group as an empirical exercise whenever it is needed. It may be unwise to assume that a group is goal-seeking, or rational, or cruel, or kind, without empirical evidence for this. However, views usually have to be formed by less than thorough sociological studies and some markers can be helpful.

There are many potential ways of classifying groups. An obvious way is by size. Common sense suggests that size will be an important determinant of many features of a group. Other things being equal, it is reasonable to expect poorer communications, and therefore less cohesiveness, in a larger group than in a small one. As a response to this there might well be more complex rules in the larger group. The larger group is more likely to have an extensive division of labour, and so on.

Another basic classifier is the extent to which the group is hierarchical. Rules widely observed in the group might be set up to ensure that each member of the group has a boss who has a boss, and so on till the top person is reached. Military groups are near enough of this kind. Other groups may have no such rules, or perhaps have such rules only within sub-groups of the group, so that there are many top people. Neighbourhoods are usually of this type. Naturally one can expect, again other things being equal, a wider dissemination of power, greater overt conflict, fewer accepted and enforced group rules and less predictable behaviour, from the second kind of group.

Groups are of different levels of maturity and this provides another means of classification. Some groups are created to accomplish a specific task after which they disband, so that they are designed not to be durable. Others flourish and die quickly. Some endure for thousands of years. The young group is less likely to have developed a complex culture than the old-established one. Culture often develops in response to group experience in an evolutionary manner. It may change in response to group wishes including the wish to survive as a group. (A group set up to accomplish a specific aim will sometimes continue, even when the aim is accomplished, because the group members value continuance. New aims may be postulated in order to justify this.) The young group probably also has a smaller core culture of its own and a more easily changed one. However, much of its culture may have been imported from some larger older group, or by a powerful individual perhaps with experience of similar groups elsewhere. The imports (or indeed any other part of the culture) might well be hard to change.

Finally, two other frameworks within which many groups can be viewed and usefully studied deserve mention.

First there is the systems theory framework. A system is a collection of parts whose behaviour is more than the sum of the behaviour of the parts. Most groups are systems, of course. There is a well-developed theory for describing the behaviour of systems which suggests that the theory might well apply to certain human groups. Thus, groups will often believe that such-and-such a state of affairs would be better than the present. They will seek actions which their beliefs tell them will ensure this state of affairs. In other words they will have goals and seek them. Sometimes these goals will be internal to the group. Thus, a lawn tennis club's goal might be to provide excellent lawn tennis facilities for its members. However, explicitly or implicitly, most goals have external effects, that is, the goals of one group, if attained, would have effects on people who are not members of the group. This is obviously true of many political groups. It may well be true of the lawn tennis club if, for example, there are restrictions about who is admitted as a member.

Now non-human goal-seeking systems and systems of such systems are subjects of system theory and more or less well understood. Perhaps this understanding extends to human goal-seeking systems. If so it may be possible to study a group's behaviour, infer its goals and goal-seeking mechanisms, and thus (assuming it is of an understood type) predict its behaviour.

While this systems theory approach can be fruitful, it has dangers. One danger is that systems theory offers the temptation so to observe a group as to depict it at all costs as a system of a type which is well understood. Another danger, as great, is the temptation systems theory presents of seeing the system and not its parts as the real entity so that, for example, system survival might be more highly valued than survival of some of the parts. Groups, though systems, are arguably not more important entities than their parts, which are individual people. A group may, indeed, be merely a vehicle for the attainment of the aims of individuals. Insofar as a group might be said to have goals, they are likely to be some complicated reflection of the culture, power pattern, politics etc. in the group and a source of frequent conflict among group members. Common goals imputed to groups, such as survival, profit maximisation, domination over rivals, and so on, may not stand up against breakdowns of consensus. That said, there will often be a sense of group goals, an understanding of which will in turn better enable the examination and prediction of a group's behaviour.

A second major framework view arises because often the only easily observable features of a group are the actions it takes. The study of groups can centre on their actions and, beyond that, the beliefs and rules which give rise to the actions. (There is here the presumption that the structure of the group, its culture, is the determinant of group action. It could be forcibly argued that individuals and interactions between them shape group actions. It is desirable to keep this possibility in mind—again it is part of the argument about keeping an open mind about a group until it has been studied. However, if individuals are shaping group actions they are by definition powerful, and the source of their power is likely to be cultural.)

An important rule in many groups is that certain actions are taken only after much reflection, a process synonymous with planning in a loose sense of the word. This soon leads to the familiar view of decision theory, namely that there are alternative actions available at points in time of which the group should choose the best for its purposes.

This view is useful in some contexts but it has its limitations. In practice, deciding what action to take is often secondary to deciding within what beliefs and rules to act. Actions of consequence often arise, not from the opportunity to act, but from the group's perceived need to act—for example, anticipating a competitor's actions. All these points can be accommodated into an action-based view. For example, groups can be pictured as continually weighing up and rejecting or accepting proposals for action, for the assimilation of new beliefs, for the rejection of old ones, for the adoption of new rules and for the rejection of old ones. In using this framework view, therefore, it is well to be careful not to assume more order than is actually the case.

EXERCISES

(1) Consider the following theories, your own sources of belief or disbelief in them and what might make you change your mind.
   (a) Financial incentives encourage hard work in most situations.
   (b) Liverpool are the most entertaining football team in Britain.
   (c) If you don't wrap up in cold weather you stand a higher risk of catching a cold than if you do.
   (d) The country called Australia exists.
   (e) Bach was a better composer than Irving Berlin.
   (f) Lead is denser than oxygen.

(2) A 25-year-old woman occupies the following roles in various groups:
   (a) A leading solo player in an amateur operatic company.
   (b) The mother of twins who have just started nursery school, and the wife of a full-time physics teacher at a comprehensive school.
   (c) A part-time chemistry teacher at the same school as her husband.

(d)   A member of the National Union of Teachers.

(e)   The best woman swimmer in a swimming club which takes part in competitive galas and the vice-captain of the club's first women's team.

Think of conflicts that might arise for the woman and ways in which she might resolve them.

Might she be a source of inter-group conflict? Again identify some of the relevant group clashes. How might these be resolved? Which would be predominantly choices for her and which matters for negotiation with others? In which might power be exercised by whom?

(3)   Take some group with which you are familiar—preferably one of which you are a member—and try to codify its core culture, listing core beliefs and core rules. Reflect on recent group actions and determine whether they were consistent with the group's culture. Does the group have a power pattern? How is power exercised? In particular, consider knowledge, command of resources and physical force as sources of, and means of exercising, power.

(4)   How might groups break up? Refer your answer to examples from your own experience.

(5)   Consider again (see question 6, page 33) a decision of some significance which you have recently made. What beliefs motivated this decision? What were the sources of these beliefs? Which were scientific? Might the decision have benefited from more research?

(6)   Suppose some small group is formed for a specific purpose, such as to suggest solutions to a pressing problem facing a larger containing group. The small group is not expected to have a life of more than, say, three weeks. Is it meaningful to say this group has a culture?

Form a small group with a life of an hour or two whose purpose is to track its own cultural development. Can you deduce anything about the dynamic behaviour of the group, about the use of power and persuasion, about the development of coalitions and their effectiveness, about conflict and its resolution, and about how beliefs are formed? Is a group culture so transient as to be meaningless in this case? If so, why is this not true of all groups?

(7)   Think of examples of concept-naming by a group which have significant implications for the group culture. (One example might be the names given to abortion by various interest groups.)

(8)   Is science merely the science of the group called scientists?

(9)   Think of groups whose culture would not be influenceable by using the methods of science, and some whose culture, in whole or part, would be. What distinguishes the two sets of groups?

(10)   What might be meant by hierarchy in a group? Is communication in a group possible without some notion of hierarchy? Is control? Is co-ordinated group action? Can a group be said to be organised if there is no hierarchy within it?

(11)   Thinking of a group with which you are familiar, identify some of the beliefs and rules which have been recently incorporated into its culture. How durable do you think they will prove? Are there recent examples of beliefs and rules whose life in the culture was compara-tively short? How would you characterise them?

(12)   Discuss the notions of organised groups as vehicles for the aims of individuals, and of organisation as a tool for achieving group aims. Exemplify the points you make.

(13)   Examine a handful of groups known to you of varying degrees of formality (e.g. your family, your workplace, an institution such as a college), and sketch out the means of communication and of infor-mation storage in each group. Note, too, any marked differences of languages (not as between French and English, say, but in the use of jargon, of shorthand ways of expressing things, of style and so on). Do these things influence the culture of the groups? Are they influ-enced by the culture?

(14)   Discuss the roles of group members' brains, paper, computers, filing systems, libraries, books (including biographies and autobiographies) as media for storing and communicating information relevant to the culture of a group. Think of examples where the balance among com-munication or information storage media within a group has changed swiftly. Discuss the problems to which this has given rise.

(15)   Many groups have rites of initiation and of passage from one status to another in the group. Identify these for some group known to you. Often some rationale for these rites is offered. Is it in the cases you have identified? Does it stand up to scrutiny?

(16)   Consider a large so-called multinational company. Is it sensible to call it an organised group? List some of the related groups and sub-groups (e.g. shareholders, bankers, employees in various countries, white- and blue-collar workers, customers etc.). Reflect on some of the con-flicts that might occur in a settled environment of steadily growing profits, stimulating but not threatening competition etc. How might these conflicts be exacerbated if there were sudden changes in the environment (e.g. a new product appeared which threatened the company's survival)? Relate these points to real cases.

Chapter 4

_____ The Nature of Problems

Those seeking help will do so because, in the common parlance, they have a problem. This chapter discusses problems as they are experienced by individuals, some common methods of solution and group problems.

PROBLEMS OF INDIVIDUALS

The word 'problem' is used to describe many situations in which an individual finds himself. These situations have three common threads.

(1) The individual is dissatisfied, or surprised, by what is happening. He might believe that his circumstances must be capable of improvement, or his understanding is at fault, or rules or beliefs which he has held inviolate are changing.
(2) The individual believes he can and/or should respond, by action or by revising some or all of his beliefs.
(3) The individual does not find it obvious what action he should take, or even if any is available, or how he should revise his beliefs.

These features of problems are subjective. They suppose that an individual perceives some normal state for himself which satisfies him and offers no surprises. Departures from this state lead to (1) above. However, he might believe that the dissatisfaction he suffers is something he can do nothing about or that whatever has happened to surprise him is of no concern to him. If so, he would not usually be said to have a problem. If not, (2) above holds. Finally, the question of whether it is obvious to him what action he should take, or how he should revise his beliefs, is equally clearly a subjective one. The individual's beliefs may dictate an obvious (to him) single precise action or, what amounts to the same thing, some action designed to elicit a precise action, such as calling in an expert to advise him or using a computer algorithm to select among possible actions.

Whether someone has a problem is therefore a subjective matter for him. Someone may feel he has a problem when another might not. He might think someone else ought to recognise that he, the someone else, has a problem, but the someone else might think he has not, and it is what he thinks that counts. (It might, of course, be possible to persuade him he has a problem of which, perhaps through ignorance, he was unaware.) Different people will view situations differently therefore: some will see a problem where others do not, others will see a problem but each for different reasons, some will be surprised that others do not recognise they have a problem, and so on.

Just as whether a particular situation constitutes a problem is a subjective decision for the individual so is the question of whether being faced with problems is of itself desirable or not. Having problems is not necessarily a problem in itself. Indeed, many people are happiest when tackling problems and many deliberately choose to create problems or actively seek them out. Some might even feel that to be seen to have problems, particularly when they have been delegated to them by an organised group, denotes a high status.

The departures from what the individual considers normal and/or his difficulty in deciding what action or belief revision to undertake are usually called the symptoms of the problem. Removing the symptoms solves the problem, lessening them alleviates it. In general terms, then, solving problems means changing, clarifying or acquiring beliefs which, acted upon, remove the dissatisfaction or surprise. Because problems are subjective so are solutions.

SOURCES OF PROBLEMS AND APPROACHES TO SOLVING THEM

Problems arise in a multitude of ways. Some of the most common ways are now discussed and categorised. The solution needs for the problems which arise in different ways are also discussed. (The discussion is still concerned with problems faced by individuals.)

Certain problems, which might be called operational problems, arise when a belief is contradicted. Thus, most people believe their car ought to start when they turn the ignition key. Suppose someone's does not and that he feels he should respond to this by taking action to get the car to start. However, he does not immediately know what to do. He has the symptoms of a problem. How does he decide what action to take? Essentially he will decide according to other related beliefs he has or can fairly easily acquire. Five possible approaches seem worth distinguishing.

First, he might simply decide, perhaps from experience or perhaps from subsidiary symptoms like the tank is empty, what to do with minimal reflection. This is a common approach to everyday problems. The human brain is good at storing relevant beliefs and pulling them out as required.

Second, there might be any of a number of beliefs he holds which are candidates to invoke to solve the problem, and he will have to decide which of these to act on. One way of choosing might be provided by the conscious accumulation of further symptoms, in the case of the car by checking whether various parts are working as he thinks they ought, and using these symptoms to narrow down his choice of which belief to involve as the solving belief.

Another possibility, the third approach, is that he might recognise the insufficiency of his own beliefs to solve the problem. He might then seek to augment his beliefs by consulting a book or asking the advice of a friend and so on. (Quite a lot of groups are formed by individuals who wish to share their problem-solving skills in this way.)

These first three ways place an emphasis on problem solution by reflection. There is no guarantee, even for such simple problems as are being here discussed, that reflection will lead to an action which will certainly solve the problem. This might be because of ignorance, or poor analytic ability or because the individual's range of beliefs, his knowledge and understanding, are insufficient. It may be necessary to adopt a fourth approach, namely to guess at the best action, try it out and, if it fails to solve the problem, guess again.

A fifth possibility, which really includes the fourth, is to guess at or otherwise develop some new belief which would, if true, solve the problem (on its own perhaps, or together with other beliefs). If the belief is testable in some simple inexpensive way it might be best to test it before invoking it. Thus, if a wire is suddenly noticed to lead nowhere in the car it might provoke the belief in the individual's mind that the wire should fit onto the discovered free terminal. He could test this belief and the implied solution straightaway by fitting the wire and seeing whether the car then goes. However, if there is a similar car nearby which is known to be working, he might check where the wire in that car goes before trying the solution on his own car.

Simple as this example problem is, the five suggested solving actions cover many of the approaches to problem resolution.

The problem is simple, among other ways, in one important respect: it is relatively clear what the individual is trying to do, namely to get his car going. It is not always clear what an individual is or should be trying to do, or, in the jargon, what the objective is. This is a common problem. It usually emerges not as a problem in itself so much as an uncertainty about how to respond to a problem. There is often a feeling that some action is necessary and an awareness of what actions are available and their likely effects. The choice among them is difficult, however, because the person choosing is unsettled in his mind which of the effects he prefers.

Another general class of problems arises because individuals sometimes believe there is some state of the world which is superior to the one they are now in and which they wish to bring about. This may sometimes take the simple form of the individual's being simply unhappy, even in extreme cases of his being morbidly depressed. He may feel there is nothing he can do. A more positive form of this problem, and an important one, is the planning problem. Here the individual is concerned with whether the better state is attainable and, if so, how. The solution effort concentrates on identifying a set of actions which the individual believes himself capable of executing and which he also believes will lead to the attainment of the desired state. The beliefs which have to be invoked here are often far from simple or few in number, and quite elaborate belief collection and analysis might be brought into play. In particular, the individual might have to form beliefs about other peoples' actions and his ability, through his own actions, to influence them.

The belief in some superior state is itself often used to solve problems in the sense that an individual advances the attainment of the state as the solution to his present problems. Thus, he might say such and such a thing presents a problem at the minute but it will disappear tomorrow when the superior state arrives. Sometimes tomorrow never comes. In other cases the individual seeks actions he believes likely to lead to the superior state rather than address the immediate problems he has. This is a seriously pursued line in much religious and political activity and a perhaps less seriously pursued one by football pools punters.

Another important source of problems is that an individual's problems might be caused by the actions of other individuals or groups. It is probable that where there is human interaction, one man's problem solving activities—his pursuit of a state desirable to him—will cause problems for other men—create states undesirable to them. Unless some state is desirable to all (not very likely), there will either be conflict—A causing B problems, B solving them only to cause A problems, and so on—or some or all of those involved will have to modify their beliefs and rules for peace to subsist. A consequence of this (already remarked on for planning problems) is that the individual might decide it is necessary to invoke, or desirable to acquire, beliefs about other people's beliefs and action rules. He might, of course, having done this perceive the desirability of collaboration with others. (Collaboration can be a useful means of problem solution. Two individuals, each faced with his own problem, can sometimes find the one's problem is the other's solution and vice versa. For example, one manager's problem may be an excess of staff of a particular kind, another's a shortage. Skilled organisational operators are adapt at matching problems in the manner here implied.)

A point closely related to one man's solution being another's problem is that other individuals might advance beliefs or consequence to someone, in that they cause him to review his own beliefs. It is often problematic whether the person concerned should adopt such a belief or not. Thus, if a person is a heavy eater of a certain kind of jam, say, and he finds that some researchers have advanced the theory that eating this kind of jam to excess causes bone cancer, he probably has a problem. (People might deliberately commission the production of problems in this way—for example, for a company, by paying for university research.)

A rather similar problem arises because events are sometimes observed which are not consistent with current beliefs, that is, they surprise the observer. An individual might be dissatisfied by this apparent flaw in his understanding and feel the need to change his beliefs to accommodate this new event. What new beliefs should he turn to? This is a recurrent problem for scientists when a theory is refuted, but it is no less a problem for others. Mere curiosity—a person extending the range of his beliefs as an end in itself—is perhaps a special case of this. The dissatisfaction he is attempting to meet is that he feels he should have beliefs or understanding about something when he does not.

Some methods of problem solving, many of which involve the selection of beliefs to invoke in solving the problem, have been touched upon. This process itself embodies problems. One such problem is that of belief manipulation. (Manipulation is here and below used in the sense of handling or managing several things at once, and *not* in the sense of giving a false appearance to the truth, or of persuading people to accept lies as true.) As remarked, it will not necessarily be easy to isolate the beliefs which solve the problem, especially if they include ones which have not been previously enunciated in their own right but are ones which follow as logical consequences of more commonly enunciated beliefs. (Brain-teaser type problems and most mathematical problems are of this kind.) Problems whose solution is reached by the development of a new belief by logical manipulation of existing beliefs might be called precise or well-structured problems.

All the above implicitly assume that an individual's beliefs and rules are consistent among themselves and are not demonstrably false. There is no reason to believe this to be the case of individuals in general. Problem solving might therefore necessitate the re-appraisal of beliefs, both individually for validity and collectively for consistency. (A problem might arise because of demonstrably false expectations. The false beliefs which lead to the false expectations need only to be replaced by better ones and the problem disappears.)

Yet a further problem arises because of the possibility of anticipating problems. An individual may believe that he is so likely to experience a problem that he will take action to have the means of solving it in anticipation of its occurrence. Two kinds of action he might take are to order his affairs so as to avoid problems (as, for example, by wearing a belt and braces or by taking out an insurance policy), and deliberately to accumulate beliefs which he believes might come in useful in some possible problem situation (as, for example, by attending car maintenance or first aid classes, or by thoroughly briefing himself on a competitor's responses to various actions of his own). How far an individual should go on these anticipatory actions can be a problem for him.

None of this should obscure the fact that problem solving frequently calls for creative thought. The beliefs necessary to solve the problem, and especially those necessary to solve the problem caused by a surprising event, may not be at all deducible from current beliefs. Some totally new concepts might need to be developed. Information which is none too easily available might be desired. How is it to be got? The beliefs might need to be guessed at. It will often be a problem whether to risk the solution suggested by these new beliefs. Tests of the solution, and/or the beliefs before it is implemented, might be called for.

It is easy enough to talk glibly about solving problems, but it is well to recognise that only rarely does solving a problem mean an end to it. The chances are that the solution has overlooked interactions caused by factors not perceived to be related to the problem at the time it was tackled. This point has already been touched on when it was noted that one man's solution may be another man's problem. To expand a little, it is perhaps sufficient to note that one man's solution may be his own next problem.

MESSES

What has been defined as a problem includes much more complex states than those easily described by some single simple statement like 'the car will not start'. Often a problem is one large mass of symptoms which it is very difficult to unify into a single entity. Rather, the individual sees a collection of problems and his method of solution is piecemeal. Often he tries to pick out one or a few problems at a time. This process of picking out problems to solve is usually called defining problems. (It will often involve, of course, what has previously been called structuring.) In many of these complex assemblages of problems, the individual has no alternative but the piecemeal approach because he believes it is impossible to conceive of an action, or set of actions, which he can take to solve the whole assemblage in one go.

These complex assemblages of problems are sometimes called 'messes'. Another word sometimes used is 'problematique'. In contrast to precise or well-structured problems these assemblages might be called unstructured problems. Defining problems might then be viewed as imposing some structure where none is evident at the outset, and, with luck, determining one or a few relatively well-structured problems whose solution will go some or all the way to solving the whole assemblage.

PROBLEMS OF GROUPS

A group has a problem, as a group, when sufficient of the individuals comprising it (making due allowance for the power pattern) think it has and seek to act accordingly. Groups have all the problems of individuals and more besides. Group problems which are a straight extension of the kinds of problems faced by individuals might arise when there is a relevant consensus in a group. In that case, for the problem in question, the group can be viewed as an individual. It is left to the reader to reflect on and to consider what, if any, changes of view are needed when such problems are referred to groups.

The problems faced by individuals and their means of resolving them are often group related and to that extent are group problems. The group might well help the individual solve his problem. An individual might find conflict between his own problem solution and the culture of the group, and he might find the culture of the group something he needs to understand and take account of in deciding his problem-solving actions. These difficulties might occur in surprising ways. Many difficulties stem from the group's requirement on an individual to play a specific role in the group. Thus, the chief executive of a firm might be led by his personal belief to take certain action as an individual, yet he finds himself forced into other action because he is compelled to toe the firm's cultural line. However, whilst having a group dimension and often being transformed by mutual help into a problem on which the group as a whole acts, such issues are essentially problems of individuals.

A source of problems for groups, as opposed to individuals, is conflict among some or all of the individuals who form the group. (This might, by the way, be about some facet of a problem about whose other facets there is a consensus. A risk is always taken if a group's problem is treated as an individual's in that the relevant consensus might unexpectedly break down at some point of the problem-solving process.) If a group feels a desirable state is that there should not be major disagreements within it about beliefs, this is likely to be a never-ending source of problems. Most sophisticated groups recognise this and have rules which allow an acceptable means of settling differences, perhaps by creating new rules. However, the rules in themselves embody group beliefs and the rules may in turn be questioned. A common occurrence is that a core belief in a group suddenly starts presenting problems because it is vigorously challenged by individuals or groups within the group. The challenge is either killed off or the old core belief collapses to be replaced by the new. This process, and how it can be affected, is a common group problem. Also common is that some members of a group feel they have a problem, or that the group has a problem, but others do not. If those with the problem seek group help in solving it, or feel strongly that the group should act to tackle the perceived group problem, conflict may ensue.

Another special problem of groups occurs when the group's performance is less than desired and it is widely felt that the organisation of the group is in some sense to blame. Perhaps a particular individual is inadequate for the role he is occupying or perhaps the division of labour is inappropriate. A review of relevant beliefs, and possibly the development of new ones, might be called for.

Those managing groups, that is, those delegated power to act on behalf of the group, will also have special problems. They might take the view that they should act merely as individuals, but more usually they will seek to act in the group's interest rather than their own. Determining what this means might be a problem. They are likely also to have some perception of the normal degree of support their actions should enjoy in the group. Faced with an issue, they may find difficulty in choosing an action which enjoys the measure of support that they and the group members would find desirable. Sometimes the situation is so extreme that the problem really boils down to no more than the search for a single action which enjoys reasonable support.

Broadly, the approaches to problem solving in groups are similar to those that an individual might adopt, with the added advantage that the group will usually have greater resources at its disposal and the advantage of being able to divide labour. It can, therefore, deploy effective problem solvers to problem solving and furnish them with appropriate tools such as an individual may not be able to afford.

However, there are important extra dimensions. The group often has the power so to rearrange its own affairs as to reduce the number of problems faced by the individuals in it. An obvious example is that an individual's dissatisfaction might be met by satisfying his needs at the expense of some or all other members of the group in such a way as to leave the others either satisfied or not sufficiently dissatisfied to feel they should respond to their dissatisfaction. Another possibility is to introduce rules that so constrain individuals that for certain kinds of problem they cannot see any action available to them to solve it. The group might be able to resolve conflicts between individuals by the imposition of rules which somehow dissipate the conflict or even remove the reason for it. Groups also often develop means of problem suppression in sometimes not very transparent ways. It may be that the powerful interests in a group suppress problems by restricting the action of certain group members or disguising the symptoms of these people's problems from other group members, or even by expelling 'trouble-makers' from the group.

Plainly, the social setting of a problem is of great importance. If the relevant parties all agree that there is a problem, and also what its general nature is, life is comparatively simple. However, there may easily be extensive disagreement about these matters. (Examples abound. Many public issues arise because some people see a problem where others do not, or because many people see a problem but disagree about its nature. Interest groups are often a banding together of people who perceive a problem which is not perceived by society generally.) This is the group equivalent of a mess.

As remarked, power in some form or another might be used to determine what constitutes problems, or at least to determine which problems are addressed. In other cases extensive negotiation might be embarked on simply to decide what problems will be addressed, a process which could easily absorb more resource than is devoted to solving the problem. Most often there is a mixture of many processes—politics, research, publicity drives, and so on—in deriving the list of problems to be attacked. In the same way, of course, all these considerations apply to the solution process and to the solution itself.

It will usually pay someone if asked to help solve a problem to gain a reasonable understanding of its social setting. He should at least be clear who 'owns' the problem, that is, who is responsible for action on it; who are the other parties who are affected by the problem; and whether powerful interests take different views about the problem and about appropriate solutions or methods of solution.

CONCLUSIONS

Enough has been said to make it clear that the word 'problem', as generally used, has a wealth of meaning. The above by no means exhausts the types of problem that exist.

It would be possible to give the word 'problem' a much more precise meaning and some writers on OR do so. There could also have been more precision, not so much in the definition of the word 'problem', as in specifying those problems which are of concern in discussing OR. Again many writers take this stance. The preference here expressed is to allow all problems as potential candidates for an OR contribution to their solution and to let this contribution be assessed case by case. However, it would be foolish to suppose that the skills of OR workers do not have greater relevance to solving some problems than others; and it would be equally foolish to overlook the implications of these skills having to be deployed within the group context. These issues are discussed next.

APPENDIX I: ABC AIRLINE—A MEMORANDUM

From: Personnel Director, ABC Airline
To: All other Directors

Subject: Pilot Recruitment and Training Policies

(1) I think it might be timely to review our pilot recruitment and training policies.
(2) As you know, we have three classes of pilot, A, B and C, corresponding to A, B and C duties, and trainees, which has always been our only recruitment grade. The trainees are trained to undertake C duties, the C pilots to undertake B duties and the B pilots to undertake A. Traditionally we have had seven salary scales, T1, T2, C1, C2, B1, B2 and A. T1 is for trainees who have not yet completed C duty training, T2 for those who have successfully completed the training but are not yet carrying out C duties, and so on. Our promotion policy has always been one of simple progression up the scales by seniority as places fall free. Some men refuse promotion, which we have always accepted, and we have always demanded an exceptional level of fitness for A duties, which means we have had to refuse promotion to some men in both B1 and B2 scales as well as retire some A men early.
(3) We face a problem in that over the past decade we have recruited on the assumption of rapid expansion. Alas, in the last two years, and as far as we can see into the future, planning for expansion is not appropriate. Moreover, even if the number of passengers flown increases, our recent decision to go for high-capacity aircraft means we shall need fewer pilots anyway.
(4) Unfortunately, however, this is not just a numbers problem (which is a pity, as we could solve that by stopping recruitment of trainees and letting numbers reduce by wastage and retirement). The A pilots have an average of ten years to go to normal retirement and we need no more of them. The B scales are full and nearly all B pilots are or shortly will be on B2. We have too many C pilots, and they are practically all on C2, and we seem to have T2s all over the place. In consequence, all our pilots are getting impatient for promotion, which they can see is never coming, or anyway not as quickly as they wish or expect it.
(5) The real problem is therefore to keep upward movement going and I can see no alternative but to seek means of early retirement, carefully phased, for class A pilots. I am sorry to have to suggest this as these men are among the most loyal and dedicated members of our staff but the future lies with the younger men whose goodwill we shall lose without putting my proposal into operation.
(6) I have discussed this matter informally with most of you and I know some of you share my distaste for the proposal while accepting its necessity.
(7) This memorandum gives notice that I now intend to raise the matter formally at our next board meeting.

APPENDIX II: SERVICE PROVIDERS

Service Providers is a job agency which provides labour for casual domestic chores—cleaning, baby sitting, light gardening, etc. It is a private firm owned by one man, Mr James Avery. Avery started the firm himself when he left the army about 20 years ago and it now has branches in 10 large towns in Southern England. It receives as many as 15000 requests for services in a busy week. It attempts to meet these requests from the names of people on its books. The hiring is done on a day-to-day basis (that is, the client hires and pays for someone afresh each day even if the job lasts several days) except in special cases, which are a negligible proportion of hirings, mainly ones where the client is a business organisation (e.g. a restaurant) and is known to have a good credit rating. The basic unit of hiring is a day, being 8 hours in the normal working day and $5^1/_2$ hours in the evening. Shorter jobs are charged at the full rate for a day. Arrangements are usually made by telephone and/or letter, payment by letter. Apart from the first time a person puts his name on the books there is usually no face-to-face contact between Service Providers, their clients and their employees.

There is a hard core of 5000 names on the books which is pretty permanent and consists mainly of housewives who do not want full-time work but are happy to earn some money as occasion allows. Throughout the year there are usually a further 5000 names which are temporary and are mainly young people who for one reason or another do not want or cannot get settled work. When the students are on vacation there is a further 3000 or so names added to the list. Many employees telephone in to say they are available and to ask for a job that day; others wait to be contacted. They are at liberty to refuse a job and indeed most of them are selective as to both location and type of work. However, persistent refusal for no very good reason leads to the person's name being dropped from the list.

Emma, a student on vacation, enrols at one of the firm's branches. To her surprise she is contacted next day and asked to call on the Managing Director, Mr Fell, whose office happens to be at the branch at which she enrolled. Mr Fell tells her that he wants her to help with one of his problems. She will be paid the normal fees for the work. He is himself rather busy but his assistant can spare her some time and all the documentation relating to the problem is at her disposal. She agrees to undertake the task and is introduced to the Assistant Managing Director, Mr Arthur Robertson.

Mr Robertson briefly introduces the problem. The Chairman's wife, Mrs Avery, wanted some gardening done. She had, naturally enough, approached her local branch of Service Providers and a young man was sent to her. The man had done a good job and Mrs Avery had suggested to him that he might be willing to spend the remaining two days of the week on similar work. He, not knowing who Mrs Avery was, had said he would be more than happy to do this, but he would rather do it by private arrangement. This, he said, would be greatly to Mrs Avery's advantage because instead of costing her £21 a day, £6 of which would be pocketed by Service Providers, he would happily do her the favour of working for £18 a day. She had ordered the man off the premises and immediately telephoned her husband to ensure that the man's name was struck off the firm's list never to be reinstated.

Mr Avery had taken a wider view. Perhaps this was a general practice which was costing his firm a lot of money and which was giving it a bad name. He was not running an introduction service. Here was so obvious a loophole that he could not understand why it had not been plugged before. As long as it was there to be exploited he was quite sure that some of the less responsible of the people on the books would exploit it. It must be stopped.

All of this had been said, with some heat, to Mr Fell, who was worried because he could see no simple way of stopping the practice. However, he raised the matter with all the Branch Managers and two of them claimed to have found a solution.

One of these, the manager of the Southampton branch, says he has got round it by charging £9 commission on the first day's work (i.e. the client pays £24 to Service Providers) but balancing this by charging a much-reduced commission of only £1.50 (i.e. the client pays £16.50) for the second and subsequent day's employment of the same person by the same client. He reckons this has two advantages. It effectively removes the incentive for private arrangements since there is so little in it for either party that no one would be prepared to act dishonestly for the trifling sum involved. More importantly, it has greatly increased the branch's revenue by encouraging longer jobs. This also has the effect of cutting the administrative costs of placement per job day since each job costs something to set up. He introduced this system without reference to head office but, in view of the high performance of his branch, he hopes this minor misdemeanour will be forgiven.

The manager of the Brighton branch has had a different idea. He selected six men from his own list of job applicants, fitted them up in chauffeurs' uniforms and hired a car for each of them. They tour round each day knocking on the doors of a sample of people who employed someone from the agency the day before. They choose cases where, according to the branch's books, the employer has no one working for him that day and the employee is not working either. When the householder comes to the door he is asked if, as the girl who keeps the records is new and inefficient, he will confirm whether he is employing the same person today as he was yesterday. Dishonesty is seldom admitted or discovered. However, people's natural feelings of guilt when they have been so approached while behaving dishonestly are sufficient to deter the practice complained of by Mr Avery, even though the firm cannot legally stop the practice. Most householders who use the branch at all regularly have been visited at least once. The Brighton manager is convinced that the practice has been squashed in the Brighton district.

Mr Fell has got a few facts and figures from the Southampton and Brighton branches and from two other branches, Hastings and Portsmouth. All these figures are at Emma's disposal. Hastings and Portsmouth were chosen because market research carried out earlier in the year had shown that, in terms of type of client, type of job and composition of the list of people wanting work, Hastings was very similar to Brighton and Portsmouth very similar to Southampton.

Mr Robertson explains that he and Mr Fell are very busy and Mr Avery is spending a few days yachting. No other staff are available so Emma will have to work on her own. Nor are any other data readily available. What he would like Emma to do is to write the best report she can with the information available and leave it for Mr Fell and himself to read tomorrow evening. He is not expecting wonders, just some help to clarify his, Mr Fell's and, with luck, Mr Avery's thoughts.

In answer to Emma's questions, Mr Robertson confirms that the matter is urgent. He and the Managing Director have an appointment with Mr Avery early the day after next. He will be surprised if they find Mr Avery at all tolerant of anything but a firm recommendation. However, Mr Robertson does not regard Mr Avery as a man who is totally unreasonable, just as one who thinks highly of decisiveness. Further questioning reveals that Mr Robertson can see no reason to prefer the Southampton solution or the Brighton solution on such grounds as company image and the like. In his view it should simply be the one that is most effective.

Just as he is leaving Mr Robertson is struck by the thought that Emma might suggest a solution which is more in the interest of her fellow students, and indeed herself, than in the interest of Service Providers. He expresses the hope that she will be as objective as possible in arriving at her conclusions.

SERVICE PROVIDERS: SUMMARY OF AVAILABLE INFORMATION

A market research exercise carried out by a reputable firm six months ago suggested that the potential market in terms of job days per week was:

Southampton	24 000
Brighton	18 000
Portsmouth	20 000
Hastings	12 000

The following table gives the percentages of actual jobs started in the last half year of different durations. In this table duration means successive days of employment of the same person by the same client through the agency.

Duration (days) Branch	1	2	3	4	5	6+
Southampton	32	33	17	8	9	1
Brighton	33	32	16	11	6	2
Portsmouth	46	23	15	8	7	1
Hastings	47	22	15	9	6	1

(Jobs lasting 6+ days have an average duration of about 9 days)

The next table shows, for the same half year as the previous table, the branch revenue (i.e. the firm's commission, being £6 per day flat everywhere except at Southampton) and the direct and indirect costs of each branch office. The direct costs are staff salaries (including that of the Branch Manager and the commission element of his pay), together with an estimate of telephone and stationery costs. Indirect costs include office accommodation, advertising and various standing charges. The Brighton direct costs include the wages of the chauffeur-clad men and the costs of hiring their cars.

Branch	Revenue £	Direct costs £	Indirect costs £
Southampton	465 252	199 518	141 786
Brighton	337 308	140 673	113 550
Portsmouth	313 728	124 098	122 373
Hastings	237 774	100 740	108 936

Finally the number, in thousands, of **job days** in each quarter of the last four years is given below. The number of separate jobs is not recorded. The Southampton scheme was introduced in quarter 3, year(n-1), the Brighton scheme in quarter 4, year(n-2). All Branches quoted here are of long standing.

	Year (n-3) Full year	Year (n-2) Full year	Year (n-1) Quarter				Full year	Year n* Quarter				Full year
			1	2	3	4		1	2	3	4	
Southampton	120	141	38	48	23	46	155	56	66	35	64	221
Brighton	121	116	27	35	21	32	115	27	35	22	34	118
Portsmouth	79	103	21	38	22	31	102	21	29	20	32	102
Hastings	74	75	17	22	14	19	72	16	17	17	23	73

* For the purposes of this exercise assume that 'now' is January of year(n+1), i.e. there are no later figures than given here.

EXERCISES

(1) In what sense might Mr Bird (pages 1–3) be said to have a problem? (Refer to points (1), (2) and (3) on page 49) Construct at least five plausible problems which Mr Bird might have consistent with what the case tells us. How could you decide which, if any, of these was the 'real' problem? Is there such a thing as 'the real problem'?

(2) Consider some everyday problem situation, e.g. car parking on a university campus. Think of a few people on whom this problem impinges. Include at least one non-car user. What might each think his problem is? What might each think is a good solution? How far do the respective solutions cause or aggravate the problem for others?

Pursuing this example, think of how solutions might be chosen in theory and in practice. Reflect on the possible use of negotiation, power and organisational politics, in reaching and implementing a solution.

(3) Consider the memorandum about ABC Airline given in Appendix I on page 58.
   (i)   The memorandum gives very little quantitative information. Is this relevant in judging whether the airline has a problem? Is size of problem a meaningful concept?
   (ii) Does the memorandum make clear whether the Personnel Director feels he has a problem? Does he think ABC Airline has a problem? Does he think anyone has? (Note: he uses the word 'problem', but does he mean it?)

    (iii)   List some of the individuals and groups with an interest in this issue. Explore their probable perceptions of the issue and whether they are likely to feel they have a problem. How might solutions for some generate problems for others? Does any actor (e.g. ABC Airline itself) have the possibility of a solution which allows it to divide and rule? If so, discuss the pros and cons of its adopting this solution.

    (iv)   A stakeholder could be defined as someone or some group with an interest in a problem and in the fact and manner of its resolution. Start to list the stakeholders relative to this problem. Is it possible to stop listing without missing out someone or some group? By what criteria might relevant stakeholders be defined? In what ways should our problem-solving activities take account of the stakeholders?

    (v)   The final question in (iv) above can be addressed as a moral or ethical question or as a pragmatic one. What is your preference? Would this preference make you more or less helpful, and to whom, in addressing the question?

(4)   A group is perceived, including by all its members, to be underperforming. An independent observer suggests actions which might improve group performance. All the group's members agree with him. By considering the following contexts, list some of the reasons why the actions might not be taken:

    (i)   The group is an amateur football team who has lost all this season's matches and the action is to replace the goalkeeper.

    (ii)   The group is a class of secondary school children who persistently fail to hand in their French homework and the action is to offer free tickets to the school disco for those who hand in most this term.

    (iii)   The group is the salesmen for a medium-sized company making and selling paint who never reach sales targets and the action is to reduce basic pay and increase sales commission without reducing overall pay on average.

Are solutions as well as problems culture-dependent? What makes a solution feasible?

(5)   The desire or need to collaborate with others in addressing problems is the main reason for group formation. Discuss this statement.

(6)   Contrive to assemble a small group for an hour for *no apparent purpose*. Does the group acquire a purpose? Does it find problems and seek to address them? Is life, and particularly social life, an exercise in problem solving? Are problems the spice of life? In this last connection, are all great novels accounts of problem solving? What about plays, films, opera?

(7) Time is said to be a great healer. Do problems go away if left unattended? Why?

(8) Is science problem solving? Whose problems does it solve? Why does it do so?

(9) For some group with which you are familiar, list what appear to you to be the group's current problems? Is this listing consistent with the group's apparent problem-solving activities? How are the group's problem-solving activities expressed? (For example, is there an overt agenda of concerns?)

If it is the case, why does your list differ from the group's? Examine what processes lead the group to its current agenda of problems. Does this tell you anything about the group (e.g. the power pattern in it, its degree of cohesiveness etc.)?

Are the problem-solving activities of a group the single most important way of quickly learning about its culture?

(10) A multi-activity group (e.g. a firm which manufactures several kinds of things for different markets; a social club which provides a variety of facilities for its members) has choices about how to organise itself. Commonly sub-groups answerable to some controlling group are established.

Discuss organisation in this sense as a means of solving group problems and as a means of generating them. Would you expect different organisations to generate different problems? Would they generate more or less, or is the number of problems largely independent of detailed organisation? Illustrate your answer with examples.

(11) Consider the Service Providers case given in Appendix II on pages 59–61.
    (a) For each of the named participants in the case, list at least one problem he or she has. Rate from 0 to 5 the extent to which the problems are of importance to those having them.
    (b) Assess your degree of cynicism in answering (a). Did you, for example, include as a possible problem for Mr Avery: how can he keep his wife quiet? Did you include for Emma: should she refuse to do the work? Is a healthy degree of cynicism desirable?
    (c) Discuss the politics of 'passing the buck', that is, of someone making another person responsible for a problem for which he should really be responsible himself. Is Mr Fell the villain of the piece? Is Emma the fall guy?
    (d) What might Mr Robertson mean by asking Emma to 'be as objective as possible'? Can she be objective?

Chapter 5

_____ Operational Research

The topic to be explored in the rest of this book is the activity called operational research, commonly abbreviated to OR. This may be broadly defined as an activity which seeks:

(a) To help groups (or individuals) to solve their problems;
(b) By using methods that would enjoy consensus support among scientists.

This chapter delineates some features of this activity and indicates thereby how the rest of the book will develop. Alternative definitions are also briefly discussed. The chapter draws as necessary on earlier chapters. (Needless repetition of earlier material is avoided as far as possible, but some reference to it seems appropriate in places.)

THE GROUP'S ATTITUDES TO PROBLEMS

The group the OR worker is trying to help, and which it will be presumed is paying him, will have a culture which categorises problems. One particular categorisation will be according to the relevance of the methods of science in solving the problem. Another categorisation of obvious importance is by the value attached to solving the problem. (Here and below phrases and words like 'suitable for scientific attack' and 'value' are used relative to the culture of the group in question.)

The group will believe that some of its problems are quite clearly suitable for scientific attack. This covers several stances the group might adopt. For example, the group might accept the belief, derived from some wider culture, that such-and-such a problem is suitable for attack by scientists, in the sense of scientists as recognised by society in general. In relation to the group the scientist has the role of an expert over this type of problem. As a second example, the group might believe that some problem it has, though not scientific in the everyday sense, is nevertheless one which is capable of being resolved by appeal to facts, by debate within the group about theories, and so on.

On the other hand, the group might believe that some of its problems are quite unsuitable for scientific attack. The group's relevant beliefs might be so firmly entrenched that no challenge to them, whether based on facts or otherwise, is acceptable; or it may be that the powerful members of the group will not tolerate open discussion of the relevant beliefs; or again the rules and/or beliefs of the group might be such that a particular problem can be settled only by exercise of authority.

For most groups, many problems fall into a middle ground: the group accepts that some facets of them are suitable for scientific attack and others not.

This categorisation of problems is important to the OR worker because, in deciding his own actions, he must be sensitive to the extent to which the culture of his employing group will accept a scientific approach on some issue. Sometimes he will wish, and indeed need, to extend this acceptance beyond that readily available. It is to be expected that groups will seek OR help on those problems which they perceive or hope to be wholly or partly scientific, save for those on which some scientific expert is already engaged.

THE POSSIBLE OR CONTRIBUTION

Some aspects of problem solving to which the methods adopted by scientists are plainly applicable have already been mentioned. (They all fall under the general heading of structuring the issue in hand.) They delineate the possible OR contribution to problem solving.

First, there is the manipulation of beliefs, especially to infer some new belief which is a logical consequence of them. Most reasonably sophisticated groups will accept the rules of logic and therefore logical/mathematical manipulation of beliefs. There would not normally be any reluctance in most groups to accept that some or all of the beliefs manipulated were not scientific in the group's eyes. Acceptance of the results of the manipulation would, however, be likely to depend on the strength with which the manipulated theories were held—indeed it might be a test of this strength.

Second, there is the checking of beliefs for validity and mutual consistency. Presuming the OR worker would wish to do this by reference to facts and by the public (within the group at least) discussion and challenge process, he is practically certain to be restricted in this activity to beliefs which the group subjectively accepts as scientific, or can be persuaded so to accept.

Third, and with the same group restrictions, the OR worker might generate new beliefs or revise/adapt old ones using the methods of science.

The possibility of anticipating problems, or at least being prepared to act quickly should problems of a particular kind arise, has also been mentioned. Corresponding to the response to immediate problems, there are methods by which the capacity to tackle problems as they arise might be developed.

These correspond, in large measure, to the sets of theories and codified experience which scientists, and perhaps more especially technologists, keep accessible to meet issues as they arise. These ideas can be related to the three points made above.

First, it might pay to be continually manipulating beliefs in order to check that there are no untoward consequences of current beliefs. (This could be relevant if some of the beliefs change—for example, those about some feature of the external world, in a way which of itself causes no problem but whose implications might.)

Second, the validity and mutual consistency of a set of beliefs might usefully be kept under continuous scrutiny. Or, closely related to this, mechanisms might be set up which allow the quick checking of these things should the need arise. (It might pay, for example, to keep relevant information in a readily accessible form to avoid the trouble of gathering it on need. Beyond that, this information might periodically be used to check the validity of current beliefs.)

Third, it might be worth a continuous activity directed at acquiring relevant new beliefs and revising/adapting old ones as circumstances change. The changes might be changes in the world or in perceptions of it as new information becomes available.

It is unlikely, of course, that anyone would do any of these latter three things unless frequent problems to which they are relevant are expected, or unless they relate to issues of great importance to the individual or the group he is serving.

THE NATURE OF OR

The picture, then, is of OR as the intersection of two cultures: the culture of the employing group and its subjective perception of the relevance of scientific methods to its problems, and the culture of science from which the OR worker draws his methods. To have any effect on the employing group's actions the OR worker must therefore understand its culture to the point of knowing at least its receptivity to scientific methods. Moreover, of course, he must understand its culture well enough to make his contribution to those problems where it is called for; and to have means of finding out, and gaining access to work on, those problems. The range of skills necessary to carry out all of this successfully has already been mentioned. It includes the skills to diagnose and understood both physical and social aspects of context, to relate effectively to other people, and to analyse and structure issues.

The OR worker's cultural link to science is often more tenuous than his link to the employing group. True, he will generally use methods which he believes would be approved of by scientists, but he is often not allowed by the group's rules to expose his theories to the community of scientists at large. Perhaps to some extent he can overcome this difficulty by exposing his theories to other OR workers employed by the same group, but sometimes all he can do is to search his own mind to be sure he is reasonably confident that, if he did expose his theories for other scientists to challenge, they would not be easily refuted. Very often, however, he will be allowed to air his theories publicly within the employing group for debate, challenge and possible refutation. Some combination of these approaches is often felt by the employing group to confer a measure of objectivity on OR work.

It is to be presumed in all this that the employing group places some value on problem solution, or at least the solving of certain problems, and that this is to be aimed for. However, most groups value, to a greater or lesser extent than problem solution, solutions to problems about problems. Thus, solutions to the problem of how to alleviate problems, how to avoid them or to get warning of them, might be highly valued. The OR worker will in most groups be expected to be responsive to the group's values and to deal with problems in ways which attract the highest value to the group. This might be alleviation or suppression of the problem rather than some perfect but long-term solution. In short, OR has a value system akin to that of technology.

Different groups can be expected to have markedly different value systems. A commercial firm might value profit highly and, if profit flows from the solution of analytic problems, they will value the solution of such problems. A community group, uncertain of its wishes and ill informed about its environment, might prize solutions that amount to little more than a clear, understandable statement of its situation. Moreover, OR is not a free activity. Whether explicitly paid for or not, it absorbs resources, including the time of the relevant members of the employing group. The cost of doing the OR is to be set against its value. Most groups will look for approaches to problems that get as much of the value as quickly and as cheaply as possible.

THE TWO FACES OF OR

It will be seen from the above that OR has partly to do with helping to solve particular problems as they come along. When the group feels it faces a problem on which OR can help it may be appropriate to *define* the form that help is to take. In order to help it is likely that the OR worker will have to *collect data* about the relevant facts and about the beliefs and rules in the group, and often these data will have to be *analysed* to formulate other beliefs. There is usually more than one belief relevant to the problem in hand and the assembly of relevant beliefs is called a *model*. The model will often be used as a help to exercising *choice* among possible actions to help solve the problem. (The words in italics are the topics of the next four chapters.)

The preceding paragraph describes (albeit briefly) the process of OR applied to an individual problem. However, it is clear that OR has another face which manifests itself not usually in the course of work on one problem but rather through the stream of work which it undertakes on many problems. There are several considerations here. The OR work might develop new beliefs or rules which are not merely invoked to solve a single problem but which become part of the general group culture. Similar problems might thereby be avoided in future or solved without recourse to OR. OR might, in this and other ways, therefore change the employing group's culture. In particular, OR might extend the group's subjective perception of what problems are suitable for scientific attack.

To the extent that OR seeks to affect the employing group's culture, it might well have considerations other than short-term value in its choice of problems to attack. However, in discussing OR applied to a single problem, the thought will usually be of working within the present culture. Towards the end of the book there is a discussion of the more general issue of OR as an agent of cultural change and, among other things, how this stance might affect relations between OR and its employing group, and what impact it might have on the management of OR.

THE OR PROJECT

It would be usual to find the work of a group of OR workers organised into projects. Each project would probably comprise one or more well-defined tasks. There would usually be an associated plan of work with dates, an intended schedule of resource consumption, etc. Projects provide a convenient way of organising work, defining responsibility, exercising accountability, and generally administering the work of the OR group.

The project is, therefore, the natural unit in which to discuss the management of OR. It is not, however, necessarily the natural unit in which to discuss the OR activity. In many ways, it is more natural to discuss the activity in terms of OR engagement on issues or problems. Some projects will relate to many engagements. (For example, a project may relate to keeping a particular set of beliefs under review, the set being invoked to help deal with a variety of problems.) Perhaps more commonly, there will be many projects related to one engagement. The projects may sometimes be being worked in parallel, sometimes they may form a sequence, often there will be elements of both. (It would not be uncommon, for example, for a first project to reveal the extent of desirable engagement, leading to another project which in turn suggests some revision of the desirable engagement, and so on.)

At the risk of some simplification, it is reasonable to say that the remainder of this book is about engagement and only about projects where this is expressly stated.

Whether this matters in practice to someone engaged in OR depends, of course, on how projects are defined in the environment in which he works. Some OR groups will try, and this may very well be good practice, to define projects so that they are related to engagements as closely as possible, perhaps defining a succession of sub-projects within the larger project as the means of management. However, even then there are differences. Unless the project is very generally defined (which probably reduces its effectiveness as a means of management), the engagement will almost certainly and desirably diversify from the project plan. When this happens, it will usually be better to let the engagement develop and not stick slavishly to the project. (Of course, nothing is intended here as an argument against projects as a means of management. The argument is rather for well-defined tasks forming projects, or for a ready flexibility to consider redefining projects as circumstances change.)

In any case, the notion of a project has implications of a pre-defined task or set of tasks. There is some presumption of a start and a clear end point reached by a sequence of stages, such as defining the problem, collecting data, building a model, testing it and so on, culminating in getting a solution accepted and then implementing it. Life is never like that. Sometimes it is nearly enough like that to make no difference. More commonly, however, activities like defining the problem, data collection, model building and so on are more usefully regarded as continuous, concurrent activities. There is, in much practical OR, a sense of learning, of revising earlier ideas with new information, of re-defining the problem, of going back to collect more data and so on. Nor, in practice, is there usually an awareness that a solution has been reached. These practical points mean that the notion of engagement better reflects practice than the notion of project, insofar as project has some of these narrower connotations.

The notion of engagement seems also to capture other features of OR in practice. Associated with most problems is some sort of social process, that is, a variety of people interacting in ways caused by the existence of the problem. Very often they would be interacting in the absence of the problem, either in the field where the problem lies or perhaps in other fields. They might, for example, be some management team who are in daily interaction with each other to ensure the effective running of a part of a business. Someone invited to help with the problem, say an OR worker, is being invited, among other things, to join in that social process. The invitation is presumably issued because it is supposed that augmenting the social process will improve its handling of the problem.

Because the social process related to the problem is often the particular manifestation of a continuing social process, it is often said that the helper is intervening in the process. In some ways 'intervening', or 'making an intervention', are unfortunate words, as they carry some connotation of interference or officiousness, of poking one's nose into other people's business. Their use in this context is usually, however, intended to have a more neutral interpretation.

OTHER DEFINITIONS OF OR

The definition of OR given at the head of the chapter is not a very common one. It defines the methods to be deployed only very generally and the problems to be addressed as those the culture allows. It is more usual to define OR either by some more precise definition of methods used, or by a list of problems suitable for OR attack, or some combination of the two. This kind of definition is the one most commonly used for defining expert roles in any organised group. The definition given above does not offer OR an expert role but rather a 'help where the group thinks your general skills are useful' kind of role. It defines OR as (relatively) paradigm-free—the methods are those which scientists use, the problems those the culture allows. (Definitions of an activity which define the activity's methods and the problems it addresses are called paradigms.) There are many other possible paradigms and some are listed below. (Doubtless the reader can think of others.)

All those listed are included within the given definition, but are more—in some cases much more—restrictive about what constitutes OR. Some crucial questions (which are left to the reader to ponder) are:

(i)   Is any paradigm limiting or can it adapt as cultures change?
(ii)   What is the OR worker's response if a group's culture rejects a paradigm-based OR?

The *problem* paradigm says OR is useful for tackling named kinds of problems, for example those of allocating resources, scheduling, congestion, etc. It is often linked with the *techniques* paradigm: OR is the deployment of certain techniques, for example linear programming, simulation, etc. There are *views-of-the-world* paradigms which identify OR with a particular way of looking at the world and, therefore, of addressing problems; for example, OR is the systems approach, or OR is applied microeconomics, etc. (These views-of-the-world paradigms define problems and methods more subtly than the problems/techniques paradigms but no less surely.) All such paradigms are fine if that is what the person concerned wants to do, but are clearly limiting and invite a narrow expert role. The *optimisation* paradigm ('OR tells you the best way of doing things') limits OR to issues where there is a relevant consensus about what best means, which boils down to few and often rather trivial issues.

The *quantitative* paradigm ('OR is concerned with the quantitative aspects of a group's problems') is, if linked with some such statement as 'as defined by the group culture', very close to the given definition. However, it seems that quantitative methods, whose use this paradigm presumably implies, are unnecessarily restrictive: science deals with falsifiable statements which might be qualitative as much as quantitative.

The *modelling* paradigm ('OR works on modellable problems using modelling methodology') is, if qualified by linkage to the culture of the group, perhaps the most serious contender to the given definition. However, while many would agree that models are central to OR (particularly if viewed as testing devices or assemblages of relevant beliefs—see Chapter 8), there must be some doubt whether modelling is the OR paradigm. Rather, it would seem to be a paradigm for thoughtful problem solving which the group culture might or might not want, at least in an explicit form. OR might well have to contribute to problem solving by other means. (Often, the modelling paradigm is intended more narrowly than it is interpreted here, that is, specific kinds of model are intended. Moreover, the definition is sometimes narrower in the sense that modelling is depicted as culture-independent. These narrower definitions seem unsatisfactory.)

Finally, there is the *objectivity* paradigm ('OR takes an objective look at things'). Here 'an objective look' means a look which would be the same as taken by any member of some such group as scientists. The look is presumably intended to be helpful by illuminating some issue of interest. There is no doubt OR is prized by some managers as being objective in this sense. This paradigm can perhaps be criticised only for its narrowness. It is part of the given definition, but there will be times when the group's culture will value more highly contributions of other kinds from the OR worker.

MULTIPLICITY OF ROLES

The tighter the definition of an activity, the clearer the role of the person engaged in it. A consequence of the definition of OR given above is that, except at a general, abstract level, the OR worker's role is not well defined. At the general level, the OR worker is simply a helper or consultant of a particular kind, as noted earlier. However, in any particular manifestation of the OR activity, the OR worker is likely to be occupying, or be perceived to be occupying, a particular role. From the above it can be seen that roles such as modeller, researcher, change agent, etc. might be appropriate at different times.

The absence of a well-defined role for the OR worker has a mixture of good and bad effects—good because it allows the role appropriate to the circumstances; bad because it can prevent access to issues where the perceived required role is not associated with OR. It must be hoped that the good outweighs the bad in this balance, but if this view is accepted it means that ingenuity has sometimes to be deployed in order to get into issues where OR can help. Often the OR worker has to resort to getting in by exploiting one of the expert roles (e.g. model builder) and broadening his contribution from that base.

The particular role the OR worker adopts, or is forced to adopt, in relation to any problem is likely to be the consequence of negotiation. Usually, but not always, the OR worker will be a party to that negotiation. It will be for him, or others acting for him, to assess and advance the contribution he expects to be able to make to the resolution of the problem. His skill in weighing up the relevant cultural factors and in negotiating an appropriate role may well be the biggest determinant of the contribution OR can make. Sometimes the culture will press towards a role for the OR worker which limits his contribution unduly, perhaps even to the point of excluding him. This exclusion may not be deliberate but simply an oversight. This and related points are returned to later.

EXERCISES

(1) Consider the different dietary habits of two groups (e.g. families) known to you, including in diet the consumption of tobacco and alcohol. List some of the beliefs about diet which seem to distinguish these groups. For each group, classify the beliefs according to whether, for that group, they are
    (i)   Unsuitable for challenge by scientific means,
    (ii) Adopted for reasons which are not scientific but changeable by scientific means,
    (iii) Adopted for scientific reasons.
    Imagine each group was offered free OR consultancy to adapt the beliefs you have listed. What might each programme of OR work look like? Generalising the argument, two in-house OR groups in different companies in the same industry might have very different programmes of work. Discuss why this might be.

(2) Give examples of (a) belief manipulation, (b) checking of validity and mutual consistency of beliefs, and (c) generation of new beliefs or revisions of old ones, which might help Mr Bird (pages 1–3 and 10–12). Could the examples you quote be addressed scientifically? How could you assess whether Mr Bird would accept a scientific approach to your examples? Repeat this exercise for some decision you recently made. With hindsight, could you have made the decision

in a better way? Again, repeat the exercise for some decision you have yet to make. Does the exercise suggest better ways of making the decision than you might otherwise have used?

(3)   An ill-defined activity has no chance of making an impact in the world. Discuss this statement in relation to OR.

(4)   List characteristics of groups which
      (a)   Might be susceptible to OR,
      (b)   Might strongly decline OR help.
      Obtain what information you can about the use of OR in various companies, government departments, etc. to test your answer. Think carefully about any surprise the information reveals. Is it that your answer is wrong, or that you have false perceptions about OR or about the companies etc.?

(5)   Is OR just the considered application of common sense? Could any reasonably intelligent, educated person do OR? Why do organisations employ OR specialists?

(6)   Is it conceivable that an OR group employed by an organised group could work itself out of a job?

(7)   Among possible roles for an OR worker implicit in this chapter are those of a technical expert, a scientist, an agent of cultural change and a servant of a group's management. Is it possible to occupy more than one of these roles at the same time? Can they be switched about as an OR engagement develops?
      How important is it that the particular role the OR worker is playing should be made explicit to all concerned?

Chapter 6

_____ Defining Problems

This chapter addresses the question of defining the problem. It is not self-evident what defining the problem means. Possible meanings of the phrase are discussed followed by ways of carrying out the activity. In broad terms, it will be argued that defining problems means deciding on a course of action designed to alleviate the problem. If the OR worker is invited to engage in this activity, it is assumed he will do so in the spirit of determining the best course of action judged from the viewpoint of whoever has the problem, and not with any specific thought of defining work for himself.

THE REAL PROBLEM

People often talk about 'defining the real problem'. This is a potentially mis-leading phrase. What people who use the phrase are usually thinking of is defining some action which removes the present symptoms and stands a low chance of quickly generating new symptoms. This is an attitude to problem solving attaching high value to solutions of a particular kind. Clearly in this sense it is better to solve the 'real' problem, or at least as 'real' a problem as possible, other things being equal (costs and other resources may not be). The way to do this is to have sufficient understanding of the system under study to be able to anticipate the consequences of actions (including adverse consequences) and to be able to judge the likelihood of getting acceptance of actions—to aim to solve the 'real' problem might be a recipe for doing nothing, as the necessary solving actions might be unaccept-able to the relevant groups.

It is assumed here, as everywhere in the book, that the OR worker is interested only in problems which he believes to be real in the everyday sense of the word, that is, problems that worry real people in the real world. The phrase 'defining the real problem' is often used to mean finding what about the real world is causing concern as opposed to someone's guess about the cause which he has based on reflection or some imagined state of the world. This seems to be a legitimate use of the phrase, that is, the words can, in this context, be taken at their face value.

PROBLEM DEFINITION

Even so, it is not altogether problems that are defined so much as what it is intended to do and how it is intended to do it. Thus, in some messy problem situation it is not the problem that is defined so much as a problem on which it is proposed to work. Broadly speaking, this means defining some activity to engage in which it is thought will contribute to the easement of the problem.

The activity might take many forms. One form, when great clarity of definition is possible, is to choose a question which it is thought can be answered and which, if answered, would solve or alleviate the problem. This case would arise, for example, if the symptoms pointed to a single cause and there were a set of actions which would clearly remove this cause. The question would be simply: what action is it best to take? This simple case is so appealing that it might pay to reflect on means of making it useable in cases where it is not obvious how to proceed. Indeed a useful general rule in defining a problem is to ask: what questions would it be useful to know the answers to? Sometimes the activity will be directed to answering these questions. On other occasions it might be more useful to concentrate on constructing the means to answer them. And then again much time might have to be spent deciding which questions are usefully answered.

All the above applies to anybody in any role. It applies to an OR worker helping, perhaps as a team member, to define a problem. In actually working on the problem, answering the questions, the OR worker can, of course, expect to be engaged on those questions which, in the context of the group culture, it is appropriate for him to address.

METHODS OF PROBLEM DEFINITION

Suppose, then, that a problem is defined once a question can be posed which it is believed can be answered. How can this defined problem be reached from the symptoms?

It seems worth isolating four ways. First, there is the irrational but often correct process of relying on some mixture of intuition and experience: I have been in this situation before and it's usually this that is wrong. The question then is simply how to rectify the wrong.

Second, there is the 'suck it and see' approach on which experiments with different defined problems (and sometimes their solutions) are made until the right one is found. In this approach the problems may be tried in a completely arbitrary way or the solver may follow a well-defined order of testing. Thus, if someone's motor car stops suddenly he might just test every part in a haphazard way or, if he knows what he is about, he will follow a well-defined path of testing. Such ordered lists are usually based on considerable experience and it is quite noticeable that they are followed by professional problem solvers like those attending broken-down motor cars. They are, however, particular to given situations, and are really useful only in dealing with problems which recur many times over.

This second approach starts with a list of problems with which the symptoms are consistent and eliminates problems from the list one by one. Even where it is recurrent problems of the same type that are being dealt with, this approach would not be especially efficient if the number of possible problems were large. This suggests the possibility of a third approach, which starts from the symptoms and constructs the set of possible problems from them. If this set has one member it is the defined problem. If not, the procedure helps decide what question(s) to ask in order to discriminate further between possible problems, and so on. This is essentially the method of diagnosis as followed in medical practice.

This third approach can usefully be undertaken in a systematic way. The power of a systematic approach, even if it is based on exceedingly simple principles, should not to be underestimated. If the approach is any good, it will force logical action and the sensible ordering of thoughts, neither of which is always natural. Such an approach might, for example, require a clear written statement of when and when not the symptoms occur, where and where not, how frequently etc. This will often eliminate a surprising number of possible causes. Often it will reduce the number of causes to a manageable number, which can be decided among by answering one or two more simple questions.

The fourth approach, which is more sophisticated than the other three and probably cannot be fully implemented except in simple cases, is so to design a system that there is a one-to-one and obvious correspondence between all possible sets of symptoms and the full list of possible problems. In an engineering design context, this might mean investing in extensive monitoring facilities at the manufacturing stage. In a managerial context it means having a system of management control which is such that any given set of departures from desired behaviour has a unique explanation. Such systems do exist in certain rudimentary management situations. For example, if actual cash and the totals recorded on the cash registers do not match up in a supermarket, the problem would in many cases be automatically reduced to what cashier X is doing wrong. However, more ambitious attempts to design self-diagnosing systems, while they commonly help in the process of problem definition, do not always complete the process. In some cases, they might be mistaken: the existence of problems which do not self-diagnose may be suppressed and difficult to recognise.

RISKS IN DEFINING PROBLEMS

Progressing from symptoms to a defined problem carries a number of risks. One is the obvious one that the wrong problem is defined, or putting it another way, it is decided to do something which is useless. There are many reasons why this trap might be fallen into. Common ones include over-ambition about people's (including the person's own) ability to produce useful results or the rate at which they can do so; mistaken assumptions about what the implicit rules of the relevant group culture will allow to be done (and there are often plenty of people around ready to use these rules to frustrate someone working on a problem in ways they dislike or distrust); and mistaken assumptions about the status of the problem as it is perceived by the powerful members of the group facing the problem. This last point can be a great time-waster. Someone persuades the OR worker that the group has a problem. The OR worker works away at a defined problem relevant to it and he offers a solution which the person who said there was a problem is powerless to act on. Too late the OR worker will sometimes find that those with the power to act did not even think there was a problem in the first place. It is a good general rule (by no means only in OR) to consider involving all those people whose power to act might be necessary to solve the problem (the possible problem owners), to participate in defining it (and prior to this, if necessary, to secure their agreement that there is a problem). This might be extended to securing, at the outset, the powerful person's or persons' commitment to the defined problem and to its foreseeable action implications. Both the problem and the defined problem are subjective and might well be influenced by the power structure in the group. It is sometimes desirable to accept this. At other times the OR worker might perceive a deeper or different problem than the power structure defines and choose to challenge the powerful.

Another risk is that time spent defining a problem is that much more time for the problem to persist (generally speaking—there are obvious qualifications to this statement). Likewise, it is that much more time for the problem to change—so that the right problem for the then-observed symptoms is the wrong problem for the symptoms that might now be observed. As a general rule, symptoms should be monitored, which means keeping a check not only on the data which constitute the symptoms but also on the group's continued dissatisfaction with the symptoms, while defining the problem and while working on it. Problems disappear as a consequence of changes in the real world or in people's concerns more often than is sometimes thought.

All these risks are worth a little care to avoid. An ideal approach to defining problems would do so. It would define the right (in every sense) problem quickly. But it is impossible to produce such an approach of universal validity. Different approaches give different weights to these risks. It is up to the individual to decide what weights he desires.

WHY ARE YOU THERE?

Assuming an OR worker is invited to help someone or some group with his or their problem, the invitation is of itself an interesting fact. Those issuing the invitation presumably had some reason or reasons for doing so. If the OR worker can determine what these are, he may be helped in deciding his contribution both to defining the problem and to working on it. (Of course, the invitation might be conditional on his doing a specified thing. He might accept it on those terms, but if he finds the specified thing is useless or judges it unethical or otherwise unsatisfactory, he will presumably seek to renegotiate his position or even, in extremes, withdraw altogether.)

Obviously those with responsibility for addressing the problem (assuming they invited the OR worker in, or, if not them, whoever did) are a natural group with whom to discuss definition of the problem. Their reasons for inviting him might take many forms. They could simply be desperate and looking for help from anybody. They may have vague feelings that research of some kind will help. Or, perhaps most likely of all, they have some prior perception that work of a kind they know he can do will be useful. The true reason may take some digging out. It is a commonplace that actions are often taken for different reasons than those openly declared. In this context, for example, the OR worker must be wary of an undeclared political motivation hiding behind a professed quest for objectivity. In other cases, the person who issues the invitation may be looking for help which he is too proud to admit needing, and his declared reasons for inviting the OR worker in may again disguise his true motivation.

PROBLEMS OF CONFLICT

Much or all of the above, and most of what follows, assumes it is the problem definer himself, or some individual person for whom he is acting, who has the problem (or, if a group, that there is such a consensus within the group as to make it as if it were an individual). An important source of problems is simply disagreement within a group. If this disagreement is about some matter which all parties agree would be settled by research into the facts, the problem is easily defined. The appropriate response is the necessary research. If the disagreement is more basic or over value beliefs—for example, about corporate objectives—again the problem is not hard to define, but it might then be asked whether OR has a role in its resolution.

There appear to be two sensible ways forward here. The first is for the OR worker to accept one of the arguing parties as his client, and to address the problem from that party's standpoint. The defined problem might then be a question whose answering will help the client's case or his (or their) beating off of the opposition. A second way forward is for the OR worker to negotiate—or, more likely, to have negotiated for him—a role which is acceptable to all who are arguing. This role is likely to be one of clearing the ground of unnecessary factual disputes and/or structuring the debate so as to facilitate its sensible resolution. Thus, the OR worker might work in a research mode to clarify matters of fact, or in a modeller (see later chapters) mode to assemble the relevant beliefs, who holds them, which of them can be checked against facts and/or which are inconsistent among themselves. Rather similar remarks apply, with obvious amendment, to disagreements between the OR worker's own employing group and other groups. (Of course, unless the OR worker is prepared to make the compromises implied in this paragraph, he stands a fair chance of being excluded from such problems.)

Needless to say, there is no generally right or wrong way to enter and act in these or any other problem situations. The skilful intervener will be the one who, more often than not, makes the right choices in each particular case about:

(i)   The role he should adopt.
(ii)   The question to address.
(iii) The approaches to adopt.
(iv)   When to withdraw.

SPECIFIC APPROACHES

Many problems will, however, have around them a reasonable consensus about the existence of a problem, about the desire to do something about it, and about belief in the relevant theories or how they should be constructed. Experience suggests that some approaches to defining such problems are better than others. Three possible approaches are discussed below. Before this discussion, however, it is timely to recall that defining problems is heavily culture-dependent. What follows does not labour this point but it should be read with it in mind.

Approach 1 (best suited to operational problems)

Suppose everyone concerned with a problem agrees that the symptoms are clear-cut and quantifiable (or attributive); the nature of the system is that its cause and effects are well understood and agreed by all (qualitatively at least); and the general nature of possible causes (i.e. possible problems) is well known and agreed. These assumptions are often true of the general running of a plant or factory, for instance. Then it is a fair guess that a clear statement of effects will allow the cause to be identified. (By definition, the converse is true unless everyone is united in error.) The defined problem is then work related to how to act so as to rectify the cause. (It is obviously helpful to problem definition if these assumptions are true. If it is thought a system is likely to be a continuing source of problems it might pay to mount research effort designed to make the assumptions true, by, for example, constructing a detailed model of a factory and logging and analysing the problems that do occur. More generally, such an approach might lead to the important possibility that problems could be anticipated and contingent solutions be made available.)

Such thinking leads naturally to the idea that a list of effects (including non-effects) should be systematically drawn up and possible causes tested against them. The true cause will be the one that produces the listed effects, *however far the list is extended.* A possible procedure is as follows.

(1) Pick one of the effects observed.
(2) For this effect note when and when not it was observed, where and where not, its extent in space and time and its non-extent.
(3) Select a further effect observed and repeat 2 for this effect. Repeat 3 until all known effects are exhausted.
(4) Postulate a cause. Does it account for *all* the effects and when and when not etc. they were observed? If it does not, repeat 4 with another cause. If it does, turn to step 5.
(5) Are there other causes which also account for the effects? If so, think of another effect which would distinguish between them. Repeat 5 until only one cause is left.

For example, sales of a certain product were badly down this year compared with last. Comparing month by month they were down in June–September inclusive but not in other months; in June–September they were down in London but not elsewhere. We must therefore, look for some cause which distinguishes between June–September in London and any other combination of months and places. *Any suggested cause which does not make this distinction is likely to be wrong.*

A point which is frequently important in this type of problem is that change often causes problems. In analysing when the symptoms occurred it is often helpful to look for changes in the system that correlate in time with the symptoms, making allowance for relevant time lags.

Approach 2 (best suited to problems of organisation and control)

Symptoms of a control or organisation problem can be said to occur when the component parts of a system (e.g. individual decision makers, individual physical processes) are behaving as desired but the total effectiveness of the system is *not* what is desired. It can thus be inferred that cause and effect in the system are not understood. It is natural to seek to understand them as a means of discovering the cause of the trouble.

As an aid to defining problems in this context a procedure along the following lines might be pursued:

(1) Establish the true measure of effectiveness of the system, i.e. what those responsible for the system believe they are really trying to do—it might be necessary to debate with care what this is, as it is often not easily articulated by those concerned. (A possibly redundant step, but worth doing as it might 'destroy' the problem if everyone is getting worked up about nothing.)

(2) Draw up a logical schema of the way the system works at the moment. The precise form of this will vary from problem to problem but it should show clearly:
  (a) The decisions and subsequent actions which might be taken at various points in the system;
  (b) Their relationship with one another, in two senses: the order in which they are taken and the effect any decisions have on subsequent ones.

(3) Is there any decision untaken, action unspecified or question unasked, which should be in order to ensure effectiveness? (The questions unasked often include ones about the environment or about other groups, including competing groups.) If *yes*, a problem is defined, if *no*, go to 4.

(4) Are there any decisions and actions being taken which the formal system does not recognise? If *yes*, are they the cause of the problem? If *yes* to this, the cause is obviously identified and the problem is one of redefining the procedures to take account of this (often involuntary or institutionalised) decision taking. If *no*, then carry on.

(5) Inspection might now define a problem, but if not then for each decision and action step, answer the following questions.
  (a) What would be the effect of omitting this step? (Why, therefore, is it in?)
  (b) What would be the effect of speeding up this step?
  (c) What would be the effect of changing the placing of this step in relation to other steps (as appropriate)?

(6) From the answers, can enough be inferred to define a problem? If *yes*, the problem is defined, but if *no* the cause must almost certainly be

looked for in the system being controlled: this is probably being mis-understood in some fundamental way and the misunderstanding is leading to wrong answers somewhere in step 5.

For example, a company is concerned about its capital investment proce-dures. All stages of the process work well: there is no shortage of ideas for new investment; they are selected between in a thorough, workmanlike way; and those chosen for implementation are quickly and effectively implemented. Nevertheless, the company has a poor return on capital invested.

Taking the steps one by one, it might be found that the true measure of effectiveness is indeed return on capital invested and this is poor; steps 2 and 3, however, might elicit that while each individual investment is thor-oughly analysed there are important interactions of which account is not taken (e.g. investment A is very good if investment B is not undertaken, but poor if it is). Suppose, however, steps 2 and 3 revealed nothing. Step 4 might reveal that the attractiveness of some investment opportunities is being exaggerated because competitors are known to be active on similar lines. Step 5, if reached, might show, for example, that the selection process is so lengthy that competitors steal a march on the company and thus reduce the company's returns. Finally, if step 6 is reached and answered 'no', it might be that the kinds of things here instanced as determined at earlier stages were not known and need to be found out.

Approach 3 (best suited to policy problems)

Most groups have rules called 'policies'. Policies usually presume cause and effect are understood and seek to take advantage of this presumed under-standing so as to constrain, for the common good, choice-making freedom in the group. The constraints are often referred to as policy decisions. Three common kinds of policy decision are:

(a) An increase in A causes an increase in the objective function (e.g. 'If productivity is up, so are profits'). Choice makers are invited to increase A as their criterion.
(b) For choices of type X no alternatives but one—the policy—are allowed (e.g. uniform priorities in recruitment rules between factories).
(c) All choices of type Y will be made after the performance of the same mechanical steps (e.g. a uniform scheme for appraising capital invest-ment decisions). ((b) pre-empts the choice, (c) says how it will be made.)

Normally policy decisions are not lightly taken and it is a fair bet that they are (or were, when taken) right in some sense. However, they are sometimes imposed by the powerful members of a group without consensus support, or what consensus support there was at the time they were taken might break down. In such cases the policy decisions may be questioned. Four common reasons for questioning policy decisions are:

(i)   It was (and still is) simply wrong, i.e. made in error;
(ii)   The premises upon which it is based are no longer valid;
(iii)   It is inconsistent with responsible and/or flexible management or restrictive of reasonable freedom—too rigid, too authoritarian etc.;
(iv)   The critic has some personal axe to grind, or the criticising sub-group find the policy inconsistent with their personal desires.

If asked to re-appraise a policy decision it is well to know on what grounds it is being questioned. It is also well to be sure of the status of whoever is asking for the re-appraisal in relation to the policy-making process. Care should be taken over (iv): it is usually invidious to be put into the position of grinding another man's axe for him, unless accepted consciously.

Again there may be merit in approaching this kind of problem systematically. A possible broad procedure is sketched below.

(1)   Be sure of the grounds of criticism. (People often do not like to admit to (iv) above and some care may be necessary to avoid being misled.)
(2)   Be absolutely sure why, by whom, and in what circumstances the policy was established. (Surprises can occur here: policies are often adopted for very non-obvious reasons. Quite a useful question here is what would have happened if the policy had not been in place. In general, a good device for understanding why something is the case is to imagine it were not, or its converse were, and to work out the consequences.)
(3)   Are the reasons valid as of now? If *yes*, there is no problem. (Some of the reasons may have been subjective and the right current person should be asked if he subscribes to these same subjective reasons.) If *no*, list carefully what has changed and *go to 4*.
(4)   Do these changes call for a revision of policy? This is perhaps best tackled negatively: what harm is the present policy doing? There are questions at two levels here: is it harming the group's performance (e.g. by causing serious undesirable resource misallocation, by 'tramlining' the organisation and preventing innovation or obscuring the need for change); and is it jeopardising the group's cohesiveness (e.g. by causing a significant number of the group's members to act in ways which as individuals they find undesirable).

The questions at step 4 often call for careful thought if profound points are not to be missed. A lot of talking can be useful at this stage. It is sometimes helpful to diagnose every word of a policy statement, asking where, when, how etc. of it. For example, a company may have a policy: 'We will manu- facture our own plant spares.' Ask why we; who else might; what are the pros and cons of we versus others; how will we (what investment in machine tools is required); why do we have spares anyway? It may also be helpful to list the various interested parties and to analyse the policy from their points of view.

By now a problem is usually defined. A few suggested steps in its reso- lution follow.

(5) If a revision of policy is called for, be bold in thinking of alternatives. The harm the present policy is doing will point to better alternatives, and the detailed questioning suggested in 4 will encourage boldness.
(6) Choose the alternative and expose it widely to those it will concern, at least as far as confidentiality allows. Listen carefully to any criticism, and be sure that any criticism can be answered (or explained away) and accommodate it if necessary.
(7) If possible test the policy out in a limited way first.

A FOURTH TYPE OF APPROACH

Approaches 1, 2 and 3 are appropriate where there is a relevant consensus and the problem is reasonably well understood or it appears to have the potential of being. Other approaches may well be appropriate for ill-under- stood problems involving several parties among whom there is not an obvious consensus. In such cases some possibly important considerations, all already mentioned, in problem definition include:

(a) Ensuring that the problem owner(s) is/are committed to the line of action it is proposed to take to tackle the problem.
(b) Ensuring that other interested parties are identified and their views understood.
(c) Obtaining a clear understanding of why the parties feel there is a problem—what dissatisfies them, what options they see, why they are experiencing difficulty in choosing actions. Some of these issues may be political, all are likely to have a social dimension and many will be subjective. Some will be rooted in history.

Various ways of proceeding in circumstances when these considerations matter have been proposed and used to good effect. A common thread is to have all the interested parties—or at least those powerful enough to com- mand a place—together for some more or less structured discussion about the problem. An outsider acts as leader and stimulator of the discussion. Commitment tends to be high and, given skilful leadership, issues are revealed which might otherwise remain hidden.

The emphasis of this approach is on guided self-help in defining problems. The discussion leader is often referred to as a facilitator. A common outcome is a programme of agreed actions (i.e. a defined problem) which might all be undertaken by others than the facilitator. The same approach persists through to the solution point (that is, of course, the point when it is decided it is not worth going on).

This approach might be used to define any problem of any kind, particularly if the joint commitment of several parties is required to solve the problem. (It may be the means by which approaches 1, 2 and 3, or parts of them, are actually carried out.) However, it might be felt that the approach should be used relatively sparingly as it can be costly in people's time. Generally its use is likely to commend itself where getting the people together is of itself desirable as a means of making progress, and where the issue addressed justifies the expense. Reshaping company strategy might satisfy these conditions.

This approach can take many different particular forms. Many of these forms presume that the participants come with goodwill, or at least can be induced to display it. Any such approach can break down if sufficiently powerful participants are set against it or the directions in which it is leading them. Their opposition may not be made explicit, of course. They may stall, or even lie, in a superficially co-operative manner.

APPENDIX I: THE BARTON MEMORANDUM

Milkomatic are a firm which manufactures and hires out automatic milk-selling machines. When a buyer puts in the right coin, the machine fills a plastic half-litre container from a pool of containers held in the machine with milk which comes from a refrigerated reservoir of milk also held in the machine. The container is automatically sealed and fed out to the buyer. If either the pool of containers or the reservoir of milk is empty, the machine automatically switches a light to empty and returns inserted coins.

There are currently about 8000 Milkomatic machines installed throughout Great Britain. Each machine is the subject of a three-way contract between the hirer (typically a cinema manager, a garage owner or a shop manager interested in out-of-hours sales), a milk supplier (sometimes a local farmer but more usually a large milk retail firm) and Milkomatic. Milkomatic receive a fixed hiring fee and are responsible for mechanical and electrical maintenance which is done by rota or, if necessary, when breakdowns are reported. They also decide when to replace old machines. Milkomatic have no responsibility for filling the machines with either containers or milk, nor are they responsible for cleaning the machines, though the contract does specify that the hirer and supplier, as relevant, must do these things according to rules set down by Milkomatic.

Milkomatic's organisation is a simple one. There is a Chief Executive, who is also the Company Secretary and nephew of the owner, who is retired. The manufacturing takes place on one site under the Works Director. There are small Scientific and Financial Departments under the Scientific and Finance Directors respectively. The Marketing and Maintenance Departments, each of which has a Director, are the biggest activities and are regionalised. The Marketing Department, as well as seeking new hirers, also puts suppliers and hirers into contact if necessary. Supplier's standards are monitored by five supply officers who are in the Marketing Department and between them cover the country. Displayed on each machine is a prominent notice which says 'In case of complaint write to the Chief Executive, Milkomatic ....' and the address.

Very few letters of complaint have been received. Until a month ago, the record was 13 complaints in a month. The complaints have always been met by a standard letter, apologising, promising to look into the matter and enclosing five tokens suitable for use in Milkomatic machines (and cashable by the hirers with Milkomatic). 'Looking into the matter' means simply noting on the appropriate maintenance man's sheet which machine is complained of so that he can check it thoroughly when next he calls. If the letter does not specify which machine is complained of—and about half do not—no action is taken.

Last month, 485 letters of complaint were received. Not surprisingly, the Chief Executive is worried about this. Jack Barton, recently taken on as his general assistant, has been asked to get to the root of the problem. Here is his report.

Memo from Jack Barton to Chief Executive

(1) I have looked through the 485 letters of complaint received in the last month. The letters seem to come from all over the place. Most complain about the milk tasting strangely. This is unusual as, prior to this month, most complaint letters were about machine malfunctioning. I therefore believe we are faced with a totally new problem.

(2) I should say straightaway that there is no obvious cause. All I can do in this report, therefore, is to list possible causes. This I have done, together with the comments of the relevant managers and the actions they plan to take. With any luck these actions will cure the problem or at least help to define it.

(3) **The weather.** As you know, parts of the country have had hot, humid, weather and it is possible this has turned the milk in some machines sour. The scientists are going to carry out laboratory tests to see if this is the explanation. Meanwhile the Chief Designer is closely examining the design of the reservoir linings and the refrigeration unit of the machines to see if they offer any clues.

(4) **Suppliers.** Perhaps some of our suppliers are letting us down. All the supply officers have been told to work seven days a week to check on this possibility.

(5) **Maintenance and/or cleaning.** I find our maintenance men have been falling badly behind schedule owing to illness and holidays. They are now practically all at work and have been asked to work unlimited overtime to get back to schedule. I think this is the most likely explanation of the problem, though the Maintenance Director cannot see any direct link between maintenance and the taste of the milk. Closely related to maintenance is cleaning. We have recently authorised the use of a new sterilising liquid, but the Scientific Director tells me this is absolutely safe and cannot be the cause.

(6) **Markets.** I checked to see whether we have moved into any new markets recently. We have expanded so rapidly that I thought our salesmen might have

been keener on their commission than on vetting hirers and suppliers. However, the Marketing Director assures me there is nothing to worry about and the statistics, which give number of installations by region and type (e.g. cinema, shop, garage, etc.), remain in the same proportions as ever.

(7) **Manufacture.** If there had been any change in manufacturing recently this might have been the cause, but the Works Director tells me new machines and spare parts are all being made in the same way and from the same materials as for the past five years.

(8) I am sorry we have not yet got to the bottom of this, but I hope you will agree the actions we are taking, which I assure you are being most energetically pursued.

APPENDIX II: BROWNS BROTHERS' DISCOUNTS

Browns Brothers is a large department store in a major shopping centre. Each section (e.g. men's outerwear) is run by a section head who places orders for replacement stock. The orders are countersigned by the head of the relevant department (e.g. clothing). There are about 50 section heads, each of whom reports to one of the 10 or so retail department heads. Orders are made out on standard forms and are placed through a central order office, who 'file' copies of all orders on a computer system.

Goods are received into Supplies Department who stock the goods by sections in a well-laid-out and equipped store. Each section head visits the store weekly and inspects the goods delivered for his or her section. If the goods are satisfactory, the section head signs a goods received note (g.r.n.) which has previously been made out in Supplies Department; if not, Supplies Department return the defective goods to the supplier. Goods with a signed g.r.n. are taken by Supplies Department staff to the counters as needed. Sometimes recently received goods are needed at the counters before a section head's weekly visit to the store. If so, the section head can sign a g.r.n. brought with the goods to the counter. Signed g.r.n.'s are sent to the order office for computer filing.

Invoices from suppliers go direct to the order office. There the invoices are checked for price against the supplier's catalogue and the details of the invoice are entered into the computer system. The system next checks the arithmetic of the invoice. Each item on the invoice is then checked to be sure that it was ordered by matching it to the related copy order. Finally it is checked to see that it was received by matching the related g.r.n. (This last check is a frequent cause of delay as an invoice can be received before the g.r.n. by which this check is made.) If the prices and arithmetic are correct and all items were ordered and are known to have been received in satisfactory condition, a cheque to cover the invoice is printed and passed to the firm's accountant, who authorises payment which is usually made that day or the next. Any queries about an invoice are taken up by the order office and no invoice is passed for payment, in whole or part, until it is fully query-free. Often the resolution of a query entails waiting for a new invoice.

Many invoices offer discounts for prompt payment, typically 5% for payment within a week, or perhaps $2^1/_2\%$ for payment within a month, compared with net payment within three months. A lot of these discounts are being missed.

The accountant has pointed this out to the other senior managers over lunch and all have agreed that he should take any reasonable steps to reduce the delays in invoice settlement. It is clear to the accountant that the present system is highly likely to miss weekly discounts, particularly if the supplier is posting the invoice at the same time as he dispatches the goods. It is also likely that monthly discounts are being missed quite often simply by the tempo of the invoice-checking procedure and the occasional build-up of backlogs of invoices awaiting checking.

The accountant therefore orders the following actions:

(i) All invoices which offer a discount are to be marked on receipt and to be given prompt treatment at every stage;
(ii) The order section are to take on a temporary clerk whenever a backlog of uncleared invoices builds up; and
(iii) Section heads are to visit the stores daily so that g.r.n.s are signed on the day of receipt of the goods.

EXERCISES

(1) Look again at the ABC Airline case (page 58). From the point of view of ABC Airline, see whether approaches 2 and 3 of this chapter offer any help in defining the problem. List two or three key questions you think need answering. Could answers be found quickly enough to be helpful? What questions need answers before the preceding question can be answered sensibly?

(2) Consider the case in Appendix I above. Has Jack Barton acted sensibly? If you think not, what should he have done? Is there, in any case, a good argument for trying everything and getting everyone involved?

(3) Consider the case in Appendix II above.
   (i) Make your own analysis of the situation described. Does Browns Brothers have a problem? Are the actions the accountant is taking useful? And if so, to whom?
   (ii) If asked to work on this issue by the chief executive of Browns Brothers, what questions would you want him to answer before you started? Would it be worth considering radical change? Does this alter the questions?
   (iii) The accountant appears to have acted with minimal quantitative analysis. Discuss what figures he might usefully have obtained? How accurate need these have been?
   (iv) Does the way a company is organised affect the problems it perceives? Does it affect the solutions it finds? Illustrate your answers by reference to Browns Brothers.

(4) Identify a problem you have which you are willing to discuss with friends. Persuade a few friends to sit with you to try to define the problem. Reflect on the process afterwards. Was it useful? How could it have been made more useful? Could the process have benefited by the

presence of someone with specialist knowledge? When, in the process, did you realise this? How might you decide whether it is worth buying specialist advice as an aid to defining problems?

(5) Is 'problem owner' a helpful concept? Try to decide who is/are the problem owner/s in the various cases so far given in the book. Would the concept have helped with those?

(6) The case often arises that a group accept there is a group problem but the members of the group would define it differently. Reflect on the Browns Brothers' case (pages 88–89), on Mr Bird's dilemma (pages 1–3), and on Service Providers (pages 59–62). List, in each case, different problems the different actors might define. How is such a case to be treated? Should a course of action be sought that meets everyone's concerns, or should negotiation of some less embracing action be attempted? Who should take responsibility for doing what? Illustrate your answers by reference to one or more of the cases.

(7) Think of a situation in which you believe someone has a problem but the person does not appear to think he has. Why is this so? If you wished to persuade the person that he has a problem, how might you go about it? In particular, is defining a problem a means of drawing attention to the existence of the problem?

(8) Assuming Emma agrees to do the work, what problem should she work on in the Service Providers case (pages 59–62)?

Chapter 7

——— Data Collection and Analysis

The process of observing things in the real world and describing them in words or numbers, written or spoken or thought, is usually called data collection: summarising the data collected, and determining patterns and relationships among the data, is usually called data analysis. The greater part of this chapter offers advice about collecting and analysing data, but first a number of general points are made.

DATA AND INFORMATION

The view is sometimes expressed that there is a distinction between data and information. According to this view, data are the impressions someone receives, in a whole variety of ways, about the part of the world of interest to him. They include sense impressions, casually generated facts and figures, recorded or not, and also purposefully collected facts and figures. Such data can be expected to reveal specific things, such as the temperature at some named place at a named time, or the price of a particular share immediately before a change in fiscal legislation. However, it could well be a tedious process to answer questions on the basis of the probably haphazard assembly of impressions, facts and figures, which the data are. The data become information when they are assembled into such a form that any reasonable and relevant question can be answered quickly. What constitutes a reasonable and relevant question depends, of course, on context. In this sense it might be said that data become information when they are made useable and useful in a context.

The assemblage of the data which transforms them into information could take many forms. One such, for example, would be simply to have the data written down in some orderly manner. Another may be to store them in an easily accessed relational database on a personal computer. There is also the possibility of analysing or summarising the data in some useful way and making the results available on paper or on a computer, and so on. Information in this sense might be called structured data.

This distinction between data and information can no doubt be helpful in many contexts, and no doubt the words are used in various parts of this book in ways which imply that distinction. However, the distinction is one which is not easy to uphold operationally. It seems easier to use the words 'data' and 'information' nearly interchangeably, with, where relevant, the degree of orderliness or structure of the data being explicitly indicated.

DATA COLLECTION

Data collection is not, of course, a totally controlled or controllable activity. Unless someone is peculiarly insensitive or purposely isolates himself, data are continually collecting themselves, so to speak, for his attention. In that sense anyone is, or has the potential to be, collecting and analysing data for all or much of the time. This is not a trivial point. The data wanted in most contexts include not only the numerical information which the word 'data' commonly invokes, but also information about the culture in which the problem of interest is set. This latter information may not (for many reasons) all be purposefully gatherable; it might therefore pay to be listening and looking all the time. Nevertheless, some considered process of data collection can be expected to be superior to its accidental acquisition, and this chapter tends to imply purposeful data collection.

Note also that data collection is not usually (if ever) something to be done before moving on to the next stage. (Data collection is sometimes presented as one phase in a sequence of phases making up an OR project. This is dangerously misleading.) Data collection is the means by which an understanding of what is going on is maintained as well as acquired. In turn this allows the sense, or otherwise, of what is being done to be kept under continuous review. It must be viewed as a continuous activity. The world changes all the time. It does not stop doing so because data have been collected about it. (Thus, in discussing problem definition, it was suggested that symptoms should be monitored so as to keep the relevance of the defined problem under review. The relevance of data also changes as ideas develop, as understanding increases and as theory conjecture is essayed. Even in a relatively unchanging world it should be expected, perhaps arguably encouraged, that important data will be challenged, necessitating more data collection, followed by more challenges and so on.)

Data are usually intended to serve a purpose. The attainment of the purpose is presumably valued and hence data have a value. Data which frustrate a purpose are not likely to be highly valued by those who value the attainment of the purpose and vice versa. It would be nice to think that scientists valued the pursuit of truth and that to them data were valued for their power to discriminate between rival theories. This is not always so.

Scientists sometimes become highly attached to their own theories and value highly data which corroborate them and vice versa. Other people can be similarly unscrupulous. Commonly, people dispute data which appear to refute cherished hypotheses—they deny their accuracy, argue they are not typical etc.—but do not look so critically at data which seem confirmatory. Such behaviour is sometimes transparent, but it can be insidiously disguised or subconscious. Everyone is prey to such behaviour.

Collecting and analysing data is heavily belief dependent in other ways. A person measuring the length of a pencil commonly invokes numerous beliefs (that his eyes can be relied on, that the ruler is suitably calibrated etc.) which he would not usually think of checking. In more complicated cases, what constitutes the right data is belief laden. Thus, suppose the capacity of a piece of equipment is requested. As a concept this has numerous definitions. The choice among these definitions would probably be made by some value belief connected with the purpose in collecting the data about capacity. Someone intent on suing the supplier for supplying a defective machine might use output per hour under normal working conditions, including time broken down; someone else, out to strike a hard piece-rate bargain with the equipment operators, might use output per hour attainable by automata and assume totally reliable operation. However, even when a person has chosen his definition, he may not be out of the trap of his own beliefs, for suppose he chooses to assess the maximum possible output per hour of the machine. He might do so by finding the maximum output recorded in any hour of the last year—embodying the beliefs that the maximum has been attained and that the records are reliable among many others. Or he might postulate some ideal method of working the equipment, based on numerous engineering and organisational beliefs, and manipulate these beliefs to determine capacity.

Much of the above is intended as a reminder that data collection and analysis is not a neutral activity. The data do not speak for themselves, they speak for the data collector, analyst or user. These points will not be laboured further but they should be borne in mind in reading what follows.

KINDS OF DATA AND DATA SOURCES

At the risk of some simplification, there are three kinds of data of potential interest to the OR worker.

(1) *Physical data*, e.g. how a system works physically, how big a thing is, what its capacity is, how much something costs, etc.—put another way, data about which there is a relevant consensus that it is measurable.

(2) *Data about the organisation surrounding an issue and the organisation's behaviours*, e.g. who reports to whom, what information flows, what the choice-making mechanisms are, etc.—that is, the organisational aspects of any relevant culture, including power patterns.

(3) *Data about policy and about the limits and constraints relevant to an issue*, e.g. constraints and behaviours imposed by corporate policy, by other cultural norms or by aspects of the environment including relevant history, etc. (but not all physical constraints many of which would come under (1))—that is, the wider rules and value beliefs of any relevant culture, including the goals and aims embodied in it.

In order to gather data, various sources can be utilised. Again risking some simplification, five sources are relevant to the OR worker. There are, in any large group, usually two readily available sources, namely

(a) *Recorded information*, e.g. the accounts, written descriptions of processes, files, data banks, operators' log books, etc.

(b) *Personal knowledge*, e.g. simply asking people what information they have, interviewing them or asking them to fill in questionnaires, etc. A case where this is really the only source of data is when the subjective opinions or beliefs of the people concerned are the required data. These opinions might be 'what do you think of ...?', the answer being a value judgement, or they might be the beliefs that lie behind decisions and actions, themselves recorded or observable, which the person is taking.

It is as well to expect that much, perhaps most, information in and about an organisation will not be written down, in a codified, accessible manner. Information about how things work and about how things get done, often, perhaps usually, resides in people's brains. So also, very often, does the means of accessing written-down information and interpreting it, as to both meaning and validity. To this extent (b) is often a precursor to (a), or a successor to (a) so as to be sure about what (a) has generated. This important point is also relevant to much that follows. A third source of data is

(c) *Measurement and observation*, e.g. field work in which the someone actually goes out and observes, counts, measures, etc.

There is a rather hazy line between (c) and (a). If summary statistics about a process are available on a sheet produced every week as a routine, this would probably be best regarded as an (a) type source, but if the summary statistics are required, are not available and can be got only by the examination of crude source data, the collection might be thought of as coming in the (c) category or perhaps in some notional (a)/(c) category.

Kinds of Data and Data Sources

Sources (a), (b) and (c) are meant to imply a passive role for lector and for those for whom the data is to be collected. A fou: data is what might be called

(d) *Stimulated data*, that is, data generated by setting up some situation which will produce data not normally or readily available, e.g. holding meetings for discussion of beliefs, changing work practices experimentally, etc.

A fifth, and in some ways less obvious source, but one nevertheless of importance, derives from the OR worker's relationship with

(e) *The sponsor*, here viewed as a source of data particularly about the culture.

It will be convenient to make a few comments on each of the sources of data. However, some general points which refer to all sources are made first. The discussion could be extensive but instead is restricted to some of the more important points which appear to present difficulties in practice.

The first general point is that the sources of data are likely to incur different costs of data collection, with (a) usually the cheapest. It is well, therefore, to think about which source is appropriate to the needs. The balance to be struck is between the cost of collection and the value of the data once they are collected. This value may depend on source, because one source may provide (say) more accurate data about something than another source. The value might also be time-related, typically the quicker, the better, other things being equal. It is difficult to be more specific on this point without a context. The comments below do, however, offer some hints about the use of sources (b) and (c), implicitly relative to (a).

A second general point stems from the frequent need to sample if costs of data collection are to be kept within bounds. It is not too difficult to sample uneconomically or misleadingly. Four common errors are:

(i) To use completely random sampling. This is almost always the least efficient sampling method (as opposed to stratified sampling, quota sampling, etc.). (Look at the theory if unsure about it.)

(ii) To give insufficient attention to sample size. Samples much too big and samples much too small for the accuracy required are commonplace. Sample size, *not* the proportion of the population sampled, determines accuracy. (Again look at the theory if unsure about it.)

(iii) To use the wrong sampling frame. By this is meant to sample from a population which is not the true population of interest. There is little to do but urge caution here. Particularly insidious traps are:

(a) To mistake the part for the whole. (This mistake is one against which scientists generally have to guard. It is often associated with a so-called selection effect, which makes some untypical part of the population most easily observed. Stars visible to the naked eye, for example, may be untypical.) This mistake is easily engendered if records are kept in certain ways. Thus, members of a Parent Teacher Association might be mistakenly equated with the population of parents at that school; or the times spent waiting to enter hospital by people needing a particular operation might be confused with the waiting times of those who enter hospital for that operation; or the difficulty of observing personal behaviours of some set of people might lead to conclusions being based on those who volunteer information. If the data are to be collected by asking people, the data collector must be wary of thinking the people he knows in the population, and can therefore easily contact by telephone, say, are representative of the population.

(b) To be misled by definitions. For example, as discussed earlier, the capacity of equipment has many possible definitions; or passenger ships using a port might cover ships carrying any passengers at all, or even ships capable of carrying passengers, whether they are or not.

(c) To construct false analogues of the true population, a mistake that must be especially watched for when it is impossible, for some reason, to sample from the true population. For example, it is impossible to sample the effect on performance of an activity by some change in the way it is performed, since it cannot be known what would have happened without the change: a 'before and after' comparison uses improvement as an analogue of effect, but other things will often have changed; or the buying behaviour of the customers at an existing store may be used as an analogue of those at a projected store, without careful thought about the implicit assumptions being made in doing so, such as their demographic and economic comparabilities.

Of course, these traps are there in principle whether the data are to be sampled or collected in full (i.e. a 100% sample).

A third general point is that data production, in the sense of causing data to be generated so that they may be collected, should always be considered. It may be expensive but may be worth the expense. Many of the key ideas are embodied in the theory of the design of experiments. This theory can be viewed as the study of how to get most information for a given resource expenditure. It deals also with, and a knowledge of it is a reminder of, the possibility of interactions between various factors which can distort data collection. Commonly, some piece of data—the numerical value of the difference in performance of two motor cars, say—will depend on the values of other influencing factors—the weather, the state of the roads, the service each has received, and so on. Well-designed data collection may reveal, through subsequent analysis of the data, whether such influences (or interactions as they are often called) exist or matter, and what allowance to make for them.

The discussion turns now to more specific points by source. Advice of a kind which would probably be endorsed by many experienced OR workers is offered on the way.

RECORDED INFORMATION

Using records as data about physical things ought to be straightforward but a number of dangers arise which can probably be summed up by saying that written-down figures are not always what they purport to be. Laying aside simple errors, it is always worth questioning what definitions the compiler of any published figures was actually working to. It is surprising what ambiguity can be generated around even the most apparently straightforward definition.

For example, read quickly the phrase 'average number of men on books' seems a straightforward concept, but there are many definitions of 'average', many of 'men' and many of 'on books'. Sometimes the data collector himself will be the person who introduces the ambiguity. Thus, many accounting conventions serve to remove possible ambiguity as long as the data collector actually knows the conventions. If the conventions are not understood by the data collector, he might easily mistake the interpretation to be put on such a phrase as 'standard cost'.

It is also worth asking how close the compiler is to the source of the statistics. It is not uncommon to find someone whose job is to collect certain information, but who is actually fed it rather than collecting it. He may have no contact at all with the physical processes to which the information refers. Those who do have the contact may be feeding him less than perfect information, in extreme cases guessed information or even lies. (The 'someone' might be a computer, or a member of the computer section.)

Typical written-down information about organisation includes organisation charts, job definitions, terms of reference of committees, photographs, the personal details of the people concerned, statements about career structures, manuals of procedures etc. It is probably safer to work on the assumption that this information is at least partially wrong than to presume that it is completely right. Almost invariably it is what someone thinks ought to be or what someone wishes to be, and only rarely is it what actually is in any complete sense. It almost always pays to make some independent verification of such data. (It is possible that over-elaborate documentation about the organisation and the people in it is a symptom of a problem as often as it is a useful source of information.)

The most useful written-down information about limits of actions, corporate policy etc. is usually that which is negative. This is because it is, on the whole, much easier to frame negative instructions clearly and, as the recipient, more easy to obey them. Some constraints under which middle managers are asked to work are inconsistent—'decisions should be taken with a view to maximising profit with the maximum service level to customers and the maximum job satisfaction for our staff'—while others are not even meaningful—'plan to adapt to all possible contingencies'. Policy changes through time, and up-to-date statements should be sought, something often easier said than done. It can also be useful to look back at, almost browse through, any files of minutes, letters etc. bearing on an issue. This can aid appreciation and understanding of the present position.

A final general point about using recorded information is the ease with which bias can be introduced by neglecting missing information. Records which are missing, fudged or corrected very carefully, and blanks, are grounds for suspicion. Such records should not be ignored but the reasons for them elicited as far as possible, a process which is surprisingly often informative. Missing information is often found to be untypical.

PERSONAL KNOWLEDGE

It is usually a last resort to rely on people's opinions for facts which are otherwise recorded, measurable or observable. The liar, the wishful thinker, the optimist, the pessimist and the joker all exist. The man who has all the figures should be treated warily: even if he is right two or three times his figures should always be checked if possible. The man whose information, given with assurance, is years out of date is another hazard, and so is the man with an axe to grind, who wants to bias the results in favour of his pet theory or just in favour of himself.

However, to determine organisational features by asking people, while difficult and relatively costly, is often worth the effort because of what is learned that is not otherwise accessible. The main difficulties are affording enough time to get everyone's trust and to do so in a way which does not destroy the consensus view that the data collection is 'objective'. However, most people like talking about themselves, their jobs and their colleagues. They are also likely to be more informative about the political and social processes which have produced the present organisational features than written material. At the very least, they will usually elaborate any inferences drawn from written material.

The means of asking can take many forms. Some might be quite informal—a word over lunch, say, or a conversation after some formal meeting. In other cases a more formal interview, entered in diaries, may be appropriate. There will often be a good case for general discussions with relevant groups informally, to get a feel for what concerns people and how the people interact, before moving to a series of individual interviews of a more formal kind. Individual interviews are, however, usually important, since people behave differently in groups than they do alone. In any case, of course, the first contact with people is likely to be an individual interview with the client.

In interviewing, or otherwise asking people for information, the data collector should try to be a sympathetic listener. As a generalisation, it is more effective to listen, even to what might initially be mere rambling, than somewhat aggressively to impose a pattern on the discussion. (Almost always in an initial interview there will be a settling-in period, when interviewee and interviewer are getting to know each other through more or less conventional exchanges. The interviewee is also likely to say what he thinks he *ought* to say until he is fully certain of and happy about the interviewer's intentions.) Nevertheless, it is wise to take a check-list of intended questions to an interview and to check before leaving that they have been asked. It is also wise to be sure the answers are understood. People do not mind explaining several times. They would usually rather do this than have the data collector keep coming back again and again. The data collector must also, of course, try to understand and share the burdens which the inadequate organisation and incompetence of certain colleagues place on a person. (There is a delicate borderline between healthy cynicism and blame casting. A good manager is aware of his colleagues' limitations and may take pleasure in discussing them, but he will not usually blame them for his own incompetence. Someone who is always blaming others is probably not very good at his job.) Bias can obtrude, though. Some types to look for are the person whom the status quo suits and who will have an answer for any question which hints of possible change; the person who, perhaps resentfully, answers the questions but that is all; and the actual or would-be expert whose aim is to confuse or even to demoralise the data collector, and who pulls no punches as he piles on complication after complication. (In all this, it is those whose organisational claims are consistent with what occurs who are to be believed.)

In pursuing a path of interviews there is merit in reflecting before going where sent: it is sometimes better to go where advised not to. It takes a big man to draw attention to others with conflicting opinions.

To determine rules by asking is basically the search for the right person or persons. In some set-ups there is an obvious person running the show and he is the limit maker. In other cases power is more subtly or more widely spread. The manifest danger is of addressing the wrong person and, without an understanding of the organisation, the data collector can easily do this. Even the right person may not give the required information off his cuff. It may take several weeks of intermittent dialogue and questioning for him to articulate the often subconscious constraints which he is imposing on the system. Another possible trap is to mistakenly suppose that the rule maker knows what the actual rules are. He may have laid down rules which he thinks are being followed but which in fact are not. Others, including those who implement or should implement the rules, should be asked what rules they work to. It may be necessary to be persistent and patient here. The implementers may not readily acknowledge that they are breaking the boss's rules.

Data may be collected in writing or by using a written questionnaire. If even a moderately complex questionnaire is contemplated, professional advice is worth considering. In any case, the following points can usefully be kept in mind:

(i)   Make the questions unambiguous.
(ii) Take care not to anticipate the views of the respondent.
(iii) If there are several questions, build in redundancy and cross-checks to safeguard against misunderstandings.
(iv) Unless essential to do otherwise, ask for simple answers (e.g. numbers, yes/no).
(v)   Be courteous (e.g. as to time taken up, explaining why the exercise is being done, reporting on results, answering queries, etc.).
(vi) Those responding to the questionnaire (typically far from all it has been sent to) may not be representative of the population as a whole. Be sure there are the means of checking this and enough information to correct the results for bias. It may be necessary to include otherwise irrelevant questions for this purpose.

It is always, if time permits, worth piloting a questionnaire, that is, trying it out on a few people first. Their completed questionnaires and comments, written or perhaps derived from interview, are usually helpful in polishing the final questionnaire.

The telephone is another medium by which people might be asked things. Suitably amended, the remarks on written material apply. The telephone is perhaps cheaper than writing but often generates more ambiguity and, because it is more likely to be interruptive than writing, can lead to careless or even ill-tempered responses.

Face-to-face interviews are usually the most expensive medium for asking people things. However, they have many advantages to offset their higher costs. A relationship, hopefully of trust, can more easily be established between asker and respondent. Body language, a subject for a book in itself, also communicates information. If, for whatever reason, cost is no consideration, face-to-face interviews are usually best. Even when cost is a consideration, face-to-face interviews with some people are usually worthwhile. Letters, and especially telephone calls, come better from people whom the receiver knows. A first contact face to face, followed by written or telephoned questions, is sometimes useful.

MEASUREMENT AND OBSERVATION

Measuring and observing to find the value of measurable and observable things such as how a thing works, physical dimensions, numbers or products made, etc., is, obviously, a reasonably foolproof exercise. It can, of course, be costly in resource and elapsed time.

Turning to observation as a means of studying human activity, the mere fact that the data collector is observing, presuming it is known to those being observed, may affect the activity. Care is necessary to avoid the bias this will introduce. Time and resources may have to be spent in explaining the purposes of observing and early observations may have to be discounted.

Observation as a means of studying organisational patterns is in any case difficult for those not trained in this kind of observation. Basically it is an attempt to construct, by observation, some 'true' organisation chart, job definitions, etc. Some points to look for are who talks to whom about what (including out of working hours) and how emergencies are handled (a good test for identifying the real leaders and whom they trust). The place, role and effectiveness of the various kinds of formal meetings is often worth observing. (Which receive the most apologies for absence?) Some questions relating to the politics of the situation where observation is a relevant means of data collection include: where does the buck stop? (these are either the strong men or the bottlenecks); who is always passing the buck, upwards or downwards? (these are either the weak people or the good politicians); who wins arguments (i.e. gets their way) even when they have logically lost the argument? (these presumably wield power of some sort); is there some clear bias in decisions in favour of someone or some group? (again, evidence of power being exercised; check whether there is some explanation of the power).

Again, as with inferring organisation from observation, it needs a shrewd observer to infer policy, rules and values successfully from observation alone. It is in any case difficult to detect why people are behaving as they are merely by observation. The problem is further confounded by the fact that people are inconsistent between different times and among each other. Thus, the data collector may be observing the limits and constraints acting on one particular person or group at one particular time rather than anything of a more durable character. It is often helpful to watch for the negatives: 'we must not consider that alternative because....' (where the reason is not physical or financial non-viability). Some effort is usually justified to find the right person or persons (e.g. via observations on organisation) to observe, i.e. the ones who decide what the limits are.

STIMULATED DATA

Sometimes the required data are not conveniently gathered from the above sources. There are several reasons why this may be so. The data might, for example, relate to some hypothetical circumstance. The output from a machine never before used, or aspects of people's behaviour consequential on some intended reorganisation, provide examples. The readily collected data might also, and this applies particularly to those relating to people's behaviour, be of dubious validity for some purposes because they represent the typical, whereas it is the untypical which is of interest. Examples here include people's response to rare events. It may be desirable to arrange for events to occur which reveal such data and allow them to be gathered. Various possibilities are available.

One possibility is simply to ask people to note things they have not been in the habit of noting before. This may require some measure of organisation on the part of the data collector and even the provision of resources. Thus, it might be that the data of interest are the type, frequency and cost of machine breakdowns. Breakdowns are not currently noted because when they occur everyone busily engages in rectifying them. An extra pair of hands, or fairly clever computer logging, might help.

A second possibility is to arrange for monitored experiments to take place. These can be expensive and time consuming and those proposing them can expect to have to justify them by demonstrating the potential value of the data. However, there may be few, if any, alternatives. Examples, aside from experiments of a physical or engineering nature, might include rearranging shift patterns so as to determine the effect of working arrangements on absenteeism, inviting the sales force to adopt a new approach to test why customers buy a particular product, and so on. Experiments involving human beings are almost always expensive and potentially very expensive indeed. Presuming ethical questions have been satisfactorily addressed, there is the possibility of much effort spent on persuasion before agreement to the experiment is reached. There is also the difficulty that an experiment may bring untoward results (usually met by building in the means to cease it quickly, but if the results are untoward for the experimenters but attractive to the other people involved, the experiment may be difficult, if not impossible, to stop).

Sometimes the experiment can usefully be made by simulation. In order to know how quickly a first-aid team would deal with an emergency it would not be sensible to cause an actual emergency, but a simulated one might be welcomed on all sides, as good training for the team as well as a means of gathering data. Business games, often advanced as valuable learning experiences for the players, can also be useful as stimuli of some kinds of information. Given a realistic game design and an incentive for the players to take the game seriously, much might be learned about their goals and behaviours towards each other. Again, this may be an expensive tactic which requires justification.

A common source of information about any situation is information about the same or similar situations elsewhere. General reading provides much such data, and library research offers an extension of this. In other cases data-exchange schemes, or data pooling with others known to share the problem, can be usefully considered. The investment in time to build up mutual trust as well as other costs make this approach potentially expensive, and there are usually other difficulties, such as confidentiality, others' uncertainty of the prospective partners' motivation even despite the data collector's own strong sense of trust, unrecognised inconsistencies, and so on. The gains to be set against these things are not always realised. The idea attracts many in principle but disappoints not a few in practice.

Finally, the beliefs held by a group, and the extent and strength of any relevant consensus in the group, can be difficult to determine without some measure of stimulation. Meetings might be arranged in order to illuminate these matters. The meetings might encompass the whole group if that is practicable, or perhaps representatives of different sub-groups within the group. They might, of course, be an agenda item on a suitable meeting called for some other purpose.

Much skill can be needed to make such meetings useful, particularly if there are grounds for expecting conflict or if the participants are nervous or inarticulate. The conduct of the meeting is best decided on the needs of the particular case. Sometimes an informal approach will be helpful, sometimes only formality can draw any response. It is important to plan such meetings with some care, deciding what it is desired to achieve and what, in light of the particular case, are the best means of achieving it. Nevertheless, some quickness of mind may be necessary during the course of the meeting in response to unexpected behaviours. Despite these reservations, such meetings, and perhaps even more so a series of such meetings, can provide data otherwise difficult or impossible to collect.

THE ROLE OF THE SPONSOR

Most OR work has a sponsor or client (in the book henceforward these words will be used synonymously), that is, someone who has commissioned the work and who, it is to be supposed, has an interest in its being carried out effectively and efficiently. He is likely to be more deeply knowledgeable about the culture of the employing group (indeed he might be the employing group) than the OR worker. An important part of practising OR is, as this book seeks to make clear, having sufficient familiarity with the culture. This familiarity might be acquired in several ways—simply by accumulating experience, by data collection (i.e. by using the above methods to determine the culture), etc. However, one method not to be overlooked is to rely on the sponsor for information about the culture, either relatively informally or by a more formal process of sitting down with him (or them if the sponsor is a group) and putting the relevant information into some structured form (e.g. a cognitive map). (The results from any formal approach, and indeed any informal one, might need frequent up-dating.)

Informing the OR worker about the culture could be argued to be the sponsor's key role in OR. Many sponsors appear to treat it as such, to the point sometimes of imposition of the role. Some sponsors will be good at it, others not so good. Caution must therefore be exercised by the OR worker. Usually, however, a poor sponsor's ineffectiveness in this role will quickly be revealed. It might even not be worth working for him again unless the reasons for his poor earlier showing are no longer valid. (The reasons might have been, for example, inexperience or uncertainty about his boss's attitude to the work, and not necessarily any inherent lack of aptitude or inclination for the sponsor role.)

The sponsor as a source of data is important in another respect. People other than the OR worker are likely to have an interest in the problem under study. They may well be taking actions that in effect redefine the problem. The sponsor himself may be doing so. It could be argued that it is the OR worker's responsibility to keep himself fully abreast of all such things and he should certainly try to do so. However, to do so almost certainly necessitates being in on some more or less formal network of information exchange—on the right circulation list, for example. The sponsor is far more likely to know what networks are appropriate and his advice should be sought. Sometimes the network will be closed to the OR worker, or his being in it may be inefficient (e.g. attending 3-hour committee meetings for 10 minutes of relevance). The sponsor, or one of his associates, will probably be on the network and can be asked to supply the arising information to the OR worker. However, even here the OR worker can expect to have to take some initiative. The sponsor will not always see the relevance of information, or, in the pressure of events, might simply forget to pass it on. Frequent tactful reminders—for example, telephone calls asking 'whether anything happened at the meeting yesterday' followed by consequential questions—are probably wise. Again, a sponsor unwilling or unable to carry through this general role is a potential liability, and to be worked for only with caution.

Note, in passing, the considerable scope a sponsor has for making the OR worker look foolish by 'forgetting' to let him have, or direct him to, highly relevant information. One of the most effective things someone ill-disposed (for whatever reason) to OR work on a subject can do is to sponsor OR work on that subject and, subtly but surely, cause it to fail while apparently appearing blameless in the failure.

DATA ANALYSIS

The collected data will usually be useful only if analysed in some way. The analysis, like the collection, will depend on the purpose for which it is being done. Common purposes are (i) simply to gain some general understanding of a problem, (ii) to test preconceived beliefs, or (iii) to decide what it is sensible to believe about the situation. Point (i) is exploratory and not usually an end in itself; a common consequence is to collect more data. Points (ii) and (iii) are to do with hypothesis testing and development and are more suitable for formal treatment.

Statistics is, in large measure, the methodology of data analysis. Note that statistics covers the analysis of much apparently qualitative data, particularly attribute data, as well as the analysis of quantitative data. A fair working knowledge and understanding of mathematical statistics is desirable. A few remarks, which assume some such knowledge, follow.

Looking at the Data

A frequently offered piece of advice is that, as a preliminary to more formal analysis, the data should be looked at graphically or pictorially, or in some other way which might seem crudely non-mathematical. This is excellent advice. It is only because experience suggests it is so often ignored that it is worth repeating here. Many computer packages offer great scope for this preliminary 'getting a feel for the data'.

Checking the Data

In analysing data it is the data themselves that are being learned about: only if the data are actually representative of the system under study is it the system that is being understood. Any data should be handled fairly critically. It is not uncommon, no matter how careful the data collection has been, for the data analysis to reveal occurrences or effects which are unlikely actually to be in the system so much as in the data. Common examples are data which exhibit too much or too little variability—suggesting the books have been cooked—or which exhibit unbelievably high correlations—suggesting that apparently independent data are in fact derived non-independently.

Developing Hypotheses

This is a creative process, skill at which, it could be argued, distinguishes outstanding scientists, or outstanding people from various walks of life, from the rest. There are some principles, however (some of which are rather more fully discussed in the subsequent chapter on models). It is helpful to have a wide knowledge of hypotheses others have found useful including standard bookwork models (as, for example, in queuing theory). It is also helpful to try to develop the ability to transfer theories from one discipline to another—one of the arguments for interdisciplinary teams in OR. A crucial distinction to bear in mind is that between fitting new parameters to a model assumed *a priori* correct (e.g. most regression) and developing a totally new model (e.g. using data about children's heights, various other measurements and weights to develop a model relating all the statistics with no prior conception of reality).

Testing Hypotheses

Suppose the data have suggested a hypothesis. To test it, more data must be collected, preferably in a planned way which makes the test most stringent for the amount of data collected. (Again, this is what a lot of statistics is about.)

Some form of statistical significance test will probably be carried out. Significance tests do not accept hypotheses in the sense that they prove the hypothesis is true: what they do is reject them or not according as the data are unreasonably inconsistent or not with the truth of the hypothesis. If a hypothesis is not rejected, it is accepted only insofar as it is felt it has not yet been disproved. (Note that most statistical tests assume beliefs about the hypotheses—e.g. that errors in making predictions based on this hypothesis are normally distributed. The beliefs about the hypothesis, and not the hypothesis itself, may be what is being tested. As far as possible, it should be checked that the assumptions of the statistical test hold. If they do not it may help to transform the test data in some way, e.g. using logs of the raw data.)

Other tests of a hypothesis, while of a less formal kind, are not to be derided. For example, if the hypothesis is consistent with theories others have found to be valid in similar situations at other times and places, it is probably right. If it is not so consistent, it should be tested very thoroughly. General plausibility is another test. It is desirable to be clear what physical interpretation can be put on the hypothesis and that this is plausible.

Extrapolation of Data

The dangers of extrapolation are well known. Usually it is accepted hypotheses whose validity is extrapolated—e.g. this trend will continue for the next 10 years—but sometimes it is the data. A piece of data usually refers to something which happened in a particular context at a particular time and place. It should be used outside this context, time and place only with care. There are today schoolboys who can run a mile faster than the Olympic champions of the 1920s.

Misleading Correlations

The dangers of inferring cause and effect from correlation are also well known. A common example is that some effect A causes both B and C. Data are collected only on B and C, and B and C are found to be highly correlated. B causes C, or vice versa, is mistakenly inferred. Effect A will not always be known or recognisable, making the mistake particularly insidious. On other occasions, the correlation will simply be an artefact of the way the data have been collected or of the sampling frame. Thus, if heads of households are asked to list the names and other information about the occupants of their house, the incidence of spelling errors is likely to be higher for larger households than smaller, simply because more has to be written. It would be an unwise inference that heads of larger households are poorer spellers than those of smaller.

Another common difficulty with correlation is the confusion that can be caused by drawing inferences from data in restricted ranges about correlations across a more extensive range or, vice versa, inferring that correlations based on data in a wide range hold in smaller ranges. For example, the earnings of individuals, taking the population at large, correlate quite highly with measures of their academic attainments. However, if some restricted group, say very high earners engaged in some particular activity, were examined, it is quite possible that no such correlation would be found. The dangers of inferences from either case to the other are clear.

Generally correlation should be treated, if at all, as a possible indicator of cause and effect, but cause and effect should only be assumed if a thoroughly plausible explanation can be made for it.

APPENDIX: PROFITABLE PAM

PAM is the trade name of a cattle feed marketed by a large farm foods manufacturing firm. It increases the efficiency with which cows convert grass to milk and thus allows either more cows per acre of grazing land or more milk per cow. Trials over several years, on the firm's own farms and on 20 farms belonging to farmers who, for a fee, try out the firm's products, showed that PAM has no unfortunate side effects and that its use is profitable at the intended selling price. It was therefore marketed with the sales blurb, both written and spoken by the travelling salesmen, placing emphasis on the profitable results of the trials, which showed a 10% higher profit per grazing acre of the PAM-fed herds compared with the controls.

It is common experience that a new product like PAM is fairly slowly taken up and then sales shoot away as the word gets round—the familiar S-shaped curve. Two years after the first marketing, however, sales have not taken off as the firm hoped. They are increasing, but linearly rather than accelerating.

The Marketing Director feels that somehow the word is not getting round as it should and he decides to push PAM at the occasional 'open-houses' for farmers which the firm holds in important agricultural centres. He thinks that practical results would be a useful selling point, and he asks the Statistics Department to survey the results of using PAM on those farms where it has been bought by the farmer as opposed to the trial farms. The following selected correspondence tells its own tale.

Head of Statistics to Marketing Director—3 May

We have carried out a random sample survey of farms using PAM and of those not using it. The main conclusion is that profit per grazing acre is no less than 38% higher in those farms using it than in those not. It is even more effective in practice than in theory!

Marketing Director to Head of Statistics—4 May

Thank you for your note of 3 May. This is just the ammunition I need. Please pass on my congratulations to the person who did the survey.

Marketing Director to Head of Statistics—16 June

I used your 38% statistic at Ipswich yesterday. Frankly it was greeted with derision. The farmers were quick to point out that PAM is so expensive that only profitable farms can afford to buy it. Comments please.

Head of Statistics to Marketing Director—30 June

We have looked again at our survey and have sought the advice of Professor Charles, our statistical consultant. We find no fault in our sampling methods, our data or our analysis, and we stand by the figure of 38%. However, there is one small point. We thought it might be prudent to look at a before-and-after effect. We went back to the same farms and found that taking last year and three years ago as the base years, farms now using PAM have increased profits per acre by 83% and those not using it by 60%. In some ways, therefore, it is more correct to say PAM increases profits by 14% ($183 \times 100 \div 160 = 114$).

Marketing Director to Head of Statistics—4 July

Your note of 30 June is reassuring. Thank you. I now feel on very firm ground. I think 14% can be safely quoted as the profit improvement.

Marketing Director to Head of Statistics—5 August

I used the 14% figure at Salisbury yesterday and was most aggressively challenged by a Mr Wood. This Wood has been using PAM and his profits have fallen. He is only a small farmer and not a very important customer, but I gather he is prominent in local politics and in the Farmers' Union. Moreover, he threatened to report us under the Trade Descriptions Act. He seemed to have a lot of support in the audience and I am worried. Please have a look at this again. Take your time but for heaven's sake get it right. Meanwhile, I am withdrawing the PAM promotion from the Open House agendas.

Head of Statistics to Marketing Director—27 September

Together with Professor Charles and his colleagues we have had a most searching look at our analysis of PAM profitability. We stick by all our figures but have the following observations to make:

(1) There is considerable variation in profit figures. Of our sample of 73 farms using PAM, 8 had shown a reduction in profit. This variation is due to the natural vagaries of farming. Mr Wood is presumably just one of the unlucky ones.
(2) PAM has been taken up more in the West Country than elsewhere, our market penetration there being 20% of all farms compared with a range of 3–6% for other regions. For reasons quite other than the use of PAM, profitability has increased marginally more in the West Country than elsewhere. We have corrected for this and the figure of 14% is more accurately $13\,^1/_2$%.
(3) PAM has also, as with most new products, been taken up more quickly by the bigger farms. Their profits have not increased more than small farms: that is, large farms not using PAM have experienced the same increase in profit per grazing acre as small farms not using PAM. However, we should not discount the possibility that large farms using PAM are more efficient at exploiting profit opportunities than others and that it is this efficiency we are really measuring.

I cannot really think of any other analysis we can do. Perhaps the safest thing is to revert to quoting the results of the trials.

Head of Statistics to Marketing Director—1 October

I write to confirm our telephone conversation in which I told you we might have hit on the answer to the PAM problem. It seems, from a chance conversation with one of my farming contacts, that PAM users have almost all produced the same amount of milk from fewer grazing acres and put the released acreage to other uses, thus artificially boosting the profit per grazing acre which we have been using for comparisons.

My staff are working on this as fast as possible and I will let you have the results as soon as they become available. It means going back to all the farms in our survey as we originally collected only the profit per grazing acre, but we now need more basic information.

EXERCISES

(1) In the Profitable PAM case (pages 108–109):
- (i) Go through each item of the quoted correspondence critically and list the mistakes or unjustified assumptions that have been made.
- (ii) Does the case tell us anything about the importance of publishing data and exposing them to feed-back?
- (iii) Who is more to blame for the prolonged misunderstanding about PAM—the Marketing Director or the Head of Statistics? Reflect more generally on the respective responsibilities of the client and his professionally skilled adviser, and list key attributes of those engaged in these roles.

(2) A way of gathering data, discussed in this chapter, is that of stimulating a group in some way and seeing what happens. The way need not ostensibly be connected with data collection. For example, and to take a rather extreme case, a company manager might gather data about a trades union's power and role in the company by dealing direct with a group of workmen rather than via the union. Can you think of cases where such ways have been used? Is this approach different in kind from observation, asking or looking up figures, or in degree?

(3) Commonly in organisations some data are regularly and systematically collected, while others are collected only when required. Some data collected regularly are necessary for legal or quasi-legal purposes. Laying these data aside, what justifies regular collection of data? Is it possible to develop a cost-benefit criterion for deciding what data to collect regularly? In what ways might the culture of a group influence what data it regularly collects? How might the decision on what data to collect regularly influence the culture? Is what data a group regularly collects, analyses and uses, a key expression of its culture? Are decisions about it possible problem-solving techniques? (If the senior managers are known to give much of their time to sales statistics, say, might this communicate a powerful message to more junior staff?)

(4) Presentation of analysed data is commonly recognised to be value-laden. Look for examples in newspapers, magazines and television of data presentation that you feel distort the meaning or implications of the data. Was it presentation or guided inference that encouraged the distortion? Was the distortion consciously engineered? Can distortion be avoided? Could it have been in these cases?

(5) Response rates to questionnaires are often low in terms of the proportion of respondents replying. There is often also uncertainty about the quality of the replies received, in the sense of how much thought has

gone into the answers, and so on. Discuss strategies for improving response. Test these against the effect they would have on you if you were a recipient of the questionnaire.

(6) Set yourself the task of planning the collection of data about some issue where you know someone who is reasonably expert on the issue. List the data you would hope to collect, the sources for them, the means of collecting them and the resources you would expect to devote to the collection. Have the expert look at your plan and comment on it. What conclusions do you draw? Were you surprised by the fact that some 'obvious' data were not readily available? By the value of a good knowledge of data sources? By how quickly some data can be gathered and how slowly others? Is knowing one's way around the data on an issue part of the definition of an expert? Can the client be expected to help the OR worker on this point?

(7) With a few friends, find a local issue that concerns all of you (some local transport problem, for example). Give yourselves some agreed time to gather data on the issue (say a few hours). Meet and compare the data each has collected. Presumably they differ. What are the causes of the differences? Distinguish between differences owing to different perceptions of the issue, those owing to different prior conceptions of the important factors, and those owing to different changing perceptions as the exercise developed. Are the causes predominantly due to natural variability or to differences between the people?

(8) Turn again to the Service Providers problem (pages 59–62).
   (a) If you were Emma and you had an hour with Mr Avery, what information would you seek from him?
   (b) How much information provided by Messrs Fell and Robertson is irrelevant to the matter in hand? Or does the phrase 'matter in hand' simply beg the question?

Chapter 8

Models

This chapter, which is not intended to be exhaustive, discusses some aspects of models and model building. It is intended, as much as anything, to describe various ways of looking at models so that the model builder appreciates some of the limitations and strengths of his models.

WHAT IS A MODEL?

At the simplest level, a model is a representation of something. Here the word will be generally used to mean a useful representation of some aspect of the world. Models can take many forms and have a multiplicity of potential uses. Two key concepts of form and use in OR are:

(i)   The idea of a model as a device (usually for making predictions).
(ii) The idea of a model as a statement of the beliefs held, including assumptions willingly made, relevant to the issue under study.

These two meanings correspond to two key motivations of much OR work, respectively:

(i)   Belief manipulation and its pragmatic application to helping select suitable problem-solving actions.
(ii) Belief creation and codification to secure understanding and to allow manipulation of better beliefs.

These two views of models are discussed in turn.

THE MODEL AS A DEVICE

One view of a model is as a device for predicting the output from a real system, under various conditions specified by the input data, without actually using the real system to make this prediction. Output is used here in a very general sense to mean some aspect of the behaviours of the real system which is of interest. Input data is also intended to have a broad meaning.

Consider Figure 8.1. It is possible to move from data about the real system and the environment in which it is going to work, to information predicting whatever is of interest (here called output), by either of two routes. These are by following route 1 in Figure 8.1 through the real system itself or by following route 2 through the model. The model has three facilities.

(1) It transforms the data about the real system into data in a form which is appropriate to the model (step 2a). (The transformation might be 'guess a value for this piece of data', in which case the variable in question is called an exogenous variable. Others are called endogenous.)
(2) It transforms its own output in terms of the model to output in terms of the real world (step 2b).
(3) A central part which transforms the model's data into the model's output, namely the model itself.

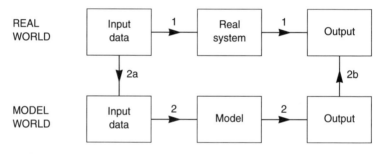

Figure 8.1

Notice that the transformations from the real world to the model world are about data and output and not about the real system to the model. The test of a model is how far following route 2 is adequate as a substitute for following route 1. (This is perhaps a controversial statement—see 2(c) below.) Model building, in this view, simply consists of constructing a device which passes this test in some measure or other. There is no reason why the model as such should represent the real system in any definite form at all. (It is easy to forget how different from reality models in common use actually are. The difference is often obscured by the fact that the same names are given to the various data inputs and outputs in the model as are used in the real world.)

Models are often said to provide an alternative medium to the real world in which to conduct experiments so that new ideas can be tried out cheaply, or be stimulated, or be 'sold' to those not sufficiently convinced to try them in real life. The simple choice—experiment on the model or the real world—tells only half the story, as it may frequently be that the 'real world' in question does not exist and may never do so. It may, for instance, be a real world which it is thought could be brought about, but whose properties it is preferred to test on a model first before deciding whether to bring this world into existence. Or the reality which is modelled might be some conjectured reality, like the past, the future or the current real world operated under different rules, so that 'what if' questions can be asked. In other words, predictions about what would happen if such-and-such were the case can be made, or statements about what would have happened had such-and-such been the case. Nor can all experiments be conducted in the real world, not merely as a matter of cost (important though that may be) but as a sheer impossibility. It is impossible, for example, to experiment on the real world to choose between alternative plans for a given time period. Sometimes also there will be obvious ethical objections to real experimentation, as, for instance, in military work.

THE MODEL AS A COLLECTION OF RELEVANT BELIEFS

Another way of regarding models is as a statement of some or all the beliefs about the real world which are held by those concerned and which they think are relevant to the problem in hand. Using the model is then viewed as the logical manipulation of these beliefs to generate consequential beliefs equally or more relevant to the problem. This is at once both a wider and a narrower concept than the model as a device, but it is a reminder that models have, or should have, a basis in knowledge or at least belief. (The possibility must be admitted that the individual beliefs embodied in the model might not of themselves be ones thought valid in the real world, but the model as a whole is something which is believed valid of the real world or aspects of it. Thus, most people would regard it as foolish to throw out a model of classical physics just because it viewed atoms as indivisible, if it gave adequate predictions of phenomena on a larger scale.)

The notion of a model as the synthesis of beliefs about the situation of interest is important, not so much as a way of describing a model as of describing the model-building process. It is arguable that building a model is more valuable than the model itself. It is, for those building the model, a means of structuring their attempts to understand reality, or possible realities, and possible actions and their effects, of stimulating and guiding the creation of new actions, and of pointing out areas of ignorance and thus guiding their research. It is a learning process which stimulates their problem definition and data collection and analysis. (Indeed it could be argued that model building is data collection and analysis, and vice versa.) They might find this valuable in the context of solving a specific problem but also, as already remarked, in equipping themselves (through understanding) to solve a wide range of problems which might occur. Even in the context of a single problem, model building is a continuous activity. A person does not start one day to build a model, finish it on another day and then move on to using it. His beliefs and views of their relevance for inclusion in the model will be under continual review and the model adapted as necessary.

This notion of a model does, as sometimes advanced, have implicit in it the view that belief and its acquisition is objective. In fact the model builder is left to decide subjectively how to start the model building and how, as his knowledge accumulates, to decide where to go next and generally to judge the model's relevance. However, he will often choose to develop and test the beliefs incorporated into the model in a way which is as objective as it can be made. Often, and perhaps usually, the OR worker will use methods which scientists use to develop and test those beliefs to which such considerations are relevant.

THE ROLE OF COMPUTERS

Many aspects of building and using models can profitably employ computers. Almost all of the rest of this chapter would be equally valid whether computers were used or not. It is much more to do with what goes into the models, the relationship of content and purpose and similar general considerations. The reader is invited to link the ideas back to computing practice for himself. However, it seems appropriate to make a few remarks about various aspects of computing.

Models often contain parts which are common to many models—at a trivial level, finding averages of, or sorting among, some data: rather less trivially, performing complex logical or mathematical manipulations. It is wise not to program these parts of a model without checking the commercial availability of appropriate software. Many excellent cheap packages are on the market, and do-it-yourself programming will be a waste of both money and elapsed time. Input and output (both alphanumeric and graphical) are well covered by commercially available packages, as are database manipulation and many standard algorithms. (It is unwise deliberately to work with a computer for which this is not true.)

Cheap computing—cheap hardware and software—bears strongly on the applicability of so-called prototyping. The following pages make much of the need to make models relevant, useful, understandable to, and acceptable by others, and all this without going too far beyond the needs of the case. Interaction between the model builder and other members of the employing group is necessary to ensure these things. A particularly convenient way of handling this interaction is to progress towards the finally accept-able model by a series of trial models. Each model is examined, or possibly used, with a view to eliciting its strengths and weaknesses, and conse-quently revised. The process is repeated until there is general satisfaction with the current model. The process might, indeed, never end, as the world and issues keep changing. The process is often called 'prototyping'.

Prototyping (which is not, of course, restricted as an approach only to computer models) seems in practice to be a very powerful way of linking the model building to the culture of the employing group, and to securing client involvement. There are points, however, to be wary of in its use. One is that the process might, by cultural pressure, be ended unduly early. Users might become so attached to an early model in the series that they are reluctant to change from it, thus losing out on the possibility of even greater value being obtained by further enhancement. (In other cases, it has to be said, users demand enhancement beyond the bounds of cost effective-ness.) A related difficulty is that the basic type of model, its place on the dimensions discussed below, is likely to be difficult if not impossible to change. This could be true whether prototyping or not, but there is a case for exercising caution about releasing the first model until the model builder has reasonably satisfied himself that it is of the right basic type. (Against this, there is a higher chance of productive work, the earlier the first proto-type is available. Here is yet another balance which will have to be struck on the circumstances of the particular case.)

CONSTRAINTS ON MODEL BUILDING

Most model-building behaviour is highly constrained. The constraints may be tangible, like limits on resources and time: these are well understood. It is perhaps less obvious that there are many intangible cultural constraints. Dimension 4 below touches on this. More generally, new concepts and new models seem always to derive from old ones—modified and adapted, no doubt, and perhaps applied in a different context, but old ones nevertheless. A consequence of this is that, insofar as models are regarded as a means of structuring perceptions of reality and of deriving actions, the model builder might be led to distort reality by his own work. For example, a model of aspects of human behaviour might be based on a highly plausible model of animal behaviour (e.g. the territorial imperative). People can understand this model well enough about animals and, if persuaded of its validity for humans, they might choose to act accordingly even though the model were not actually valid. The easily understood old concept, transferred to a new context in this way, seems to have considerable power. A famous example is the use of the phrase 'cold war', which presumes that relationships between Russia and America in the late 1940s and 1950s were modelled by the well-understood concept of war somewhat modified. How far was the coining of this model a self-fulfilling prophecy? What if, by chance, the model of 'hot peace' had been coined instead?

In this same general connection, modelling and concept formation seems often to be dictated by the current technology and general cultural scene, as well as contributing to it. People are inclined to choose representations consistent with this scene or drawn fairly directly from it, not always pausing to consider relevance. Modelling until fairly recently was heavily influenced by the deep development of classical mechanics so that many models of all kinds of processes were mechanistic models (e.g. deterministic models of human behaviour, in which men are viewed as machines) and reductionist (see page 26). Perhaps now a current modelling paradigm is the computer or the understanding of the human brain (e.g. the firm as an information processor), which are among the technologically most recent of man's achievements. There are other pervasive cultural models: the idea that all things can be weighed as if in a balance and the heaviest detected (e.g. cost-benefit analysis, fairness, as in an incomes policy, and derived ideas like the national interest); some of the important concepts of the great religions (e.g. Utopia and ideals generally); and, more locally, such concepts as 'the done thing'. Mathematical elegance, or more generally the inherent beauty or style of a model, are sometimes more highly valued than they should be. All of these things can press model building into certain directions and are liable to constrain originality and thus perhaps the relevance of the model.

It is well to remember that model building is subjective. To repeat earlier remarks, the model builder decides subjectively what relationships might be at work, he takes subjective views on data and so on. The preceding paragraphs are a reminder that these decisions can be as much influenced by general cultural values as by the nature of the system being modelled or, putting it another way, that many deeply held beliefs are not always articulated in models.

TYPES OF MODEL AND MODEL-BUILDERS' ROLES

Model building can be a costly and perhaps unrepeatable process and the subjective decisions referred to in the preceding paragraph can usually be made only once. It is, therefore, almost always worth giving thought to the choice among types of model before embarking on building one.

An important reminder is that it is impossible to construct the full model, in the sense that not all beliefs about everything that might conceivably be relevant to the situation being modelled can possibly be incorporated. There is, therefore, much choice about what beliefs to include, what subject matter to include beliefs about, whose beliefs to include, and so on. It also has to be decided how to articulate the beliefs that it is decided to include.

The ultimate criteria in making these decisions are, of course, cultural. They depend on the role the model builder perceives himself having in the group for whom he is working. He will presumably try to build models which serve the values of the group employing him. There is a wide variety of possible values, some of which are discussed a little more fully towards the end of the chapter. However, in general terms he will want to be sure that his model is relevant to the problem in hand, that it is likely to secure use by those whom he hopes will make use of it, and that it does not run too big a risk of worsening the problem which has led to its being built. He will want to achieve these and similar aims as simply as possible, that is, he will generally be satisfied when he has a model adequate for his purposes even if it is inadequate for many other purposes. Prototyping, referred to earlier, is obviously a relevant approach to consider in addressing these issues. (It goes without saying that models must be distrusted when their use is extrapolated beyond the uses intended by the model builder. It is often helpful to set out what the model is for and, implicitly or even explicitly, what would be unsuitable uses.)

One of the roles of OR workers is sometimes that of criticising other people's models—for example, models deployed by competing groups, who are perhaps anxious to persuade some third party such as the Government that a decision should be taken in their favour. The model builder might usefully remember that his own models might also be subject to this process of criticism. This is not an argument for 'objectivity' so much as a reminder that there is another criterion to remember in deciding what kind of model to build, namely it should perhaps not be one too closely tied to a belief which is easily demolishable by an informed critic.

However, the roles for OR workers of main concern in this chapter are those related to models built for the use of the group employing the workers. Commonly these roles are one or both of two. First, it is not uncommon for the OR worker to be in charge of the model viewed either as a device or as a collection of beliefs. That is, he is the person who turns the handle or who systematically collects and stores beliefs. Second, he might be the person who decides what beliefs are to enter the collection. This is rather rarer and may well be more often wrong than right. The OR worker may well be the best person to develop and collect certain kinds of beliefs—those which the culture regards as scientific—but he is not likely to be specially adept at deciding which of other kinds of beliefs should enter the model. He may well be adept at suggesting what kinds of other belief should enter, but his ideas should be offered as an agenda for negotiation, as should any ideas he might have on the precise form of such beliefs.

As previously remarked, most of the decisions made about types of model are ultimately subjective. However, there does seem to be some sort of consensus among experienced modellers about the properties of different kinds of models, and what follows is an attempt to set out some of these generally held views. This is done by defining a number of dimensions along which any given model can be thought of as having a position. Subjective decisions can then perhaps be helpfully related to decisions about the chosen position along these dimensions. (In what follows the presumed subject matter is formal models, that is, ones which are written down or otherwise articulated. However, the unconscious or unarticulated use of models is very common, or at least presumably it is, unless people choose actions without some examination of the effect of the actions and other belief-dependent considerations. The following discussion probably has application to unarticulated models.)

Dimension 1

The end points of this dimension are *actuality* and *abstract*. At the actuality end is using the real system to model itself (i.e. the process of using the model would consist of experiments on the real system). An intermediate point on this dimension would be using a scale model (e.g. a model railway to predict the effect of different modes of signalling on a real railway). Another point further along the dimension is the use of analogue models where a physical model is constructed in some different medium than the real system, but a medium which obeys basically the same physical laws as the real system (e.g. an electric network to model the flow of air in a colliery). Almost at the abstract end are qualitative models where the logic of the system is described in words, and mixed logical numerical models which are typified by simulation. Finally there are algebraic models, typified by queuing theory. On the whole, OR workers are concerned with the abstract end of this dimension, but it must be recognised that the layman's understanding of the model and his likely acceptance of predictions that the model makes will probably go down, the nearer one approaches the abstract end. It must also be recognised that the process of abstraction is often accompanied by a process of simplification: indeed, this is the merit of abstraction insofar as simplification means greater ease of use, but it is a danger of abstraction if simplification means that the model fails in its main purpose of providing an acceptable alternative to route 1 in Figure 8.1 or of otherwise helping to solve problems realistically.

Dimension 2

(2a)   Another dimension has its end points in *black box* and *structural*. In a 'black box' model cause and effect are not explicitly taken into account but in a structural model they are. Few models actually are structural in this sense. The essential difference can be illustrated by econometric models of various kinds. Black box models simply take the data generated by the economy and look for patterns in the data. The continued existence of these patterns is assumed in making predictions. A structural model, on the other hand, identifies relationships which the modeller believes hold in the real world and uses the data only to fit these relationships with numerical parameters. A black box model reveals nothing about the actual mechanics of the real system being modelled and is, on the whole, less likely to be sympathetically received by a layman than is a structural model. However, the structural model runs the risk of being highly subjective unless the causal relationships built into it are each independently verified. There are a number of dimensions closely related to this one and discussion of them follows.

(2b)   There is the dimension *predictive* to *exploratory*. At one end is a model which is good for predicting certain named outputs, but which has no tested validity beyond this. An exploratory model, on the other hand, allows the user to examine a wide range of possible realities, including realities which differ by having different causes and effects. It is sometimes thought than an exploratory model must necessarily be structural. This is not absolutely the case, as black box models can be used in an exploratory manner by conditioning the outputs. Thus, the output of a black box model of the UK economy will probably be a vector of predictions of the levels of various activities. One such activity may be the number of motor cars being made. The vector will be a random variable and, in order to know the effect of a different level of motor car output, the distribution of the other elements of the vector conditional on a fixed level of motor car output can be examined. However, this is rather abstruse, and where the aim is to encourage the exploratory use of a model by a layman it will probably be easier to work at the structural end of dimension 2(a).

(2c)   Another related dimension is *instrumental* to *realistic*. An instrumental model is, roughly speaking, one which works but no one quite knows why (e.g. a gravity model might well predict car flows between towns very accurately), while a realistic model is one which is assembled from refutable theories about the system modelled. Generally a realistic model will be structural and an instrumental model black box. However, 2(c) is listed separately from 2(a) because instrumental models of the analogy type often have the appearance of being structural without actually being so. It is not difficult carelessly to lapse into believing that towns attract traffic like planets attract moons is a genuine cause-and-effect argument.

(2d)   *Micro* and *macro* models, or crudely the amount of detail built into the model, provides another dimension. A micro model has as its entity the smallest unit of the system, whereas a macro model looks at the system as a whole, and is concerned only with global data and outputs. Often a macro model is used because it is adequate rather than best, but often also it is used because a micro model cannot be constructed either through limitations in time to collect the data, to build the model and to compute with it, or simply because the micro situation is not understood. Macro models are often superficially structural, but more often than not they are actually only implicitly structural in that they presume causes and effects which are not themselves self-evident and which usually rely on the assumption that cause and effect in the various entities can be added together in some sense. From the point of view of economy in model building and use the more macro, the better: one of the arts of model building is how little detail can be got away with without losing the model's usefulness.

(2e)   The amount of detail which an abstract model can encompass may well determine where it lies on dimensions 2(a) to 2(d). This will often be determined by the position chosen on the dimension which represents *computing power* and runs from a single person to a large powerful computer.

Dimension 3

A third dimension runs from *standard* to *purpose-built*. A standard model can be looked up in a textbook or a published paper, and a purpose-built model not. Clearly there is much to be said for using a standard model if it fits the case. The use of standard computer programs, including utilities, referred to earlier, deserves a second mention here.

Dimension 4

Absolute to *relative* provides another dimension. An absolute model is one which is valid anywhere and at any time. Some of the models of physics possibly have this quality. A relative model is one which is situation dependent (e.g. it is valid only for a particular management group, or for a particular way of doing things). Almost all models used in OR are relative ones, or are at least more relative than absolute. Consider how often what is modelled in OR is:

(a)   The here and now, e.g. assumptions are built in about the present relative costs of different modes of transport.
(b)   What someone thinks are causes and effects and he or someone else chooses parameters.
(c)   Models themselves, e.g. much linear programming work is concerned with modelling the model which the person or group who does the relevant allocation has in mind.

This is an important dimension and there are some hidden dangers in deciding a model's position along it. For example,

(1) Models are often thought to have a wide range of validity because they have been built to make predictions in a wide range of circumstances. However, it is not always the case that the assumptions made in the model building are valid across the whole range of conditions which the model builder implicitly believes them to be. In particular, implicit assumptions are almost always made about the way people behave and these can be turned upside-down in changed circumstances. In this connection it is always tempting to assume when building a model that rational decisions will be taken. This is not always the case.

(2) A second important danger is that a model may be built which is unconsciously restrictive of the kinds of change that may be desirable, or which unconsciously accepts the status quo. For example, it may be tempting to build into a model beliefs which essentially embody the values of some powerful group. Many economists believe that much economic theory is not so much science as a codification of the values of the economically powerful. Thus, the widely held view that free trade is a 'good thing' is, it is argued, a consequence of economic theory developed at a time and in countries where the interests of the powerful were being well served by free trade. As another example, a model of the effect of different tax packages might model only those kinds of taxes and tax structures which are, or have been, in existence. It might, therefore, constrain the model user from thinking of and evaluating the effect of some revolutionary change in tax structure.

(3) Sometimes an abstract model is built not of the true reality but of some analogue which is believed to be a good analogue of the true reality. This can be useful, but there can come a point where the analogue fails to represent reality and the model is rendered useless and perhaps positively misleading. The analogue may be an intermediate abstract model. Thus, a simulation model of a real system might be built by simulating a network model of the system. If things change so that the network model loses validity, so will the simulation model.

Dimension 5

Models vary according to the extent that they presume beliefs about actions that people will or ought to take. Three aspects of this deserve attention.

(a) There is the dimension *passive* to *normative*. ('Normative' is a generally used word: 'passive' is perhaps the best antonym in this context.) A passive model is, at the extreme, a model which embodies no beliefs about the behaviour of conscious beings and specifically people. (Models in the hard sciences are of this kind.) It might output the consequential effects of inputs which may or may not be under human control (controllable/endo-genous or environmental/exogenous variables respectively). It might just output useful information which amounts to little more than a sorting of, or simple calculations on, the input data. (A so-called decision support system is of this latter kind.) A normative model is one which incorporates beliefs about the way actions should be chosen and outputs the best action (the best values of the controllable inputs). Normative models are appropriate if there is group consensus about how the best action is to be determined. When there is not, or when there is doubt whether there is, it is wise to think very hard before using them. The whole model can easily be brought into disrepute because its normative aspect is disliked or distrusted.

Many models are part normative, sometimes in disguised ways. An easy trap to fall into is to incorporate beliefs which limit the range of possible actions. To illustrate this, consider a simple stock-control model for a single item bought into a firm. Certain beliefs about the costs of ordering, of holding stock and of running out and about demand are set down. Certain stock control policies (actions) are postulated to be available. A mathematical model is then built which predicts, for each possible policy, the number of orders that will be placed, the average stock and the expected number of run-outs over some time period. On the face of it, this is so far a passive model. In fact, it is already probably part normative, because it is likely that constraints have been imposed on the actions whose effects have been evaluated (e.g. attention has probably been restricted to re-order level and/or cyclic review policies: the possibility of policies for influencing demand has probably been excluded).

This model might be made fully normative by incorporating a belief that the best action to choose is the one which (say) minimises expected discounted cost, and allowing the model to determine this best action. Again on the face of it, this belief might seem uncontroversial, but it is often found that the criterion favoured by the relevant group members is somewhat less simple than can be embodied in a single belief, or indeed articulated at all. In this simple stock control example, the true criterion might be quite complicated. For example, it might be desired to choose the policy with the minimum cost but subject to restrictions on the number of orders placed, on the maximum size of stocks and/or the number of run-outs.

Even where there is acceptance of all the beliefs embodied in a normative model there need not be acceptance that it produces the best action. This is because there may be beliefs beyond those embodied in the model. More generally, all models are approximations either in what beliefs they include or in the accuracy with which they articulate the belief or otherwise. Only by chance does a normative model produce the truly best action: it produces the best action conditional on the model and what is in it. If a normative model suggests an action different from the one other methods would pursue (and it usually will) it is well to be sure that there are no hidden snags which the form of the model is obscuring. It is perhaps best to think of the model proposing an action which is then subject to criticism by the relevant members of the group: if their criticism is met by what is in the model, all well and good, but if not (i.e. there is some belief not embodied in the model) then the model will have to be recast or abandoned.

(b) A closely related dimension is that of *passive* to *behaviourial*. The passive end of this dimension is defined as above. A behaviourial model is one which incorporates beliefs about the way people will act. Many models are quite explicitly behaviourial—for example, economic models. Others are less explicitly so, but do nevertheless incorporate beliefs about people's actions. For example, to return again to the simple case of stock control, a model usually incorporates numerous beliefs about the competence of people to operate policies, about their disinclination to sabotage computer installations, etc. It is important to be aware of the implicit behaviourial assumptions for a number of reasons, most of them obvious. Among them are that change which appears merely as a different number in a mathematical model might entail a change in behaviour quite unacceptable to the person who has to operate the policy; behaviour is likely to change as a consequence of things quite unrelated to the system being modelled (thus in the stock control example it might be assumed that a clerk has sufficient powers of concentration to look up 200 tabulated entries a day and it might have been verified that this is indeed the case, but some disruption in his domestic life might render this assumption quite invalid); and, more generally, repeated use of the model might disclose that it is less useful than was originally supposed and this might be as much due to behaviourial assumptions in it as to any defect in the more tangible beliefs.

(c) Some people react strongly against normative and/or behaviourial models, partly on the intellectual grounds that they necessarily deal with issues which are inherently unmodellable (or putting it another way, issues which are unlikely to be describable scientifically), and partly on ethical grounds, the argument here being that the technocratic model builder implicitly limits people's freedom of action. A way round these objections is sometimes provided by constructing *interactive* models. In such models the relevant beliefs are split into two. First there are those which the group for whom the model is built are happy to have manipulated. Commonly this would be the passive part of the model, but it might well include behaviourial beliefs, and indeed normative beliefs if there was a suitable consensus in the group. The second kind of belief, and it is frequently a belief about choosing between various actions, is simply one that the relevant group prefers to invoke, review and reflect on before using it. The first set of beliefs constitute a model in the conventional way which is used to predict outputs from known inputs. The outputs are then fed to the appropriate choice-making point of the group (say this is an individual called the choice maker). The choice maker now decides what actions he would take in the face of these outputs and feeds these back into the model for a second run, and so on. Typically such a model might be used to simulate the development through time of some system of interest, or to achieve some desired end-point by successive approximation. Decision support systems are often used in these ways. There are also obvious possibilities for the use of such models as learning devices.

There is much empirical evidence that interactive models (which are fairly easily used with appropriate computing facilities) are greatly preferred by choice makers when there is any serious doubt about the validity of beliefs about action.

Dimension 6

A dimension of increasing importance is that of *private* to *public*. A private model is one accessible only to specified users and a public one is accessible to all. Models, incorporating as they do the knowledge and beliefs of their users and providing the capability to manipulate these beliefs and to understand better the effects of actions available to the user, almost always provide the user with extra power in a competitive situation over those without such a good model. Some people, therefore, argue that the man with a model has an ethically unacceptable advantage over the man without one. He should not keep his model private, but should make it available to at least all interested parties. This argument almost always has political overtones, in that models can be expensive to build, and it is often argued that the power of the economically powerful is thereby further increased.

Another less contentious argument is that where there is conflict there is considerable value in a common model, because the process of building it, or of working through one already built, clearly distinguishes those beliefs which enjoy consensus agreement between the conflicting parties and those which embody the conflict and must, therefore, be fought over or compromised about.

To make a model public can be a weighty decision. A public model will usually provide ammunition to enemies as well as help to friends, and it is likely to be a difficult balancing act to decide whether the bad effects outweigh the good.

Dimension 7

A final dimension worth mentioning is that of *part* to *whole*. As the real system of interest will usually be a part of some larger system, there are potential dangers in modelling it of looking at this part system as if it were a self-contained whole. Important inter-connections can be overlooked. In making predictions by experimenting on the real world these interconnections will usually manifest themselves, but, unless they are taken account of explicitly in the model building, there is a high chance that they will not be when one uses the model to make predictions. Little more can be said than that careful thought is required to avoid this danger.

MODEL-BUILDING APPROACHES

The actual act of building a model of whatever type is a creative process about which it is hard to offer guidance. It is useful to have a fair knowledge of models that have been found useful at other times and in other places, and there is much to be said for devoting time to keeping up with the literature and to developing some knowledge of the book work, at least to the extent of knowing what standard models are available. It is useful to try to cultivate the aptitude for thinking of commonalities between superficially different contexts, i.e. the ability to recognise different real systems which have similar abstract models relevant to them.

The systems approach is a useful device for abstracting a model. At one level the systems approach is no more than sitting and writing down or drawing schematically what is thought to be happening in the total system. However, it is observable that systems—collections of interacting parts—have generic properties, e.g. many are automatically goal seeking, lagged feedback is commonly built in, etc.—and are to some extent classifiable, e.g. adaptive, goal seeking or non-adaptive, open or closed, high or low variety, etc. If a system can be classified and the properties present in it determined, it might be possible, by analogy with some better-understood but similar system, to model it better. Certainly elementary errors of omission in building the model might be avoided. (Think of examples where feedback considerations were ignored.)

There is much research into the process of model building, theory construction, etc. Much of this work is concerned to develop approaches aimed at relieving inhibitions imposed culturally. Thus, there is the idea of brainstorming, for example, and indeed the whole range of ideas for team problem solving etc. is probably relevant. Many of these ideas can be viewed as reactions against a cultural system, and particularly its educational subsystem, which puts a premium on so-called vertical thinking (i.e. essentially argument by induction and an absorption with problems whose one correct solution can be derived by induction—what were earlier called precise problems), on skill in absorbing and re-producing authoritatively asserted 'facts', and on individual assessment of these skills. These concerns are not, even in the narrow context of OR, any more important in relation to model building than in relation to the problem-solving process as a whole.

VERIFICATION AND VALIDATION OF MODELS

A distinction is sometimes drawn between model verification and model validation. Verification is usually taken to mean the process of making sure that the model, regarded as a means of transforming input to output, does what the model builder intends. Thus, the verification of a simulation program would be the process of ensuring that the transformation of data to output was performed in accordance with what the model builder actually intended the model should do, unrelated to the reality being modelled. There are few systematic ways of verifying models, although sometimes there will be some set of input data for which the output is known with certainty, and it is clearly worth checking that the model does produce this known output. It is also good practice to check that the model properly analyses rare or extreme events.

Validation, which is the process of testing that the model does actually represent a viable and useful alternative means to real experimentation, is essentially data analysis and is covered briefly in the previous chapter. A point to add is that the testing should be made relevant to the use to be made of the model. The model should be at least up to what it is to be used for, but, of course, some extra plausibility beyond this is nice to have. Note, however, that most models could easily be tested to destruction if very powerful testing were insisted upon. A model can be false in detail but retain enormous value (e.g. Newtonian mechanics).

Validation is naturally impossible if the model is of something never before experienced, but this is rarely the case. It is almost certainly true that parts of the real system have been experienced before, even if at other times and in other contexts. It is also quite likely that enough analogous experience exists to make plausibility a very real criterion for evaluating the model. However, it has to be recognised that any validation of a model in these circumstances involves the extrapolation of data with all the consequent weaknesses.

MODEL SENSITIVITY

A point closely related to both verification and validation is what might be called the sensitivity of the model. Suppose it is intended to use the model to make deductions or predictions conditional on certain assumptions about the state of the world. For instance, a model may have been built to help assess the number of primary schools a local authority should make available over the next 10 or 20 years. The model predicts the size and other characteristics of the population of children in the authority over the relevant time period, working from assumptions about numerous demographic factors such as birth rate, migration to and from the authority, etc.

It is conceivable, indeed likely, that the deductions drawn from using the model may be markedly different according to the assumptions made. More particularly, they may be greatly influenced by quite small differences in certain of the assumptions. The model would be said to be sensitive to these assumptions. So, for example, it may be that the number of schoolchildren in some future year ranges widely according to small differences in the assumptions made about the ages at which women give birth to their first child. Equally, there may be assumptions which make little difference to the deductions, that is, to which the model is insensitive.

This will often be a helpful state of affairs. It will indicate what are the key factors which should influence any decision and, therefore, guide further model building towards a fuller understanding of those key factors, perhaps through further data collection, belief acquisition or refinement and more detailed modelling. If no reasonable amount of work will sufficiently improve the model, it is at least possible to make statements such as: if such-and-such is the case, the following can be deduced. Thus, if the average age at which women bear their first child is between 22 and 26, you should aim to have 28 to 30 schools in 10 years' time, if it is between 26 and 30, 24–27 schools, and so on.

However, it is quite possible that the model is so sensitive to certain assumptions as to render it nearly useless as a predictor. This would arise, for example, if predictions were so sensitive to one or more assumptions that it would be impossible to make those assumptions accurately enough to make useful predictions. Conceivably, for example, the desirable number of schools might be 10 or 100 according to whether the average age on bearing a first child was 26 years 11 months or 27 years 1 month.

Such appears to be the case for many natural systems, and much of chaos theory alluded to earlier is about such matters. Sometimes deep patterns can be found in processes which, because of extreme sensitivity to initial conditions, have the appearance of randomness and unpredictability. However, this is of small comfort in many practical situations. Often the best that can be done is to point out which assumptions are critical and, having tested and refined them as far as possible, point out the importance of continually monitoring them.

Sometimes, however, it is possible to go further and consider recasting the model, particularly if it is one which includes beliefs about the behaviour of people. This is because feedback may occur or actions other than were first thought possible may be available. These possibilities may have been overlooked or simply not thought worth considering. In the school case, for example, the local authority might have recourse to temporary school buildings or some other device which makes predictions a deal ahead less important, or young would-be parents might emigrate from the area, or think to send their children to private schools should it become clear that the local authority is failing to provide adequate schooling.

CHOOSING BETWEEN MODELS

Problems have been described as characterised by symptoms, a wish to act, and uncertainty how to act. Data might be collected and models built in order to understand better the symptoms and thereby the actions that might affect the problem; and the better to choose which action to take. Usually there will be any number of models which can be assembled by selections from currently held beliefs. Several different ones might already exist. How are the models to be chosen among? Almost any criterion might be adopted according to the needs of the case, but responsiveness to the culture of the group for whom the model is being built is, as always, necessary for effectiveness. The criteria should, therefore, be related to the values embodied in that culture. These include the values that highlighted the problem and the desire to act on it. The model should aim to address the implied concerns.

It follows that many groups will give plus points to models which are different from, to take a norm, points which might appeal to the pure scientist. An example is that usefulness will usually be prized over exactitude, usefulness here meaning doing something better now, which will be preferred to the promise of doing something perfectly in the future. The modelling process, if it can be used as an understanding generator (which almost certainly means that it must itself be understandable), might also be prized. Other valued reasons for having a model include that it helps create an image to others of a forward-looking group, etc.; that competing groups might have models which appear to be doing them good or which appear to be creating a favourable impression with some powerful party like the Government; and that a model might be a useful means of making the group's case plausible in some debate, or of strengthening the case, perhaps by predicting something dreadful if the group does not get its way. Minus points are likely to be scored by models too difficult to understand, expensive to build and use, slow of response, and so on. Thus, some models, viewed as devices, will be useless unless they can produce results to meet deadlines (as a consequence of the cultural tempo of choice making, and in particular the time between the need for choice being recognised and the need to make it). An important source of points, though whether plus or minus points depends on the context, is the choice between a model designed to be used once (specifically and quickly built) and, at the other extreme, one built for extensive use on a wide class of problems which it is anticipated might occur. The risks and gains implicit in this choice are pretty obvious.

All these plus and minus points are, of course, culture-dependent in their interpretation: what is expensive to one group might be cheap to another; a model impossible for the management of a firm to understand ten years ago might, through changes in management training, be easily understood today. The discussion of dimensions above tried to show how model form might influence the strengths of these various points. Prototyping is a way of assessing the strengths before too deep a commitment is made.

Another important case of model choice is one where two or more models can be assembled from scientific (relative to the group culture) beliefs, all of which summarise previous experience, but some or all of which would, if believed in, lead to different actions being chosen. The scientific analogue is commonplace. Some new theory (e.g. general relativity) is proposed which is no different from some previous theory (Newtonian gravitation) in summarising known information. (In fact, general relativity was better in a few respects, including describing the orbit of Mercury, but suppose it had not been.) What the scientist, in this case Einstein, does is to search for some event about which the different theories make different predictions, and seeks to perform an experiment or collect data which, by observing the event, decides between the theories (the bending of light passing near massive bodies).

Likewise, what is usually done in OR is to collect more data to decide between the models. This might be by carrying out an experiment but this may not be necessary: it might be sufficient to dig around in historical records or to look more deeply at present practices. (Unlike the scientist's, most OR models are unlikely to summarise all previous experience, in that experience will probably not have been thoroughly codified.)

A final general point is that both data collection and model building are, or can be, means to better choice making. An error of judgement easily made is to get wrong the balance between choosing actions (which can itself be a long, complicated process) and basing the choice on the right amount of data collection and model building.

APPENDIX: THE KALEIDOSCOPE PROBLEM

Your work involves you visiting a toy factory fairly often. You are on friendly terms with the Works Manager. On one of your visits he shows you a letter he has just received from the Managing Director. The text of the letter is as follows:

I am most concerned that output of kaleidoscopes has not risen as you planned it would. The following are the figures:

	Jan.	Feb.	March	April	May
Machines installed	40	60	100	130	100
Output (kaleidoscopes per machine day)	30.1	23.3	19.8	22.4	20.9
Net profit (£ per machine day)	164.5	122.0	101.1	118.4	110.6
Number of breakdowns per machine day	0.50	0.67	0.76	0.69	0.71

I am frankly disappointed. You have been given every help. From the moment we decided to increase production of kaleidoscopes no effort has been spared to get the machinery delivered. You now have 200 machines, and you should be getting five times your January production. In fact productivity is down 30%.

All the staff you need, including fitters, have been made available. I realise it takes time to train them and for this reason I have been loath to interfere. Indeed I felt we were just beginning to turn the tide in April, but the May results are so bad I feel obliged to intervene. With a capital investment of £5 million failing so dramatically I can scarcely do otherwise. Moreover, further orders are coming in and, without further investment, it seems we shall soon be losing sales and breaking contracts as well as watching profits tumble.

I want to see you first thing tomorrow, when I shall want to know what steps you are going to take to stop the downward trend in results and to get us into a position to meet demand. For my own part, I cannot help noticing how profit levels are influenced by breakdowns, and I shall expect you to be suggesting ways of improving maintenance.

The Works Manager explains to you the position as he sees it. Some big new export contracts were won for kaleidoscopes. He was told output had to be up to five times its previous level as soon as possible. Capital was raised, extra space rented and labour recruited, all at some trouble and expense. The specialised machinery was delivered as speedily as could be, the first 20 new machines arriving on 1 February and others at monthly intervals. He was put in absolute charge of increasing output. It was his big chance and he failed. In answer to your query, as far as he knows, routine record keeping has gone by the board in the rush to increase output, and no more information than the Managing Director has quoted is available, save that operators earn £30 a shift and that the kaleidoscopes sell at £10 each, material costs being £3 per kaleidoscope. However, he is very hazy about what current demand there is for kaleidoscopes, although he did hear the Export Manager say in the canteen the other day that he (the Export Manager) could easily sell as many as he could get his hands on.

The Works Manager calls in the relevant staff and they confirm the failure to keep routine records. The Maintenance Manager is strongly of the opinion that the new machines are having a lot of teething troubles and he is disposed to blame the inexperienced operators; the old machines, with the old operators, are still the most reliable. The Training Officer partially agrees. He thinks that although the operation of the machines is simple, and is supposed to be taught in a day, nevertheless it is certainly a month, and perhaps two months, before an operator is really efficient. He wonders if the machines ought to go on to three shifting (they work only two 8-hour shifts at the moment). This would increase profit per machine, even though wages might have to go up to £40 a shift for night work, he says.

EXERCISES

(1) A person finds he can buy an orange for 15 units of currency. He proposes the model

$$C = 15n$$

where n is the number of oranges bought and C is the cost of buying them.

    (i)   Comment on his data collection, data analysis and model building.

    (ii)   Where does this simple model lie in the dimensions discussed in the preceding chapter?

    (iii) If, for some purpose, you wished to build a realistic model of the cost of buying oranges, how would you go about it? Would it matter what the purpose was?

(2)   Look again at the following cases:

          Mr Bird's dilemma   (pages 1–3 and 10–12)
          The Barton Memorandum   (pages 86–88)
          ABC Airline   (page 58)
          Browns Brothers' Discounts   (pages 88–89)
          Profitable PAM   (pages 108–109)
          Service Providers   (pages 59–62)

    (i)   Case by case, would it have helped to have built a model? Why? What kind of model might it have been?

    (ii)   From the information provided in each case, can a useful model be built? If not, what is the least further information necessary to build a useful model?

    (iii) In at least one case, build a model making such assumptions as are necessary. Place it on the dimensions discussed in this chapter.

    (iv) Is any of the models particularly sensitive to any of the assumptions or estimates you have had to make? Can you do anything about this?

    (v)   Use the model(s) to answer 'what if' questions that some of the actors might have put. Is this an important use of models?

    (vi) In which cases might a standing model (i.e one kept up to date regardless of immediate use) have been justified? How much might it have been worth spending on such a model? (Express your answer relative to the costs of other activities in each case.)

(3)   Make a model of some everyday activity in which you engage (e.g. your early-morning routine). Ask a friend to make a model of the same thing based on your description of the activity and your answers to questions your friend might put. Compare the models, noting the similarities and differences. Are there similarities through shared assumptions, or are the similarities because of similar perceptions of actuality? What about the differences? Try to construct a jointly agreed model. What difficulties does this present? Was the exercise useful? Will it change your behaviour?

(4)   Consider the Kaleidoscope Problem (pages 131–132).

    (i)   The Works Manager wants your advice for the meeting and you agree to spend the remaining two hours at your disposal. What do you think his problem is? What advice do you give him? Would you build a model?

(ii)   Construct a model or models which you think might help the Works Manager. Does building the model(s) help your understanding of the problem? Would it help the Works Manager and his colleagues to have participated in the model building?

(iii)   Position your models(s) on dimensions 1 to 7 of this chapter. Would some repositioning be desirable? How could it be achieved?

(iv)   Are there any key pieces of research which would greatly improve the value of the model(s)? Were they suggested in the model-building process?

(v)   Discuss the verification of your model(s).

(vi)   Should the Works Manager maintain a model or models?

(5)   Seek information about a few models of the national economy and their predictive performance over the last few years. Of what value do you think the models have been to policy makers? Is there evidence that the models have been used politically? What has been the response to predictions of poor economic performance? Are the models getting better (as, presumably, they should be as experience accumulates)? If not, why not?

(6)   Can you think of examples where an ill-chosen model has led to grossly unsatisfactory outcomes? How did it come to be chosen? Was its weakness predictable? (Possible example of public issues might be the community charge ('poll tax') in the UK; various disastrous military campaigns; or the selection of an unsuccessful sports team.)

(7)   Consider prototyping as a means of data collection. List some of the data which might be gathered by prototyping but not easily by other means. (Possible examples are to do with the use people make of models, and, by implication, their value systems or what concerns them; and how they respond to these concerns.) How might this affect your model building? Referring to Chapter 7, should prototyping have been mentioned as a source of data or is it a special case of stimulated data? Would your answers be the same if 'model use' replaced 'prototyping' in the above? Why?

Chapter 9
_____ Making Choices

Life presents choices for everyone. Choice arises as a consequence of a problem and a wish to change to alleviate it. The choice is which change to make. This chapter discusses how OR might help. It is worth first remarking how frequently people make choices in their everyday life and in their work, including, if they are an OR worker, in their conduct of a piece of OR work. Much writing about choice conjures up images of choice at the grand level—where to site an oil refinery, how to deploy an army, and so on. The reader is invited to think, as he reads the following, as much of choice in the everyday conduct of life and work as in the more obviously striking cases of 'big' decisions.

An individual, faced with a choice, makes the choice which presumably he thinks is best for him. He might, through incompetence, make a choice which proves wrong after the event; or he might let others make the choice for him, either because he wishes them to do so (as, for example, if he asks a lawyer to act for him, or his priest to advise him) or because he is afraid to exercise choice himself (perhaps for deep psychological reasons or just because his boss dominates him); or he might not regard the choice as important and leave it to chance, even tossing a coin; or he might be so unsure of the effects of his choice as to be overwhelmed by all the uncertainties and almost paralysed into indecision.

He might also hesitate about making a choice because, while superficially the choice is his alone, he knows the potential effects of the choice will spill over to other people. Indeed, the outcome from exercising choice might well depend on the response of other people to the choice actually made. The person making the choice might hesitate while he considers, by whatever means, the likely responses of others and how he should accommodate them. In particular, the effects of the choice might spill over to some identifiable group of which he is part (his family, his political party, the other employees of the firm he works for, etc.). Indeed many choices are best thought of not as available to individuals but rather to the group constituted by the individuals. In many cases, groups make group choices, and the individual member of the group himself has to choose between acceptance of the group's choice, acceptance for now but working within the group to change it, or withdrawal from the group.

Some choices will be irrevocable, although only rarely will this be absolutely the case. Other choices are readily revocable, so that the person making the choice can change his mind with no, or minimal, effect on himself or anyone else. Such choices need concern no one. They might as well be made by trial and error. Most choices of interest fall into some middle ground. They are revocable, but at some cost and with some consequences in the future. Typical consequences may be to restrict available choice next time, to damage relationships with colleagues, and so on. (In assessing the outcomes of exercising choice in a particular way, it will be desirable to take such things into account.)

WHO CHOOSES AND HOW?

Faced with a choice, an individual or a group has to decide two things: who should make the choice and how it should be made? 'Who should make the choice' and 'how it should be made' might interact. 'Who' and 'how' could, for example, be answered, for a group, by all members of the group by a vote, the most popular choice being taken. But normally in any sophisticated group the question 'who should choose' is answered by: some individual or group of individuals within the group, as it might be the chief executive of a firm or the committee of a sports club. The question 'how the choice should be made' would be answered by the processes those who are to make the choice should go through in order to do so. The processes include how he, she, or they decide what choices are possible; by what means they choose (for example, what advice they take and what consultations they make); and what criteria ultimately dictate their choice.

Most groups have rules which answer these questions for many decisions. Thus, in many countries of the world the accepted, or even enforced, rules are that choices of national policy are made by a small elite and are made in the interests of that elite. In other countries, there is broad agreement to rules that allow choices of national policy to be made by an elite, but which keep self-interest in check by a frequent process of parliamentary votes, general elections etc. In less important groups there may be rules which hand power to choose over a specified area of the group's activities to one of the group, and the power is withheld from him if he abuses it. Thus, in a youth club, one member might be allowed to buy all the gramophone records, a privilege he might lose if he spends too much money or reveals too narrow a taste.

Sometimes it is not widely agreed within a group who should exercise choice on its behalf. Disagreement might be so widespread as to cause anarchy. In some cases, a significant sub-group might agree that other people should exercise choice than the current rules specify. If those who at present exercise choice, or those who think they should continue to do so, have no intention of changing, the group might break up—the relevant members of the tennis club will set up another club elsewhere or, on the larger scale, there might be bloody revolution. Very often, however, people accept the current rules about who should choose for the time being but agitate for their change. Thus, the people of Cornwall might feel very strongly that the Chancellor of the Exchequer in London should not decide the rate of income tax in Cornwall. All Cornishmen might, as a consequence, withhold payment of tax. But more likely they will pay tax and press for change through political or quasi-political means.

If, for any particular choice, all those affected by it agree who should make it (as, for example, if this is established by an unchallenged rule) the position is simpler than if they do not. However, even if it is agreed who should make the choice, it might still be a matter for debate how he should make it.

There will often be in a group some sense of the 'proper' way to exercise choice, to the extent that a choice not made in this way, however favourable its outcome, will be regarded as unsatisfactory. Perhaps, in relation to the group in question, there is some objective way of making the choice: that is, all members of the group would, if they were choice maker, make the same choice as the individual would (or at least believe they would, if they were clever enough or well enough informed etc.). If this is so, the choice is, of course, made as if it were an individual's choice. More likely, however, not all members of the group will agree how the choice should be made, and there will often be extensive debate about how it is to be made even though it is accepted who should make it. The debate might be about criteria to be used, the degree of consultation to be carried out, the composition of choice-making teams, or many other things. Thus, in a democracy, named officials like Finance Ministers are accorded wide consensus powers for exercising choice about fiscal options and, by and large, when they have chosen, their choice is accepted. But this does not stop numerous individuals and groups from exercising sometimes considerable powers of persuasion, usually within rules, to influence how the choice is made, nor does it stop them from arguing that it was badly made and should be changed.

How the choice is to be made also includes questions of when and where. A named time and place at which the choice will be made is often published. Sometimes members of the group who are not among the choice makers are allowed, even encouraged, to attend. Indeed a whole calendar of choice-making meetings could well be published, together with terms of reference defining what each meeting will make choices about, who may attend and who participate. Much of the routine, but nevertheless important, choice making of organised groups is, at least superficially, carried out in this way. In companies, for example, the routine of choices about company strategy, resource allocation, accountability, and so on is exercised through regularly meeting and properly constituted bodies like boards of directors, budget committees, investment committees, and so on. This apparatus will be complemented by information flows, pre-circulated papers, and much preliminary work by a range of people.

Often the choice is not exercised when or where it is advertised to be. Formal bodies often endorse choices already made, if not acted on. Sometimes they seek justification for the choice. However, if they are unhappy about a choice put to them for endorsement, they will commonly not make an alternative choice but instead ask for an alternative to be put to them next time they meet. The actual choice-making (or perhaps more strictly choice-proposing) processes will be going on elsewhere. They will often be going on in quite difficult to divine manners, at surprising times, and in surprising places. Who is involved in them could be equally surprising.

It is important in advising people how they should choose to be sure what rules, explicit or not, about who should choose and how, are current in the relevant group. It is one thing to offer advice within this set of rules and quite another to offer advice which is implicitly asking that the rules should be changed. Thus, suppose in a factory the actual rules of choice about which men work on which machines are that the men decide among themselves and force their decision upon the factory management by various unofficial and well-camouflaged industrial means. It is quite futile to advise the factory manager, who perhaps in some set of written rules is given agreed power to allocate men to machines, to use some clever work-study-based allocation procedure. Either the adviser helps him make the best job he can given the men's behaviour, conceivably suggesting ways of outwitting them without breaking the unwritten rules, or he helps him go about getting the rules changed.

The OR worker has to be prepared to find out enough about the culture in which he is working to know by whom, when, where and how, choice is being exercised if he is seeking to influence it, and to act in conscious awareness of these things. Much OR flounders on a failure to act on this point.

ANTICIPATING CHOICE

Rather as problems sometimes occur in a surprising way and, moreover, often require too quick a resolution to be solved other than *ad hoc*, so sometimes do choices. If an unexpected opportunity to exercise choice occurs which must be seized quickly (or else some default choice like 'leave things as they are' is taken) an organised group might be ill equipped to respond sensibly. Both 'who' and 'how' may be undecided. In other cases the time-scales associated with the agreed who and how will be too lengthy for a timely response. If some self-elected person or sub-group chooses, other members of the group might be retrospectively very angry; and if the choice is made by an accepted person, how he does it might be arbitrarily decided, again without consensus agreement.

For this reason many sophisticated groups plan ahead. They try to define choice opportunities that will or may be available in the future, and to anticipate how and by whom the choices should be exercised, trying also to achieve anticipatory consensus. Those choosing for such groups also often give notice of decisions they intend to make and encourage other group members to offer comment and amendments to the decision. However, none of this can alter the fact that some choice opportunities cannot be anticipated. Groups often try to meet this difficulty by having rules which allow for extraordinary action by some appropriate person or persons. Some try to meet it by rules which effectively prevent all but certain default choices in such situations.

An often advanced view, though it is probably a counsel of perfection, is that groups should so organise their affairs as to be highly adaptive (that is, among other things, to respond rapidly and efficiently to choice opportunities). Another view is that groups should not passively wait for these choice opportunities but spend much effort anticipating them, perhaps controlling them or even creating them. The mechanisms for ensuring such stances, and the means by which widespread agreement to the development and use of the mechanisms can be achieved, are not always clear.

Needless to say, any perceived need to rush at a choice could be mistaken. Many groups can easily be whipped up into a frenzied desire to choose when choice can be deferred at no loss, but this desire may be so real as to require satisfaction.

THE OR ROLE

The OR worker will himself make choices in his personal life and in his work. He might also be one of those who chooses on behalf of a group—for example, as an employee representative, or a member of some management grouping, and so on. However, the role of the OR worker as such is not usually to exercise choice, but rather to help those who do. He may be able to help in any of a variety of ways. He may, for example, be able to contribute significantly to deciding how the choice should be made, as well as helping to predict the outcomes of different choices, designing decision support systems to help the choice process, designing systems which draw attention to the need or desirability for a choice to be made, and so on. Many of these things will be accomplished, or at least attempted, via the medium of a model or some sort of structuring.

In principle the OR role is, as always, helping clients who have problems. However, there have grown up many technical aids, strongly associated with OR, which are specifically geared to the problem of choosing among options—mathematical programming, various combinatoric methods, etc. As commonly depicted, these methods assume a single choice maker (or, what amounts to the same thing, a choice-making group with a relevant consensus within it) who will make the measurably best choice. This will not always be a valid assumption. (Indeed, it could be said to be valid only for trivial problems. Many engaged in OR are critical of what they see as a presumption, particularly in courses, textbooks and other publications, that OR is useful only when this assumption holds. They feel this limits the use of OR in problems of clear interest—for example, in social and political matters, and in groups with unclear choice-making hierarchies.) More usually there will be much debate about who should choose or, if some group is allowed to choose, conflict within that group about how choice should be made. As remarked in an earlier chapter, the scope for OR in such circumstances is perhaps limited to taking sides (i.e. working on behalf of one of the debating parties) or helping to structure the issues and working on those aspects which the parties agree are suitably addressed by OR.

However, while the roots of many OR methods lie in the idea of a single choice maker seeking the best choice, many of the methods are just as relevant to helping a client who is one of a group making a choice where there is disagreement in the group, or to helping such a group structure its processes. In practice, it is this point which often gives them their value. The rest of this chapter is about these methods and the way they can help, but first they are given a context.

To define some terms, the things to be chosen between will be called options. Generally an option will be an action or set of related actions which the choice maker believes can be taken. The act of making a choice among them will be called simply making a choice. There are two important problem areas: first, to develop a list of options to choose from; and second, given the list of possible options, to choose from them.

The wider the range of options chosen from, the better is the choice likely to be (but, of course, the more difficult it is likely to be to make). Creative effort devoted to thinking up a wide range of choice is, therefore, not likely to be wasted. (Note in passing that a group will sometimes decide who should exercise choice on its behalf not by who *chooses* best (which in many cases can be reduced to a technical chore), but by who can think up the more imaginative options. Many sophisticated groups have quite explicit rules for choosing, but equally explicit rules for *not* inhibiting the advancement of numerous alternative options. Indeed there are often rules designed to force the production of numerous alternatives. Thus, in some countries a free press is encouraged and even protected, partly to allow the generation of options; public money finds its way into university research geared to the exploration and development of new options for economic and social policies; interest groups are encouraged to present evidence to Royal Commissions and the like.) Aspects of this point crop up later, and indeed it has been touched on before. It offers important opportunities to the OR worker, perhaps more through the scope his methods offer to increase the number of options considered than through his being allowed or encouraged to create new options. However, a good relationship with a client, underwritten by earlier achievement, may well encourage option creation, and from time to time it may be the recognised problem to which the OR is addressed from the outset. Moreover, the use of some of the methods discussed below may stimulate or even force the production of new options.

Turn now to choosing from the options. It is possible to conceive of an ideal state (never realised, of course) in which the effects of choosing any of the considered options can be accurately predicted, and, moreover, in which these effects are such that different options can all be ranked in order of the choice maker's preference for them. Perhaps, for example, some quantity like profit can be assigned as the outcome of each option. The choice is then easily made: the effects of each option are predicted and the preferred one is chosen. (It might be arithmetically difficult to do this, but there is no difficulty in principle.)

Another ideal case is that in which the effects of pursuing each option are predictable but where these different effects are not easily compared. Thus, each option available to a firm might have accurately predictable effects on both short-term profits and labour relations: it might be no easy matter to compare one option which leads to high profits and poor labour relations with another which leads to lower profits and improved labour relations. This will be particularly so if there is uncertainty or disagreement about what the firm's goals are, what it is trying to do: in this case maximise short- or long-term profits, for example. Perhaps most importantly, different options might have quite different effects on different members of the group: an airport at A rather than an airport at B has some effect on residents of everywhere else than A and B, but profound effects on those who live at A or B. This is the area of *multiple criteria*.

Alternatively, again as an ideal case, it is possible that the different effects can be ranked but what effects stem from pursuing each option can be predicted only statistically. This is the field of *decision theory*.

Methods are available of clear use in these ideal cases. Unfortunately, there is only one realistic case: neither can the effects of options be predicted, nor can the effects of different options be compared and thus options ranked. What must be hoped, if the methods are to be helpful, is one or both of two things. The first is that something close enough to an ideal case can be abstracted from the mess to allow the methods to be of direct value. The second possibility is that the methods might structure the choice-making process by forcing discussion, and hopefully agreement, about the key issues that influence the choice.

Clearly an ideal case cannot always be abstracted, but it might sometimes be possible, by research, analysis, negotiation and just careful thought, to do it well enough for practical purposes. Indeed, a strong case could be made for saying that the essence of good OR is precisely to reduce the difficulties of choice making. Thus, data collection, data analysis and model building can be directed to the aim of achieving the ultimate ideal state of perfect predictability and comparability of the options' effects. In some cases, careful attention to thinking up options which reduce risk might be appropriate. In other circumstances, even to attempt these things might be wasteful of time and money: it might cost more than its help to the choice maker is worth.

In some perfect world an optimum balance could be struck between the costs of preliminary research and analysis, the time it takes and the added value it gives by way of a better choice or an improvement made earlier or later. It will rarely be possible to decide what this balance is or to strike it, but the general principle is one to be borne in mind. Note also that sometimes a party to the choice might wish to delay it. An effective way of doing so is to insist on lengthy preliminary research, analysis and model building. In other cases, there may be an enthusiasm for choosing before it is necessary to do so. This is often advocated on grounds of removing uncertainty, and its presumed bad effects, from the minds of those who will be affected by the choice. These things have to be balanced with the possibility of new information and further analysis which is foregone, and the possibility of some more or less unanticipated change in the world, any of which might change the preferred choice.

The second, and probably more important point in practice, is that the various methods provide an agenda around which the choice-making process can be conducted. For example, the process might start by assuming perfect predictability and comparability for the effects of various options. A choice is proposed on that basis, but the choice-making group is unhappy with it: it transpires they do not really accept comparability. An exercise is now undertaken which exploits a method appropriate to choice when comparison is difficult. And so the process continues. The whole may well be highly interactive between the various parties engaged in the choice making, including the OR worker. This is usually desirable.

These points of potential usefulness will not be laboured case by case in discussing the methods, although some relevant remarks are made. The reader is invited, the general points having been made, to bear them in mind in his reading.

The remainder of the chapter discusses methods that might help in the various cases outlined above. Much of the ensuing material assumes that preliminary work (in terms of prediction, generating consensus about values, and option creation) has been done before addressing the question of choice. Of course, this preliminary work may, as the choice-making process develops, be elaborated. The whole process is likely to be a somewhat messy one of considering options, narrowing the list, calling for more work on prediction, reshaping the list, and so on. It is often a learning process, in that those engaged in it learn much about the issue in hand and about their attitudes to it.

GENERATING AND LISTING OPTIONS

As remarked, choice is likely to be better, the more options are being chosen from. Against this, the mechanics of choosing may be unduly laborious or time consuming if the list of options becomes too long. It would be helpful to have some means of generating options, and then making some preliminary culling of them which leaves a list which is relatively short but contains the good ones. This is easier said than done. Some possibly useful ideas for the OR worker drawn into these issues follow.

The generation of options is comparatively easily done if the available options are characterised by a handful of numbers. The list of options is then the list of all meaningful combinations of these numbers. Seldom is it as simple as that, but sometimes it is for all practical purposes. The simplest case is where the options are yes or no, do or don't. (Go to this concert or do not go.) In other cases, several numbers may be enough. Thus, to someone choosing a hotel for a business trip, the options may be sufficiently characterised by some 0/1 variables (rooms do/do not have private bathrooms, television, etc.) and other continuous ones (price, distance from city centre, etc.). In many cases, however, the available options are not so simply developed. They may differ in kind as well as in degree.

Various methods are available to stimulate options. Many entail bringing as many minds to bear on the task as possible, often in an environment designed to stimulate wide-ranging thinking. Consultative exercises by local government, weekends away for a board of directors to review policy, annual conferences of trade unions or political parties, are all in their various ways manifestations of this phenomenon. Other more or less structured approaches are used. Some have overtones of brainstorming, some are organised almost as competitions and some are simply suggestion schemes. These or similar approaches seem necessary if, in option generation, undue constraint is to be avoided. Sticking to tradition and a disinclination to think innovatively are commonly observed behaviours. There is a tendency, too, to stick with options whose effects can be analysed and predicted. Mathematical theories, for example, offer powerful analyses of certain aspects of situations, and might lead to options not covered by them being ignored. It is well to guard against subconscious exclusion of options for these reasons.

Any of these processes may lead to too long a list of options from among which to make considered choice. There will commonly be one or more preliminary cullings of the list before a final short list from which the choice is made. Putting it another way, there will be a succession of lists, each shorter than the previous one. The options omitted from list to list are not, until the final list is reached, likely to be evaluated one by one. Rather, some more or less course sifting will delete a whole batch of options of a particular kind. Various ways of doing this sifting are discussed in what follows on optimisation with multiple criteria where they are given tangible shape around an example, but they merit brief reference here.

Criteria for shortening the list of options covered below include the important one of efficiency or dominance. In a nutshell, this says all options should be deleted which are plainly inferior to another option on the list. If it is desired to choose among people for some combination of their attributes, there is no point in leaving on the list someone who is worse in every attribute than another on the list. Often this kind of thing is done rather arbitrarily, recognising that mistakes may be made but equally that the chance of doing so is small. Thus, if one of the desired attributes were 10 years' experience of computer programming, everyone under 28 years of age might be cut out if that were easier than ploughing through the list checking on programming experience. It may mean losing a few people who were really suitable, but, nonetheless, in total it is likely to be a sensible procedure.

More generally, options are often constrained out for any of a variety of reasons. Common ones includes doubts about whether the option can be implemented, fear of indirect or unforeseen consequences of the option, and so on. Other common criteria include deleting options that differ markedly from ones known to have worked well in the past, and, closely related, deleting options which appear to offer undue risk.

Finally, note that the size of the final short list may be the dominating criterion because the cost of a thorough evaluation of options is so high. While, no doubt, there will be the wish to get down to the short list by means as sensible as possible, it is sometimes necessary to act rather arbitrarily in getting there.

OPTIMISATION

Given a set of options, the act of choosing the best is known as 'optimisation'. In order to optimise, a good predictive model, or at least an adequate one, is needed. Some device for ranking the options is also necessary, that is, some function of the outcomes of taking the different options which is essentially scalar is needed. ('Scalar' is here and below used to imply comparability, that is, a function is scalar if its values can be put in order, including placed equal as a special case. The simplest example of a scalar quantity is number: so, for example, height is a scalar quantity, and, of two things, one is higher or they are equal in height. However, qualitative measures can be scalar: a piece of work might be rated unsatisfactory, fair, good or excellent, and, of two pieces of work, one is either better than the other (good versus fair, say) or they are equal.)

This function is called the objective function. If the outcome of choosing an option is intrinsically scalar, it constitutes the objective function. In such a case, any two options can be compared and the better one chosen; and, therefore, the best of a set of possible options can be chosen. If the outcome is not scalar, and cannot easily be made so, the choice of the objective function, and therefore the comparison of options and choice among them, is less clear cut.

Optimisation is clearly a subjective act. The person or group performing it chooses how to make predictions and how to assess their adequacy; and chooses what objective function to use. Different people might, usually would, choose differently.

SIMPLE OPTIMISATION

There is often an adequate predictive model and a clear scalar objective function, and all interested parties agree this is so. In this case optimisation is, in theory at any rate, a trivial step and an uncontroversial one for the OR worker or anyone else to take. It can be, and often is, automated, e.g. taken by computer. The arithmetic involved and the way of organising it may, however, be far from trivial. If there are just a handful of options these are easily compared. The methods of calculus will be relevant in other cases where the options are characterised by continuous parameters and their outcomes have particular functional forms. Difficulties can arise when the outcomes are many or infinite in number.

Much of the mathematics associated with OR is concerned with the pursuit of efficient algorithms for choosing among many possible options when their outcomes are scalar. Even in some apparently simple cases, the arithmetic necessary to choose the best is so lengthy as to be impracticable and it is necessary to be satisfied by finding a good option as opposed to the best. (Even if not impracticable, the arithmetic may be so time or resource consuming that the total balance of cost of arithmetic plus value of choice favours not finding the best so much as a good option.)

An important concept in this general field is that of polynomial bounding of the time taken to find the best option. Suppose the options and their outcomes are specified by n numbers. The problem of choosing the best option may be solvable in a time bounded by some power of n. That is, as n increases, the time taken increases in proportion to a power of n. The problem is then said to be a member of the class P. In all such cases and others, calculating the outcome of a particular *single* option can be done in a time bounded by a power of n. Such a problem is said to be a member of the class NP. (Clearly P is included in NP.) For many problems in NP, no way has yet been found of comparing all the option outcomes in a time bounded by a power of n. For such problems the time taken, as n increases, increases exponentially with n. For reasonably large n, even a polynomially bounded time could be unacceptably long. A time not so bounded can easily become impossibly long.

To exemplify these points, consider the problem of choosing the greatest of n numbers (i.e. there are n possible options and numbers A1, A2, ..., An which are their outcomes). Plainly this can be done in a time which is proportional to n. The problem is a member of P (and, of course, of NP, as calculating the outcome of a single option is just reading one number). Consider now the travelling salesman problem, which in general is specified by the $n(n-1)$ numbers in a square matrix of distances between pairs of n towns. The problem is to find the shortest way of visiting every town. If a route is specified (i.e. a particular option is given), its distance is calculated in a time proportional to n (it is simply finding and adding n distances). The problem is, therefore, in NP. However, no way has been found of choosing the shortest of all routes (of which there are $(n-1)!$) which can be performed in a time bounded by a power of n. (A little arithmetic will convince the reader that evaluating the outcome of $(n-1)!$ options becomes horrendously time consuming for reasonably large n.)

Among problems in P are linear programming (the proof of this is comparatively recent) and finding the shortest route through a network. Among problems in NP but not known to be in P are, as already remarked, the travelling salesman problem and integer linear programming.

As an aside, an interesting question is whether P and NP are the same (i.e. whether any problem in NP can be solved in polynomial time in principle, even if a way has not yet been found a way to do so). The answer is almost certainly no. Some problems—the travelling salesman is one—are what is known as NP-hard. NP-hard problems are such that, if any one of them can be shown to be a member of P, then P and NP are the same. None has been shown to be, despite much effort to do so.

The practical importance of all this is clear. Simply having a good predictive model is not enough to guarantee finding an optimum when there are many possible options, even when the outcomes of the options are scalar. The number of options considered has often to be restricted by some means or another, and not necessarily the best chosen but only the best among those considered.

OPTIMISATION WITH MULTIPLE CRITERIA

Turn now to the case where there is a predictive model generally acknowledged to be adequate, but the outcome induced by different options is not readily expressible in a generally accepted scalar form. Some different approaches to helping choose among the available options in these circumstances are discussed below. The question of performing the calculations is not returned to, but it goes without saying that if this can present difficulties in the simpler case, it can certainly do so here.

Suppose there are possible options A, B, C... Option A has an outcome (a1, a2, a3...). a1, a2, a3... are measured on scales which are not immediately comparable, at least to the choice maker. These scales will be referred to as dimensions. Thus, a1 may be profit this year, a2 may be the closing stock position at the end of the year, a3 may be the amount of recruitment necessary to implement option A, etc. Most importantly a1, a2, a3,... might be the outcomes for party 1, party 2, party 3,... (assumed scalar here, but actually more likely to be vectors).

Useful aids here might cut down the number of options that need to be considered or, what really amounts to the same thing, introduce some partial ordering among the outcomes of the options and, therefore, among the options themselves. (A set is partially ordered if the statement A is better than B or vice versa can be made for some pairs of members of the set, but not all pairs, and if A is better than B and B is better than C are both valid statements, then A is better than C is implied.) Easing the choice-making task by using these methods is not, of course, just a matter of convenience. Sometimes the search for perfection may be more time consuming or costly than is justified by the value of being right or, putting it another way, the value of improving from a reasonable or good choice to the best one.

To fix ideas, and as a peg around which to hang subsequent discussion, consider a simple case. Suppose someone has to choose one child to whom to award a scholarship. A group of children, A, B, C,... have applied for the scholarship, and have been given tests in three subjects—say, reading, writing and arithmetic. Each child is marked out of a hundred in each subject. What approaches might the OR worker adopt to help choose which child should be awarded the scholarship, based purely on the marks obtained in the examination? (This simple example is chosen merely for exposition. The reader is invited to go through approaches 1 to 8 below with other examples. A possible example might be where the options are different computer systems. Another could be one where the options A, B, C,... have outcomes a1, a2, a3,... etc. where 1, 2, 3, ... are different people, such as might be the case where the options are different routes for a by-pass.)

A sensible initial step before embarking on comparison is often to check whether the outcomes are independent one of another and, if they are not, to choose a new vector representation of outcomes which has as near-independent elements as possible. This is to prevent the way the outcome is expressed biasing choices. Thus, it is possible in the case of the school-children that reading and writing are so highly correlated that the marks in one would have to be ignored, or the average of the two used instead of both, unless verbal skill is to be given double the weighting of numerical skill. To take another example, if profit, profit margin as a percentage of turnover, return on capital employed and market share were the outcomes of following certain commercial options, careless comparison might lead to biasing the comparison in favour of financial return, even though it was intended to give equal weight to market share. (More generally, careful consideration should be given to what outcomes positively to include in making a choice. What follows rather assumes that all outcomes are pre-dicted and some chosen to work with: more commonly, some are predicted and important ones sometimes left out. In this connection, see the remarks on cycling below.)

Some possible ways of helping to compare the available options are now discussed, in general terms and around the specific example. As will become clear, the methods described are almost as much about exploring the choice of objective as about the choice of option. They are aids to choice making, not means of making choices.

1. Efficient Options and Dominance

The first thing to be done in comparing options, once it has been decided how to represent their outcomes, is to restrict the list of options to be con-sidered to those which are efficient. An efficient option is one such that there is no other option which has a higher ranking in one of the outcomes and at least as high a ranking in any of the others. Thus, if there is one of the schoolchildren who has scored (65, 60, 58) he is obviously to be pre-ferred to any child whose score is (x, y, z) where $x \leq 65, y \leq 60, z \leq 58$ and at least one of $x < 65, y < 60, z < 58$ holds. Equally he is inferior to any child whose score is (u, v, w) where $u \geq 65, v \geq 60, w \geq 58$ and at least one of $u > 65, v > 60, w > 58$ holds. This point can be put graphically in two dimensions (suppose it were just writing and reading) as in Figure 9.1. In this figure the x's denote the individual children's results. The ringed x's are the 'efficient' children. If there is only one efficient option, it is presumably chosen.

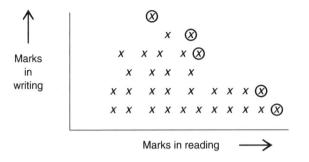

Figure 9.1

This is introducing a partial ordering by using the ordering in individual dimensions. The idea of dominance has been used. (Option A is said to dominate option B if it is better than it in one dimension and not worse than it in all others.)

If $(x, y, z, ...)$ were the scalar outcomes of an option for a number of individuals, note that an efficient option is one for which the outcome cannot be improved for any single individual without worsening it for at least one (and usually more, if not all) of the others. Such an option is said to be Pareto optimal.

If the choice maker does not accept restriction to efficient options, and assuming he understands the point, the overwhelmingly likely reason is that there is some further measures of outcome that has been overlooked, but which matters to the choice maker. Its overlooking might be inadvertent or deliberate, the latter particularly if it is one which the choice maker would be reluctant should be known influences him. Thus, in the schoolchildren example, suppose a school were awarding the scholarship and it was keen to preserve its reputation for music or sport, say. The school may wish the public perception to be that the scholarship is awarded on academic merit, but may nevertheless wish to take the other relevant attributes into account.

2. Ignoring the Problem

As an aid to choosing an option, the options might be ordered on only one of the outcomes. This amounts to ignoring the multidimensional nature of the problem. (It is possible to go further than this and ignore the outcomes altogether and pick an option in a purely arbitrary way.) To rank on the basis of one dimension is not necessarily a silly thing to do, particularly if it is treated as a first step. For example, the options might be ranked on profit while making explicit the values of the other outcomes. It might then be proposed that the choice maker or choice-making group choose the option with the highest profit which is acceptable in the other dimensions. This forces consideration by the choice maker of what he is really trying to do, or what his objective is.

This idea extends naturally to ordering in one dimension (the most important) and within that in a second (the next most important) and so on, as in a dictionary. The ordering of importance among the dimensions would presumably have been a matter for discussion and decision beforehand. There is an implicit idea of a kind of weak dominance here. Option A might dominate option B in what is considered the most important outcomes without fully dominating it, but for practical purposes the proposal is offered that A should be regarded as dominating B. In the scholarship example the children might simply be ranked on ability in reading and the scholarship awarded to the best reader. Or they may be ranked in order of reading ability as an aid to the choice maker, with the proposal that he takes the best reader whose marks in other subjects are 'satisfactory'. The ranking may, of course, be on a less simple basis (e.g. classify into those with 3 marks over 70, who out-rank those with 2 over 70 and 1 between 60 and 70, who out-rank those ... etc., and rank within classes by total marks).

Another related possibility is to list possible objectives and say (if possible): if your objective is..., then you should choose option... In the schoolchildren case, at its simplest, this might be to say: if you want the best reader, choose the child with the best marks in reading, and so on. What might be more interesting is that there may be, or it may be possible to construct, a model which relates marks in this examination with subsequent performance at various levels (say, GCSE, A-level, admission to higher education). It may then be possible to say: if you want the child who is going to do best at GCSE, choose X; if at A-level, choose Y; if at gaining admission to higher education, choose Z. The choice maker's thinking is, again, thereby concentrated on what objectives he is pursuing. (In general this approach might be called conditional optimisation.) ('Ignoring' is perhaps an over-strong word to describe these approaches.)

3. Scalarising the Problems

A stronger thing to do is to introduce a complete ordering to the set of options by reducing all the dimensions to one. This may be achieved, for example, by using monetary value as the common denominator for all the dimensions (e.g. cost-benefit analysis). There are an infinity of ways in which can a scalar can be constructed from a vector, and which of the ways is ultimately chosen is at the heart of the problem. It is what the choice is about. Some prior research is possible—for example, posing questions like 'how much would you pay to avoid having to recruit?' and other more complicated comparisons. A simple thing to do in the schoolchildren example would be to use the average mark; a slightly more subtle thing would be to standardise the score in each of three tests and then take averages; another possibility would be to take a weighted average of these standardised scores reflecting the varying weights the examiners put on different subjects—for example, greater weight could be given to reading ability than to skill in arithmetic. There are many more subtle approaches to introducing full ordering. One example is provided by the idea of goal programming. The idea here is that there is some acceptable level for the outcome of each variable and the option is chosen whose outcome maximises the least excess, in any one variable, of outcome over desired level. Another approach is that of utility theory, described below in the discussion of choosing between gambles.

A particular form of scalarisation is the use of so-called proxy variables (of which crude cost-benefit analysis is an example). This arises most commonly when the outcomes are numerous and/or their relation to some presumed 'true' objective is obscure. Thus, the question 'what should be the level of expenditure on the health services?' might be analysed by predicting any number of outputs for various levels of expenditure. However, the 'true' objective is some generalised abstract concept like the health of the people. Some scalar combination of the outputs which it is believed correlates highly with the true objective (e.g. a weighted combination of infant mortality, man-days lost in industry, waiting time for minor operations, etc.) may be proposed as a proxy objective function: it stands proxy for the true one. (More generally a proxy variable is a measure which stands in lieu of some other unmeasured variable where the unmeasured one is the one of importance.)

Naturally, these and similar techniques have no absolute validity. To use any means of introducing full ordering is, in effect, to be making trade-off decisions between the various dimensions, and this is necessarily a subjective exercise. Indeed, to use such an approach in practice is likely to be useful more as a means of stimulating thinking, discussion and negotiation about the appropriate scalar, or in other words the objective or goal being aimed for, than to lead directly to a choice.

4. Constraining Option Choice

A common way of narrowing the field of options from which to select is by introducing constraints which have the effect of rendering some (preferably many) of the possible options unacceptable. Thus, in planning the flows of goods from factories to customers, a constraint that says at least 80% of the present flows must persist may be invoked in order to restrict the set of options which are acceptable. (In the example given, the constraint may have been imposed because the costs of change are felt to be worth taking into implicit account. Some such rationale will usually guide the constraining, with doubts about implementability as a common criterion.) To use such an approach concentrates attention on the constraints, their validity and, when appropriate, ways of removing or weakening them.

Possible constraints in the schoolchildren problem would be that anyone who scores fewer than 40% in any one subject would not be accepted, nor would anyone who scores more than half his total marks in one subject, etc.

5. Establishing Equivalent Sets

Sometimes it may appear easier to express indifference between certain options than to order others. If, for example, the whole set of options can be reduced to two exhaustive and exclusive sub-sets such that the choice maker is quite indifferent between any two members of one of the sub-sets, the problem would be reduced to choosing between a pair of options, the one arbitrarily selected from the first sub-set and the other arbitrarily selected from the second. More generally, it may be possible to group the options into a few sub-sets and so reduce the problem of choice. Administrative hierarchies sometimes work this way. The top level of the hierarchy choose among certain very broad sets of options—the sub-set labelled growth, the sub-set labelled no redundancies, the sub-set labelled prevent take-over etc. (i.e. in this example the top level is indifferent between any option which guarantees growth). They communicate which sub-set they have chosen down to the next level, which then chooses among the options in that sub-set. (In the example quoted it is far from obvious that an option would be in one and only one of the sub-sets. In order to guarantee this it may be necessary to be quite subtle in setting up the sub-sets. For example, in this case a sub-set growth without redundancy would almost certainly be needed.) Cluster analysis is a possibly helpful technique in this kind of approach. Such approaches tend to concentrate the choice-making process very directly onto a choice among goals, the respective goals corresponding to the sub-sets.

In the schoolchildren example the choice maker may elect to be indifferent between the efficient children whose marks in all subjects lay below 80% (the good all-rounders), and indifferent between efficient children whose marks in at least one subject exceeded 80% (the specialists). (Some of these sub-sets might be empty.) It would then be necessary to look at just one all-rounder, one specialist reader, one writer and one arithmetician, and choose among them. The exercise would then be forcing a view of consistency of mark attainment.

6. Satisficing

A different approach would be to name a minimum standard and simply work through the children until the first one to satisfy it was found and that child selected. Thus, the first child on the list whose marks are 65% or better in every subject might be selected. Such an approach is known as satisficing.

Most people would regard this as an unsatisfactory way of awarding a scholarship. It offends natural justice and in this example case seems to have little merit. However, it might even in this case have merit if the examination papers were difficult, laborious or expensive to mark. More generally, it might be difficult to develop numerous alternative options to choose from, or it might be expensive to cost out even a single option, or to predict and evaluate its effects. In such circumstances it is common, and may well be thought right, to find any option which does such-and-such and to choose that option. (This is another reference to the general point that most people do not want to spend more time and resource on making a choice than it is worth.)

7. Incrementalism

Suppose the child selected last year was an efficient all-rounder, the final selection from efficient all-rounders having been made by any process, and that his subsequent performance has been satisfactory. The child might be chosen this year who has the same or most similar (defined in some simple way) marks to those of the winning child last year. Alternatively, last year's winning child's subsequent performance, while very good, has suggested slightly stronger reading and writing than arithmetic. Perhaps this year a little more weight should be given to arithmetic and the choice made, say, from the most efficient all-rounders whose marks in arithmetic exceed 80%.

This procedure of choosing based on earlier choice, slightly modified to take account of any dissatisfactions with the earlier choice, is often called incrementalism. It finds many applications, not so much in option choice as in option generation: the present option is taken as the starting point, a set of options differing slightly (in what are thought desirable ways) from it are generated, and it is proposed to choose from among them. In this connection, it is perhaps most appropriate where feasibility is desired as an important goal.

CYCLING

It is probable that having gone through one or many of the above processes, those charged to make the choice will have failed to do so, or have made a tentative choice with which not everyone is happy. Such deadlocks might be resolved in any of a number of ways. One way is to transfer the responsibility for the choice, for example, to the electorate by calling a general election, to a judge by ordering a public inquiry or to chance by using some more or less arbitrary chance mechanism, like dice, for making the choice. Another way is to abandon making the choice (or, what mounts to the same thing, choosing to do nothing or to leave things as they are).

Perhaps the most common way, however, is to invoke some other measure of the options and to cycle through the choice process again in its extended form, either in the same way as before or differently. Or, if some method has been used which assigns weights, to go back and think again about the weights and perhaps change them. (This intention might, of course, be made explicit from the outset—another variant of prototyping.) This might be called getting the option you wanted all along by cooking the method accordingly. It takes numerous forms, too many to discuss. However, it is well to be wary of too much cynicism. Often people cannot quantify or even articulate all the things they want to take into account in exercising choice. There is no reason to suppose that a feeling which cannot be articulated is nonetheless valid; nor that unexplained choices are not explained because the choice maker is ashamed of, or otherwise wishes to disguise, the real reasons for his choice.

More positively, the cycling process, even if it is an exercise in choosing the option that was wanted all along, will often help make explicit why that was the option that was wanted. The explanation, as opposed to justification, may help those concerned see more clearly what were previously even subconscious considerations, and thus make objectives more explicit. In turn this may be even more helpful if similar choices are to be made in future. The method has helped to structure the process.

To repeat a remark already made about one of the approaches mentioned above, none of these approaches to optimisation has any absolute validity, except perhaps 1. Numerous other approaches are possible. The approaches are presented as a list of ideas, some of which may be relevant in a particular circumstance. The main thing is consciously to recognise the problem and to have some awareness of the strengths and weaknesses of the various approaches.

PREDICTIONS

So far it has been assumed that the outcome of each option considered is perfectly predictable. This will seldom, if ever, be the case but will sometimes be near enough so as to justify proceeding as if it were. However, there are cases where explicit account must be taken of the inaccuracy of prediction.

Even when adequate prediction is impossible, it will sometimes be possible to make adequate predictions conditional on the state taken by some key variable which cannot be predicted. (In the language of models, viewed as prediction devices, the model is a good one, but its output depends on the value of an exogenous variable which cannot be predicted too well.)

Thus, someone might be totally confident of his ability to predict the result of a football match, but only if he knows whether it will be raining or not when the match is actually played. Different values of the key variable which conditions the predictions of outcomes—the weather in the case of the football match, the state of the US economy or the pound–dollar exchange rate, or which party will win the next election in other cases—define what are commonly called 'states of nature'. (Note that the states of nature may be the outcomes themselves. Thus, it may be possible to predict that the outcome will be A, B or C, but without knowing which. This can formally be treated as the outcome will be A, conditional on the state of nature being A, etc. This is important because it allows simple uncertainty to be included in any theories that might be developed.) So one kind of choice situation is that in which the outcome of an option can be predicted given various states of nature.

Beyond this there are numerous other difficulties of prediction. One worth special mention arises because of the difficulties of predicting the effects of options over time and, to a degree, over space. Often it will be possible to predict quite accurately the immediate, local, effects of choosing an option, but not so confidently the longer-term effects. For many choices, including personal ones, the longer-term effects are those that really count. So another question is how might choice be exercised, given uncertainty about the possible long-term effects.

A particular difficulty arises here because only rarely is making a choice a single unique event. It is often one of a sequence of choices, made by the choice maker or others, and the choices yet to be made will influence the outcome of the option under consideration. This leads naturally to the idea of looking at sequences of choices, or at least taking cognisance of the fact of there being a sequence. It leads also to the idea of taking account of the possible options which others may exercise, either as competitors seeking their advantage and the choice maker's possible disadvantage or as potential collaborators with whom he might choose jointly to mutual advantage.

Ways of handling the difficulties described above are now discussed. The general field is often called decision theory or decision analysis in those cases where no explicit account is taken of the choices of other people: where it is, the titles 'game theory' or 'options analysis' are often used.

UNCERTAIN STATES OF NATURE

Suppose the various available options can be listed and their outcomes, which are scalar, predicted against an exhaustive list of the possible states of nature. If only one state of nature is likely, the choice problem is a 'simple' optimisation problem. Even if several states of nature are possible, it may be possible to find an option which is better than all others for all states of nature. If not, a new criterion must be developed. Can the OR worker help the choice maker to do so? There are various possibilities which divide themselves into two broad classes.

The first possibility arises when the choice maker cannot, or does not wish to, attach probabilities to the states of nature. Several criteria have been suggested for this situation. Among the criteria are *minimax*—choose the option whose worst outcome is best; *Laplace* or *Bernouilli*—choose the option whose average outcome, assuming all states of nature are equally likely, is best; and *minimax regret*—choose the option whose worst regret is best, regret being the loss of utility in the event compared with the utility attainable had the future been known with certainty.

All these approaches are controversial. All can be shown to be 'obviously' right or wrong by judicious choice of examples to suit the case. Their value lies principally in helping to structure the exploration of possible decisions and their outcomes. Few people would actually choose by any of these criteria alone, so much as be influenced by considerations implicit in them. Consideration of the approaches, and the choices they suggest, helps clarify what criterion the choice maker is really interested in and helps him articulate his real goals.

As an illustration consider a simple example. It has to be decided whether to install 1, 2 or 3 new units of production. Various levels of demand $D1,...., D6$ are the states of nature and the table of outcomes is:

		Demand					
		D1	D2	D3	D4	D5	D6
	1	10	15	15	15	15	15
Option	2	9	14	19	24	24	24
	3	6	11	16	21	26	31

(For example, the value of having pursued option 1 if $D1$ arises is 10, etc. This value is often called the utility of option 1 if $D1$ arises. The option of installing nothing is assumed to have a zero utility in this example, and so no reasonable criterion would suggest it. In general it is an option that should be included. It is often the best choice.)

With no assumptions about the probabilities of demand the different criteria would suggest choosing option 1 (minimax), option 2 (Laplace), and option 3 (minimax regret). The kinds of thoughts these results might stimulate in the choice maker are a recognition that option 1 is pretty reasonable whatever happens, but that option 2 is decidedly better against a majority of eventualities. Can those eventualities be brought about, or more information gathered which will help decide their likelihood? The fact that the choice maker would have regrets if he did not choose option 3 but $D5$ or

D6 occurred might make him think quite hard about what he is really trying to do. If a single option had been best on all criteria, would he have
chosen it?

Second, the choice maker may feel he can attach probabilities to the various states of nature. This makes it possible to work in terms of expected
outcomes, to present the probability distributions of outcomes, etc. The
choice would now be a choice between gambles. (Note the distinction here
between risk, where the probabilities have some objective basis, e.g. the
states of nature are the weather and historically based probabilities are
available, and uncertainty where no objectively based probabilities are
available. To treat uncertainty using subjective probabilities as if it were the
same as risk is most properly thought of as a possible criterion to be considered in the absence of probabilities. Arithmetically, of course, it is the
same as risk.)

Suppose it were thought possible to put probabilities on the states of
nature, that is, the various demand levels, in the ratio 2:3:5:5:3:2. Option 2
has the highest expected utility (19.75), suggesting that it should be chosen. In more complex cases the frequency distribution of outcomes might
be considered, and choice made by different criteria than the expected
value. Someone who enjoyed gambling might do something which
reflected this taste. He might, for example, prefer option 3 to option 2.
(Why? This example does not make the point very well since the implicit
gamble would probably appeal to no one but a pathological gambler, but
little ingenuity is required to construct a more pertinent example. Consider
lotteries.) All of this is perhaps more useful in clearing the choice maker's
mind about his attitude to risk than in more directly helping him choose.

Returning to a point made earlier, this last example covers the case
where only statistical predictions of the outcome can be made. The possible
outcomes are themselves the states of nature. Thus, action 3 can be viewed
as having outcome 6 with probability 0.1 (i.e. 2/20), outcome 11 with probability 0.15, etc. (More subtly, the reader might like to convince himself that
the theory can cover the case where the outcomes can be predicted only
statistically, but are different for different states of nature.)

IMPROVING PREDICTION (OF STATES
OF NATURE)

Although the assumption was made earlier that as much effort as was
thought worthwhile had been given to prediction, a short digression on the
value of improved prediction is perhaps worth while. Note that in all the
cases in the example on page 156, the choice maker's ignorance about the
states of nature makes him not better off, and generally worse off, than if

he could predict which state nature would take up. If he knew for certain that demand would be $D4$, for example, he would choose option 2 and be 9 units better off than by adopting the minimax approach. Presumably, however, the improved prediction would have cost him something to make. The best improvement in pay-off he could ever get by choosing option 2 or 3 is 16 (being $31 - 15$). It could, therefore, never be worth him paying more than 16 units of utility to improve his prediction. (It is, of course, doubtful whether he would think it worth paying as much as 16.)

An important concept in the case where probabilities are attached to the states of nature is the expected value of perfect information. This is the increase in utility that could be expected if demand could be predicted accurately. Assuming that the outcome of accurate prediction is $D1$ with probability 0.1, $D2$ with probability 0.15, etc., the value is:

$$0.1 \times 1 + 0.15 \times 1 + 0.25 \times 0 + 0.25 + 0 + 0.15 \times 2 + 0.1 \times 7 = 1.25$$

(These figures arise in the following way. There is a probability 0.1 that $D1$ would be the accurately predicted demand. In this case option 1 would have been chosen instead of the choice actually made, option 2, based on expected outcome. This would have increased utility by 1. This explains 0.1×1 and the remaining terms are explained by considering $D2$, $D3$,... in turn.) This gives 1.25 and this is the expected value of perfect information. It may be thought sensible not to spend more on information gathering or analysis to improve prediction than 1.25 units of utility.

By extension of this kind of argument it is possible to assess whether some means of improving, as opposed to perfecting, predictions about the states of nature is worth while.

CHOOSING BETWEEN GAMBLES

In certain cases the choice is between clearly defined gambles. (As remarked earlier, choice where only statistical predictions are possible can be viewed as choice between gambles.) This is one case of choice where prediction is uncertain for which a mathematical treatment of a convincing kind has led to a theory of how a person ought, in some sense, to choose. (To some people the mathematical treatment provides a model of how mathematics can help to make choice and points the direction in which theoretical extensions should be made: to others it reveals the futility of mathematics in this context.) In order to illustrate the kinds of assumptions made to develop a normative mathematical theory of choice under uncertainty, and related criticisms, this topic is explored at some length.

To begin with, assume that the choice is indeed between 'clearly defined gambles', that is:

(i)   The outcomes of following each gamble, given each of the possible states of nature, are known.
(ii)   The probabilities of each of the states of nature arising are known.
(iii) The parties concerned agree these figures.

In practice it would never be as clear-cut as this and the choice would be between ill-defined gambles with subjective estimates of outcomes and probabilities, but the ideal case will be assumed. Note, however, that a *certain* outcome is not excluded: it is merely a gamble with one outcome whose probability of occurring is one.

To put flesh on these bones, the reader will find it helpful to think of an example. He might, for example, think of an investment decision such as a supermarket chain might take: whether, and if so, how big, to build a superstore at a named site. The gambles are the various sizes of store; their outcomes are profit; and the states of nature are combinations of the state of the economy, whether or not a housing estate is extended, and who occupies the store planned for a neighbouring site. In this case, it seems plausible that a smaller store will correspond to a gamble with a high chance of success, but a modest return, while a larger store will correspond to a gamble with a number of outcomes, ranging from a large loss to a large gain, with various probabilities. (Are assumptions (i), (ii) and (iii) above reasonable in this case?)

Now it is an observable fact that people sometimes choose in ways which stand little logical analysis. This need not prevent the offering of advice about ways of choosing, any more than the fact that people swim badly should deter a swimming coach from trying to improve swimming styles: the advice can always be rejected. However, it is true that the swimming coach would find it difficult to make much progress if there were total disagreement about what constituted a good swimming style. What is perhaps needed in the case of choosing between gambles is, therefore, to decide what constitutes a good choosing style. The logical implications of adopting this style can then be explored. It can then be pointed out that if those exercising choice believe the style is right, to be logical they must accept the implications.

Are there, then, rules about choosing between gambles with which no reasonable person could disagree? A plausible set of such rules follows.

(1)   All gambles can be compared, so that of two gambles a person prefers one or the other or is indifferent between them.

(2)   If a person prefers one gamble to a second, and the second to a third, he prefers the first to the third.

(3)   If one gamble is preferred to a second, consider a composite gamble which gives a chance of the first but otherwise the second. The first gamble is preferred to the composite gamble, which is preferred to the second.

(4)   No gamble is so attractive that a gamble which gives any chance at all of taking it is preferred to any other gamble. Nor is any gamble so unattractive that any gamble is preferred to one which gives any chance at all of the gamble in question.

(5)   A person is indifferent between gambles whose outcomes and associated probabilities are the same: how the gamble is presented is irrelevant.

It can be shown that if these rules, or rather a more precise formulation of them, are acceptable to a choice maker, then *numerical* values can be assigned to alternative gambles which are such that

(i)   The choice maker should always choose the gamble with the highest value, and

(ii)   The value of a composite gamble is formed in the following way. Let the value of gamble 1 be X and of gamble 2, Y. Consider a new gamble whose outcome is gamble 1 with probability p, gamble 2 with probability $1-p$. Its value is $pX+(1-p)Y$.

These 'values' are *not* to be interpreted in the everyday sense of the word 'value', namely as a sum of money which will give the choice maker no more and no less satisfaction than the gamble. Instead, let us call this sum of money the certainty equivalent. Then the value of the gamble is the same as that of the certainty equivalent, but there is no reason to suppose *a priori* that value is linearly related to certainty equivalent: the value to a person of £2 million is not necessarily twice as much as the value of £1 million. The value here being considered is often called 'utility'. The marginal utility of cash is often supposed to fall as cash increases.

Utility can be measured only indirectly by establishing preference and inferring utilities. Thus, to say something about the utilities a man ascribes to a pint of each of three types of beer (A, B, and C) he might be asked: Which would you rather have, a pint of A or a pint of B? If he answers A, the inference is that $U(A) > U(B)$. Successive questions and answers might be: Which would you rather have, a pint of A or a 50/50 chance of a pint of B and a pint of C? (Answer: B and C, inference: $0.5U(B) + 0.5U(C) > U(A)$); and for what value of P would you be indifferent between a pint of A and a $p\%$ chance of a pint of B and a $(100-P)\%$ chance of C? (Answer 25, inference: $0.25U(B) + 0.75U(C) = U(A)$). In all cases enough of such questions will allow the utilities to be deduced to within a linear transformation.

(There is always this arbitrariness of scale and origin.) In this case the three questions above are enough. B and C can be assigned utilities 0 and 1 giving $U(A) = 0.75$. If it were thought that having no beer were a more convenient bench-mark to be given zero utility, a further question: For what value of Q would you prefer a pint of B or a Q% chance of a pint of C? (Answer 80 inference: $U(B) = 0.8U(C) + 0.2 \times 0$) allows utilities 80, 95 and 100 (say) to be ascribed to B, A and C respectively, where now only the scale is arbitrary. (As a digression, it will be seen that utility theory offers scope for scalarising outcomes more generally than just in choosing between gambles. People can simply be asked to imagine gambles whose outcomes are the outcomes to be scalarised and asked preferences, as above. Alternatively, questions can be asked directly about the outcomes. The difficulties to be discussed below bear on these cases.)

The rules themselves can be criticised in a number of ways. For example, if it is supposed they are rules which would be followed by any reasonable person choosing between well-defined gambles at a particular point of time, then rule 5 implies that no allowance is made for the person who prefers one form of gambling to another which is identical in terms of money and odds. Note, however, a rule that is *not* in the scheme: it is always right to refuse a gamble when all the outcomes are worse than doing nothing. There is thus no explicit exclusion of the person who likes to gamble for its own sake even when he is certain to lose.

More fundamental objections arise in trying to use this theory. Among the more important of these are the following.

(a) A person's preferences may change from time to time, from place to place or according to his financial circumstances. This consideration does not destroy the theory so long as the person sticks by the rules. All it does is force the recognition that it may be necessary to reassign values to gambles each time a choice is made. Thus, in assigning values to the chance nodes in a decision tree, account might have to be taken of the fact that the choice maker's financial position, given that the node is ever reached, is different from his starting financial position.

(b) How are these preferences going to be measured? In the case of an individual it is conceivable that he could be presented with successive pairs of gambles and forced to choose and enact one of each pair. But it is really rather unlikely that anyone would allow himself to be the subject of meaningful experiments of this kind. Hypothetical questions might, therefore, be resorted to, but this too is unsatisfactory for different reasons. The problem becomes more acute when the choice maker is not a single individual but a group of people. In such cases, even if a way to measure the values of different gambles to the individuals making up the group could be thought up, it is obviously doubtful whether there would be general agreement about the best gamble for the group to choose as a whole. In practice, of course, recourse is usually made to a very crude method of choosing, for example, by appointing a dictator, or by some such principle as 'one man, one vote'. (The acceptability of 'one man, one vote' relies to an extent on similarity of preferences, or at least willingness to compromise, among the voters: if a majority were continually using their voting power to force the group as a whole to accept choices which were highly preferred by the majority but strongly disliked by the minority, trouble might ensue.)

(c) It is far from obvious that a person will be willing to say which of two gambles he prefers even in cases where he admits he is not indifferent between them. In some ways, the theory rests on the assumption that a pistol can be pointed at someone's head to force him to choose. However, life does not usually present such dramatic choices. Thus, if a manager is asked to say which gamble of one concerned with a pricing decision and one concerned with labour relations he would prefer to take, it is not obviously unreasonable that he should answer 'I don't know' or even more strongly 'they are not comparable'.

In summary, then, there are certain rules which it seems reasonable should be followed in choosing between gambles. Insofar as someone departs from these rules, he might reasonably be said to be behaving oddly and his inconsistency is probably worth drawing to his attention. However, there is a great difficulty in applying the rules and following them through to their logical conclusions.

But note the advantages if the rules are adhered to, to the point that a person never acts or wishes never to act inconsistently with them, and if utilities can be inferred. Use of the results (i) and (ii) on page 160 allows that person always to make the best choice given knowledge of all the relevant probabilities. Result (ii) tells him exactly how to calculate the utility of any gamble involving outcomes whose utilities are known, and result (i) tells him how to choose. It is these results that justify the manipulative rules for decision trees.

SEQUENCES OF CHOICES AND BOUNDING OUTCOMES

Only rarely is a choice a single thing. It is usually one in a sequence of choices, so that the outcome of this choice depends on choices yet to be taken, by the choice maker or by others. Moreover, either linked with this or separately from it, the outcome of the choice may be difficult to bound either in time or in space. (This is saying no more than that modelling is not easy in such circumstances.) There are various ways of helping choice makers faced with these considerations. The most important help could be ensuring that the choice maker is actually aware of the existence of the considerations, and this should certainly be done if he is not and it is of real importance. It is assumed from now on that the choice maker is aware.

The problem of sequences of choices can be structured by dynamic programming and (a special case of dynamic programming) by decision trees. Neither is widely applicable, owing either to computational difficulties or to the simplifications necessary to circumvent these. However, with certain well-structured sequences of choices, either approach—and particularly decision trees—can be useful at the very least as setting out the choice sequence clearly. The difficulties of bounding in time can be alleviated by discounting or by fixing a definite time horizon, perhaps linking this with constraints on the situation that one predicts will hold at that time horizon. The difficulties of bounding in space are usually resolved arbitrarily.

Most planning problems suffer from the kinds of difficulties referred to here. Consider the case of road improvements. The dangers of choosing to make a specific road improvement in isolation from all other possible road improvements are well known. In particular, the effect of a specific road improvement depends on improvements which it is subsequently decided to make, while their effects in turn depend upon the improvement currently under consideration. These interactions go on into an indefinite future so that theoretically the choice now, interacting as it does with all future possible choice opportunities, should be examined as part of a very large number of possible sequences of decisions stretching over a very long period of time. Practical considerations usually prevent anything approaching so thorough an analysis. Probably the best that could be done along these lines is either to discount or to examine the programme of improvements over some definite time period, with the aim of choosing the best programme (best according to whatever criterion is relevant) which leaves an end position which is capable of an appropriate measure of improvement in some time period immediately after the time arising. For example, consider a situation in which traffic through a town centre is thought to be increasing at 10% per year. Among proposed road improvements, the one which minimises the expected cost of handling the appropriate volume of traffic over the next five years, the expectation being taken over the estimated probabilities of different levels of traffic, might be chosen. However, choice might be restricted to those which, at the end of five years, would be capable of extension to cater for a traffic flow of named size at a cost of no more than a named figure in the five years immediately beyond the planning period.

A similar discussion could have been developed about effects in space—a road improvement here increases traffic congestion there and so on. It is often tempting to ignore the difficulties of bounding geographically or in any dimension other than time. For example, in the present case it may be tempting to assume that all traffic will continue to use the city centre whatever congestion results, whereas in practice undue central congestion might divert large volumes of through traffic through the suburbs. Little more can be done than keep an eye open for such things.

An alternative approach is to appeal to the concept of *robustness*. Broadly this is trying to keep as many desirable options open as possible. The idea is to try to choose now in such a way that the least number of possibly attractive alternative sequences is prevented. Although not an easy concept to formalise, robustness is perhaps the approach nearest to that of the good practical decision maker.

The principle of robustness might be particularly appropriate in the above example. Suppose there is some set of layouts of the road system which it is thought will be acceptable in ten years' time. Any choice made now cannot increase the number of layouts in this set which are obtainable but may, of course, decrease it. The concept of robustness suggests that the option chosen now should be the one which causes the least reduction in the number of attainable satisfactory ultimate layouts.

This is a concept which can be tinkered with in various ways. In particular some weights can be attached to each member of the set of ultimate layouts (perhaps some function of its cost), and an option's robustness can then be defined in terms of these weights. A useful secondary criterion that can be applied in this sort of situation arises because of the risk that, for reasons beyond the choice maker's control, the programme of road improvements may be cut short before any satisfactory final stage can be reached. This leads to the concept of *stability* being applied to the initial choice of option. The choice is said to be stable if it does not lead to an unsatisfactory state of the system, even though no further choice were to be exercised. Stability thus corresponds to avoiding making a road improvement which actually worsens the short-term situation, simply because it leaves open lots of desirable future sequences of road improvements. The concepts of robustness and stability will often be great aids, and sometimes the clinching considerations, when introduced to a choice-making process.

CHOICE UNDER COMPETITION

Sometimes someone is exercising choice in circumstances where opponents are also making choices and where the outcome is determined by the choices all parties make, not just his own choice. The word 'opponent' might have a literal meaning, or it might simply be some other person with no malevolent intent, or even someone with whom the choice maker wishes to co-operate but can communicate with only in a limited way. (It is, of course, always the case that what others do could influence the outcome of someone's chosen option. The choice maker will almost certainly be aware of this. It is just that sometimes he can ignore these effects, or thinks he can, without loss.)

This kind of choice can be regarded as ordinary choice making with some changes of emphasis. Thus, the options available to opponents might be viewed as states of nature in ordinary choice making, perhaps incorporating nature as a further opponent, probably one that does not think. Probabilities might then be assigned to the opponents' choice of option, perhaps allowing the possibility of their choosing options rationally according to various criteria. Alternatively the existence of opponents might be accommodated in predictions. (Recall, by the way, that prediction is always an alternative to examining the outcomes against various states of nature by direct prediction of the states of nature.) To do so it would be necessary to assess the options the opponents might adopt in response to each option available to the choice maker, and to predict accordingly.

Various structures have been suggested by which to view and to discuss such issues, and to help those engaged in this kind of choice making. The most famous is the theory of games. This is (at least in part) a normative structure. Two other approaches are the theories of meta-games and hyper-games. All are concerned essentially to improve understanding of the effects of choices. In general terms, they may be used to help the choice maker deduce whether competition is worth taking explicitly into account; and, if so, how he might best do so.

In an ordinary game each player is assumed to choose options in ignorance of the choices made by the other players. In a meta-game other possibilities are allowed such as negotiation and/or sequential choice. A hyper-game is a game, or meta-game, in which the players do not necessarily share the same perceptions of the game. (These are simplistic explanations intended only to set out very general ideas.)

Thus, to take a simple example, suppose A and B are two firms competing to supply electric motors to a washing-machine manufacturer. Each must submit a tender. A has two options: A1 a tender to supply motors in any quantity at a flat rate, and A2 to supply a smaller number at a higher flat rate. B's options, B1 and B2, are to offer up to a certain number very cheaply, and any number at a higher rate. The effects on profitability to the two suppliers of the manufacturer's choice of supply, called the pay-offs, are known to each and set out below.

This may be viewed as two players, A and B, joined in a game where each has two options A1, A2, and B1, B2, respectively. The pay-offs (known to both players) are:

	for A			**for B**	
	A1	A2		A1	A2
B1	10	−50	B1	10	20
B2	20	15	B2	−50	15

(For example, if A chooses A1 and B chooses B2, A gains 20 but B loses 50. This is not, of course, a so-called zero sum game which is one in which A's gain is B's loss and vice versa.)

If A and B have to choose in ignorance of each other's choice they would probably settle on A1, B1 respectively—the theory of games choice. From A's point of view, he judged what would happen if B did his worst and chose the option for which this worst is best, and vice versa. Neither A nor B could obtain a better result by changing his chosen option unilaterally.

However, both could obtain a better result by choosing A2 and B2 respectively. Neither does so in the conventional theory of games because each fears the other will not co-operate. However, it is quite plausible to imagine A and B getting together and agreeing to make these mutually beneficial choices. Meta-game theory (and the related analysis of options) explores games to find bases for agreement or negotiation among the players which lead to these improved benefits. It is a reminder that choice need not be made alone, and that there might be advantages in choosing options jointly with others.

Suppose the game is to be played many times over and there is an agreement to co-operate at every play, so that A2 and B2 are the exercised options. If either A or B breaks the agreement he is instantly punished by his opponent also switching his option. However, note that either player could improve his own position on a single play if he changed unilaterally. This could lead to a breakdown in co-operation if it was known when the series of plays was to come to an end. Note also that, again in a series of plays without explicit co-operation, the players can, in a sense, communicate with each other by their successive plays, and in particular by their response to the opponent's previous play. In this way the result can be as if there were explicit co-operation without there actually being so.

Consider now another possibility. Suppose A and B are playing this game, co-operatively or not, but each has different perceptions of the game. They might, for example, take different views of what their opponent thinks the pay-off is, they might be unaware of all the options available to their opponent or of the criteria to which their opponent is working, etc. (Perhaps the grossest misperception of all is that one of the players does not realise he is in a game and consequently ignores the fact that the other player's choices of option might have any bearing on his choice. This point, and the other misperceptions, can be thought of as particular cases of ignoring feed-backs, a danger which was alluded to in earlier chapters.)

In these circumstances, either player or both might be in for quite a shock when the game is played. Suppose, for example, A did not know that B had option B1 available. Assuming A and B are fighting each other,

A1 seems to A to be a very attractive option—he gains 20, his opponent loses 50. When B plays the surprising B1, however, the players come out equal. Or suppose again A does not know B has B1 available and B persuades A that he, B, is anxious to co-operate: he asks A to play A2, promising to give A the 5 that he, A, loses by not playing A1 (or even more). This seems plausible to A, as the pay-off as it appears to A is much better for B and not worse for him. A therefore agrees only to find B playing B1—A's misperception was not only about B's available options but about his criterion, too. This kind of thing is the subject matter of hyper-game theory. It is a reminder that in predicting the outcomes of choices someone might be badly wrong unless he fully understands the interests and perceptions of all relevant parties, with or without the joint exercise of choice.

APPENDIX: COX'S ICE-CREAM VANS

You are a student spending your summer vacation working in Cox's ice-cream factory in a large Northern conurbation. Cox's is an old-established family business run on homely lines. Bert Cox, the boss, is a man of about 60 who directs the ice-cream making. He often takes his jacket off and joins in the work with you, the two permanent employees and a couple of other casual workers who work on the factory floor. His younger brother, Sid, is in charge of the van fleet and of the eight men who maintain and service it. Bert's son, Ed, looks after the financial side of the business.

The business is a very simple one. Cox's own 32 ice-cream vans. The vans are of the old-fashioned type with sales being of cornets or wafers, made up from the tub by the driver/salesman using a scoop and sold at a prominently displayed fixed price. The firm employs six full-time driver/salesmen. At weekends throughout the year, all week during the summer and on Bank Holidays, casual driver/salesmen present themselves.

The full-time men are paid £20 for each weekday and £30 on each of Saturday and Sunday plus 10% commission on sales. Most work every Saturday and Sunday, certainly in the summer; and many work a seven-day week in the summer but take one, two or three weekdays off in each winter week. They pick up a van each morning and return to fill their tubs as necessary.

The casual men pay Cox's £40 per 24 hours for a van (including a full petrol tank) and £20 for a full tub of ice-cream. They can come back for as many tubs at £20 a time as they want during the 24 hours. (The regular drivers usually take about £75 from customers for a full tub.) There is no refund for any ice-cream returned with a van, although it can be easily returned to the spacious deep-freeze for subsequent use.

You know several of the drivers, both regulars and casuals (many of whom are students), and you know that they agree routes among themselves without much argument, and you know also that at least some of the casual drivers pool their takings.

The whole system of operation has impressed you, in your brief acquaintance with it, by its efficiency and its easy administration. The casual drivers apparently turn up only on days when they think ice-cream can be sold. Bert Cox has the knack of guessing sales as well as, or better than, the casual drivers. The upshot is that he always makes roughly the right amount of ice-cream and, by making good use of his fairly large deep-freeze capacity, he has never, while you have worked there, refused a man a tub when asked for it; nor has he grossly over-produced despite the sudden weather changes that are sometimes experienced in the 2 or 3 hours it takes to make the ice-cream.

One day, somewhat to your surprise, Bert Cox calls you into his small office. He presses very milky coffee on you and fusses in a manner suggesting embarrassment.

'Look,' he suddenly says, 'you know my lad, Ed. He's the sharp one of the family and he's on a modern management course at the Tech. He's got this bee in his bonnet that we're losing a lot of business. He wants to buy six new vans, the modern kind where you turn a tap and get a measured amount for each sale. He's got it all wrong and I'll tell you why. First, he thinks extra vans means extra sales. Well that's true to some extent, but you have a look at the figures. Extra vans means less sales per van.'

Bert shuffles around on his desk, throwing bills, racing papers and maps to one side, and produces a bit of paper. 'Here,' he says, 'have a look at this, Master Ed's masterpiece. Why, we will go bust if we don't do what he says. You're more educated than Sid and me, and than Ed, whatever he thinks. Sid, Ed and yours truly are going to come in this room in two hours' time and talk to you about our problem. We'll find that helpful. So you sit here, make yourself at home, and think about it.'

Bert refills your cup with more of his nauseous coffee brew, asks you to slip down to the betting shop for him, and then returns to ice-cream making.

A quarter of an hour later, a smartly dressed young man, evidently Ed, strolls in. 'Look here,' he says, between puffs of his cigar, 'I know what's going on. My old man's past it. Just have a look at these market research results. Got a chap at the college to work them out for me. We've got to have these vans, otherwise the business is just going to collapse. Dad thinks our ice-cream sells on its quality, but it's really an image we're selling.'

For the next half-hour you are left in peace. Then a dreadful rumbling cough is heard approaching and a man in a grease-stained pair of overalls comes in. You recognise Sid. 'Listen, I don't want to bias you,' he says in a hoarse whisper, 'but I hope you're on Ed's side. He's right you know—for the wrong reasons, of course. Bert's never got it into his head that we're not in the ice-cream business. We're a van-hire firm, and if we don't get some new vans soon, we'll be in dead lumber. Just have a glance at these maintenance costs. See what I mean?'

Sid departs, but not before asking you to go out to buy him 80 cigarettes. Subsequent interruptions consist of nothing more than Bert coming in to check your comfort and to offer you more coffee, until Bert asks you to join him, Sid and Ed so that they can hear you talk over their problem. The factual information you have gathered follows.

Information given to you by Bert Cox

The following table covers mid-May to mid-September of the current year. It gives the Sunday figures, Sunday being the weekly peak sales day. Sundays marked * were in Bank Holiday weekends. On all days all six regular drivers were at work.

Sunday	Vans in use	Casual drivers only				Total tubs	Tubs/ van day	Regular drivers Tubs/ van day
		No. of vans selling						
		1	2	3	4+			
			(tubs)					
1	5	–	–	5	–	15	3.00	2.67
2*	25	8	9	8	–	50	2.00	3.17
3	11	2	4	4	1	26	2.36	2.67
4	12	4	4	3	1	25	2.08	2.83
5	13	–	10	3	–	29	2.23	3.33
6	18	5	8	5	–	36	2.00	3.00
7	17	4	7	6	–	36	2.12	2.67
8	20	7	7	6	–	39	1.95	2.83
9	18	5	6	5	2	40	2.22	2.83
10	17	5	6	6	–	35	2.06	3.00
11	17	2	12	3	–	35	2.06	3.17
12	21	7	7	6	1	43	2.05	3.00
13	23	7	7	7	2	50	2.17	3.00
14	24	8	8	7	1	49	2.04	3.00
15*	25	9	7	7	2	52	2.08	3.33
16	18	5	7	6	–	37	2.06	3.00
17	16	5	5	5	1	34	2.12	3.33
18	14	3	5	6	–	31	2.21	3.17
Total	314	86	119	98	11	662	2.11	3.0

Vans in use per day averaged over the whole year is about 12, including the regular drivers. Tubs per van day for all the drivers for the whole year averages about three.

Note from Ed Cox to Bert Cox

I think we should buy six new automatic dispenser vans. This will cost us about £100 000 which we can easily afford. They will be used all year and if they sell only average amounts, we will get an annual revenue of about £400 000 from them if they are used by regular drivers and £200 000 even if we have casual drivers using them. (They will actually sell more as the tub is double the capacity of the old ones and the men will not have to waste time coming back to refill.) As ice-cream only costs us £4 per present tub and maintenance costs will be minimal on the new vans (say £400 per year) we will get a fantastic return on capital. Also we shall appear more modern. Finally we shall have enough vans to employ all the casual drivers who turn up on even the busiest days. (On ten days last year we turned drivers away so six new vans would give us at least 180 tubs extra sales from this cause alone.)

Extracts from letter to Ed Cox from Quentin Scott-Jackson, Lecturer in Marketing at local college

..... and I very much enjoyed our night out last Saturday.
(2)   Now to business and the results of the survey you asked for. These results are very reliable as we have used a carefully selected sample of 1 000 people.

(3) I have determined the general market picture in the town. Up to four years ago you had only shop competition. Since then Antonio's Continental Ice Cream has been set up by Mr Eli Birkenshaw. He now has about 20 vans of the modern type. The market has been increasing in volume. As you know, your sales have been static in volume and I find that shop sales have as well. Birkenshaw has been obtaining all the increased market.

(4) Why? We asked people over 30 and those under 30 to state their preferences for makes of ice-cream and separately their preferences between methods of sales. (The sample was about equally split by this age-break.) The results (in percentages) were:

Make	Over 30	Under 30	Method of sale	Over 30	Under 30
Cox's	38	21	Old-type van	37	18
Antonio's	21	39	Modern van	22	36
Shop	20	35	Shop	20	41
Don't know	21	5	Don't know	21	5

These figures are bad for you as 75% of ice-cream sales are to under 30s. The only consolation for you is that 80% of the sample, in both age ranges, had heard of Cox's ice-cream, whereas only 50% of the over 30s had heard of Antonio's (but admittedly 80% of the under 30s).

(5) I look forward to receiving the agreed fee as soon ....

Information given to you by Sid Cox

Our newest van is 8 years old and our oldest is more than 20. None of them has any value except for scrap and they all cost a fortune to maintain. I spend £156 000 a year on wages and overheads before we start buying parts. I have four men cleaning, greasing, spraying etc.—what you would call routine maintenance—and I realise I would always need these. But I also have four men on repairs at £160 a week each and just look at the bills for parts. Some of these we have to get specially fabricated.

Year (current is n)	n-1	n-2	n-3	n-4	n-5
Cost of parts (£)	29 312	25 604	24 820	19 296	22 716

(I have converted all these figures to today's prices, so don't think it's just inflation.)

   The vans only go out on average 150 days a year, none more than 200. So you can see it's costing us about £40 a van day, just the amount we charge. We shall be in the red next year.

EXERCISES

(1) List some of the more important choices made by a group to which you belong. Who took the choices and how were they made? Is there some sense in the group of a proper way for the choices to be made? Is it more or less important that appropriate procedures should be followed

than that the right choice is made? Were any formal evaluations of outcome or probabilities of outcomes made for any of the choices? If not, might they have appropriately been? Is there anything in the preceding chapter that might have helped improve the choices? Were any clearly badly made? Why?

(2) Mr Bird (see pages 1–3 and 10–12) has a number of options available to him. Would it help him to approach his problem as an exercise in optimisation with multiple criteria or as an exercise in choice among uncertain outcomes? Is he a player in a game? Distinguish between the values of these approaches by the stimulus they might offer to Mr Bird to understand his position, as well as by their direct choice aiding properties.

(3) Consider a case of public policy where a wrong choice appears to have been made. What went wrong?

(4) Throughout this chapter the words 'choice' and 'option' have usually been used. Some writers would use 'decision' instead of choice and one of 'action', 'strategy' or 'policy' instead of 'option'. Does the choice of words matter? Might there be advantages in using different words in different contexts?

(5) Consider some choices which groups known to you are making recurrently (e.g. for a sports club, who to pick for the team this week; for a high street shop, how much casual labour to employ each Saturday, etc.). For each, reflect whether some simple set of rules could, perhaps with computer aid, help with this choice. How much work would be involved in setting this up and keeping it going? Would it be worth it? More generally, what determines whether an aid to choice making is worth while?

(6) Consider the case of Cox's Ice-Cream Vans (pages 167–170):
   (i) Given the two hours Bert stipulates, do what you can to prepare for the discussion.
   (ii) List some of the options available to Cox's. Can the outcomes of the options be predicted? Is uncertainty worth taking into account? Can the outcomes be compared? Is it worth gathering extra information? Have you in answering (i) chosen among these options? Was it a good choice?
   (iii) Are Cox's and Birkenshaw's players in a game? Is it a meta-game, a hyper-game? Are Bert, Sid and Ed playing a game against each other? What options does each have? What are the outcomes for each? Could they or Cox's and Birkenshaw's usefully co-operate? How?

    (iv)   Should the van-drivers, maintenance men and other workers be involved in making the choice (as opposed simply to their opinions being assessed and taken into account)?

    (v)   If invited to appraise Quentin Scott-Jackson's work, what would you say? How much would you be prepared to pay him for the work?

    (vi)   If all relevant parties agreed that you could have a week to work on the problem and that they would co-operate with you and with each other, what would you plan to do? If Bert agreed to allow you to engage some assistance and to pay for it, what would you do? How much would it be worth Bert paying and what kind of help, thinking widely, might be useful?

    (vii) If you were advising one of Bert, Sid or Ed as opposed to Cox's would you do things differently? Is there any sensible way in which you can advise Cox's as opposed to the individuals?

    (viii) Do Cox's have a problem?

(7)   A recently married couple are contemplating buying their first house. Sketch out in general terms the things they might wish to consider in choosing a house. Include some consideration of the future. How do you think they should make the choice? By reflecting on choices young couples known to you have made, would your method have helped them make better choices? Does this exercise tell you anything about people's attitudes to risk, about their rates of discounting the future, or about their malleability to fashion? Are their actions severely constrained by the choices of others, such as those financing the purchase?

(8)   To whom are those exercising choice in groups with which you are familiar accountable? How can their choice-making behaviour be changed if it is unsatisfactory? In the last resort, how can their power to exercise choice be removed? By considering groups for which the answers to these questions are different, can groups be helpfully classified according to how choice is exercised on their behalf?

(9)   Take some choices you have recently or will shortly make. Is there some relatively simple way in which *all* the options available to you can be exhibited? Example ways, aside from a simple listing, are:

    (a)   An algebraic representation of the options, by $(x_1, x_2, \ldots x_n)$, the x's being values of the variables that define an option;

    (b)   A tree, where each branching represents the various (finite number of) values which the variables defining the option can take.

Set out the criteria by which an option is thought to be impossible. (Typically these might be the impossibility of variables jointly taking specified values, like x_1 must be less than $x_2 + x_3$.) Use these criteria to reduce the number of options if possible. Is this process more effective in some cases than others? Why? Is it to do with the means of representing the options or the constraints?

(10) Do you think the methods described in this chapter are in principle widely applicable (accepting that in particular practical cases they may be more trouble than they are worth)? Do they assume more rationality in making choices than is usually exhibited in real-life choice making? How many choices made by others which significantly affect your life were ideologically made?

(11) Look again at the problems you identified for the participants in the Service Providers case (Exercise 11, page 64). Taking some or all of these, list the options available. How might the options be chosen between? In particular, assuming someone (possibly Mr Avery) wishes to do his best for Service Providers as a company, how might he handle choice, given the possibly competing criteria of profitability, market share and stamping out 'cheating'?

Chapter 10

—— Implementation and Solutions

Attention turns now from methods of problem solving commonly employed in OR to the management of the OR activity. The remainder of the book, save for a concluding summary and a bibliography, addresses this topic. This chapter discusses the management of the process of OR, that is, the actual undertaking of the activity. A subsequent chapter discusses the management of the OR group so as to allow and facilitate this process.

Since OR, by practically any definition, is concerned to help tackle problems, its usefulness relates to the contribution it makes to the solution of problems. In what follows, the general nature of solutions and the OR contribution to them are discussed, followed by how the OR contribution can be made effective. This will lead to a discussion of handling relationships and working with others to cause change.

WHAT IS A SOLUTION?

Problems have been discussed as a state of dissatisfaction or surprise for an individual or a group, where a response is felt to be necessary but where the right response is not easily decided. The problem is solved when this state no longer persists. This change of state can occur for several reasons which might not invoke what would normally be called a solution. The normal usage of the word would probably suggest that the right response had been decided. However, as the word is used here, a solution would also be reached if it were decided that no response were necessary or if the dissatisfaction or surprise were to be dissipated. These latter states may arise as a result of reconsideration or improved understanding. They may simply be the result of other more pressing problems obviating or reducing the significance of this problem in the minds of the relevant people. Other ways in which a solution may be reached include by the exercise of power, either to make the choice or simply to rule that the problem is irrelevant or not worth wasting time and money on. Tiredness or a sense of futility, of failure to improve the situation, might induce a willingness to live with the problem. Changes in circumstances, either self-induced or brought about by others, could bring about a solution in this sense. A disinclination to attempt the change necessary to solve the problem might also be relevant. More or less negotiation among the interested parties might precede these various end points.

Thus, it should not come as a surprise if not all problems reach a clear-cut solution stage. Moreover, as remarked in Chapter 4, problems are seldom solved so much as alleviated. Their solution or alleviation often also gives rise to other problems. It is perhaps best, therefore, to think of problems as going away, with solution in the more everyday sense of the word being one of the ways of making them go away. To give this an operational meaning, a possible catch-all definition of a solution is that one has been reached when none of the relevant people wishes to spend further resource on the problem as such—as such because, of course, the problem might have been solved by spending resource as the solution. (In relation to a group it is, as usual, the relevant people, bearing in mind the power pattern.) The OR solution has been reached when no one wants any further contribution from the OR worker.

It will not always be easy to infer that a solution in this generalised sense has been reached. If it has, then further expenditure of effort is wasted. It is well to be sufficiently aware of the changing state of mind among the problem owners to the point of awareness of when they think a solution has been reached. The OR worker may, of course, be one of the leaders in proposing that a solution, or at least the OR solution, has been reached. He will be well placed to judge when the point of diminishing returns has been reached, when his further contribution will have too small an effect to justify it against other uses of his time.

None of this is to say that the problem will never come back. Some problems, even in a reduced form, are so important and so enduring that a solution is but temporary, and a final solution takes a long time to reach, if ever. More generally, any solution of whatever kind, is perhaps best viewed as a trial or experiment. If it works, all well and good, but if, in whatever sense or whenever, it does not, then another solution must be tried.

THE OR CONTRIBUTION TO SOLUTIONS

The OR worker, engaged to help with a problem, can adopt a passive role, helping as requested and stopping work when a solution has been reached. Alternatively, he can engage himself in the sort of social processes implicit in the above brief description of a solution. This second approach has much to commend it. OR may have a part to play in the process of deciding which problems merit how much attention.

There are several considerations here. The size of the amount of damage the existence of the problem is causing may not be carefully weighed by some of the processes alluded to above. This can cut both ways. A problem whose effects are debilitating to the group that has it might be solved in the sense of 'turned aside', because its importance is simply not perceived or, if wholly or partially perceived, the effects of possible responses are feared (e.g. the necessary change will cause much unhappiness to long-serving workers). Equally, a problem which is actually no more that an irritant (e.g. the photocopier keeps breaking down) and quickly disposed off (get a new photocopier) can consume much problem-solving time. In various obvious ways, OR effort can help to assess the size of problems and urge solution procedures appropriate to size. (Some problems, superficially no more than irritants, might, of course, be important, particularly if they are symptomatic of larger problems. Such might be the case if they recur, or occur in many other parts of the organisation, the case in hand being merely the first reported one. It might also be the case that the symptoms of the problem in hand are the first symptoms to reveal themselves of a larger problem which is as yet hidden.)

The considerations of the previous paragraph are intended to bear on the amount of resource in general brought to bear on solving any particular problem. Part of that resource may be OR workers. A second consideration which the OR worker might bring is whether and how much OR work is justified on this particular problem. At one level this is a question of the value added to the solution by various amounts (including none) of OR effort. However, there are possibly deeper issues which bear on the management of OR and which might argue for greater OR involvement than a simple single problem view might suggest. This is because large benefits from OR may be achievable only if there has been OR involvement on problems whose solution, at the time, seemed to offer minimal benefit. The argument here deserves development in its own right.

One approach to OR is to tackle only what problems come up, each one on its individual merits. This is almost certainly to deny the larger potential benefits of OR. The chance of the OR worker's contribution leading to a markedly better solution than the client would reach unaided by OR is probably not particularly high on any single issue, and it seems probable that, in the vast majority of the work OR workers do, they are, at best, making small improvements. It is by the few occasions when they make big improvements that OR is justified. (By a big improvement is meant doing something in a different way which is obviously and by some margin better than was the case. The act which causes the improvement might typically be the distillation of some new concept or enunciation of a belief which is absorbed into the general group culture, or it might be a change in the rules of the group culture to allow a different approach to an issue or class of issues.)

If these views are correct, then an important facet of the way OR is organised and deployed in a group is that the organisation and deployment should encourage a search for these big improvements and provide the flexibility for cashing in on them when they are recognised. (As an aside, these big improvements appear to arise most often either where part or all of the client group has got itself into the position of working to a manifestly false objective, or where innovation and change mean that the regular management has not had time to learn by experience. Possible examples of manifestly false objectives are: producing the best possible motor car in a performance sense when the market aimed at wants reliability, minimising the cash value of stocks when failure to supply from stock is costly, etc. Possible examples of rapid change include war-time OR, when quickly changing technology meant the relevant action theories could not be learned fast enough by experience alone.) It is not usually clear where the opportunities for big improvements lie. The search process might therefore be expedited by work on a whole range of problems. Moreover, the relationships and understandings built by the implied variety of work will probably help the effective response when the opportunities for big improvements are recognised.

A plausible further inference from this view is that the OR worker should not be over-concerned with the solution to the current problem, unless it transpires that it is one of the class which will lead to big improvements. Rather, he should be concerned to advance a solution which ensures that when the scope for big improvements comes along in the context of the current problem, it is recognised and the improvements obtained. However, the opportunity to make this contribution depends on getting in on the current problem and helping with its solution. So the quality of the instant contribution must be balanced with the more far-reaching aim.

BASIC TYPES OF SOLUTIONS

If OR work on a problem is thought worth-while, there are numerous alternative types of solution the OR worker might offer to produce, or at least aim his work towards. The solution offered by the OR worker is, of course, only going to be taken as a proposal for action by the client. The client might reject it, having weighed it or not against other possibilities, he might amend it or he might ask the OR worker to rethink and revise it. As with much of the OR activity, the OR worker must be prepared for negotiation about what is really wanted, what will work in the particular environment, and so on. Quite early in addressing the problem it is wise to talk about possible kinds of solution and certainly not to restrict that discussion to one kind. The process of reaching the solution is, in this sense, part of the solution. As the work progresses, different kinds of solution might be offered according to the changing perceptions of the problem. Some possible kinds of solution to which the OR and other work on the problem might be directed at various stages follow with comments. (If one of the solution types is offered, it is supposed backable by an appropriate justification.)

A   The best action in this case is .... ;

B   The way of deciding the best action in this and similar cases is .....
(B is assumed to include A in the sense that the solution to the current problem is explicitly stated or easily inferred as well as the way of .....)

    B1   A set of rules (e.g. evaluate proposed investments in the following programmed way);

    B2   A general model (e.g. a computer program which the OR worker can use again for similar problems without re-programming);

    B3   The means of applying the model (e.g. an interactive computer program operable by the client or his own staff);

(Note: A and B are cast in terms of solutions to problems where actions are sought. The word 'action' is to be widely interpreted here: action in the everyday sense, the action of adopting a belief, or new rule, or the action of rejecting old or inconsistent beliefs or rules, are among the ideas intended.)

C   There is no problem (or it does not matter what you do, or any further OR work cannot help you, or the cost of the further help is not justi-fied—the cost being, of course, the opportunity cost, in this case the value of the help on other issues which help on this one prevents);

D   Giving the means of solution generation—more generally giving prob-lem-solving skill, including when to call for advice. (D is a fuller version of B—it is, to a degree, B with understanding and the capacity to apply the concepts more widely.)

It is to be expected that cultural considerations, in particular the perceived role of OR in the culture, will influence whether some of these types of solutions are to be preferred to others. Indeed such considerations might mean that one type of solution is not even worth considering. The choice of type or types of solution to offer is, therefore, dictated by the OR worker's perception of the culture and his role in it. Moreover, the different types of solution may have markedly different costs and take markedly different times, both in their being reached and in their being put into effect. A type B solution, for example, could involve much more extensive research to develop than a type A one, and involve much training and/or 'hand-holding' before it is put into effect. The choice of solution type will therefore, depend on the value expected from it, which in turn will depend on the issue involved, the frequency with which it recurs and the added value of an OR contribution to the solution. All these things will be time related and weighed accordingly. The cost/value balance will often be the biggest single factor in choice of solution type. In what follows a number of points are made about other things which worth considering in choosing the type or type of solution to be advanced, but any normative advice implicit in the discussion may not be valid in any particular culture.

In many cases, B is preferable to A. A risks leaving little behind to help with the address of similar future problems. Choice among B1, B2 and B3 is not always available—for example, on grounds of cultural or technical feasibility. B1 has some merit in that the outcome of implementing by decree—which is what successful implementation of B1 implies—is predictable in principle and the objective function can be implicit. An example where B1 may be appropriate is in recurrent credit-rating decisions. The merits of B1 are consistency, the removal of bias, and clarity of responsibility for mistakes, all things which might well appeal to the client. The choice between B2 and B3 rests very largely on feasibility. In most cases, B2 is to be preferred to B3 except only on the grounds of interest and involvement by the client and his staff but, of course, these are very important grounds. B2 or B3 is probably preferable to B1 except in very clear-cut or trivial cases, because B1 removes any element of judgement from the client or his staff in their role of choice maker, discourages their understanding and inhibits their ability to make allowance for the peculiarities of particular cases, etc.

Type C is important. There should be no fear of offering type C solutions—to refuse to do so is a capital way of wasting time and resources which might be more profitably spent on other problems. Unfortunately, there are often pressures, sometimes self-induced, against the offer of such solutions. There is commonly a feeling that problems must have solutions in the everyday sense of the word, and an urge to draw out a solution, however ineffective it might be and whatever the cost of reaching it. Some people experience a profound sense of failure if they cannot offer a solution or if they feel they have only part solved a problem—even if that part solution achieves nearly all of what a full solution would. Sometimes it is difficult to convince the client of the validity of a type C solution, but to do so often generates valuable understanding about either the problem or about possible OR contributions.

A, B1 and C have something in common, namely that they all attempt to remove the client's worries—the problem solver takes responsibility, so to speak (although doubtless the precise solution will be reached by a process that effectively shares the responsibility—it would not be being offered, it is to be hoped, unless there had been prior acceptance of the methodology and understanding of it). With type D solutions, however, the client is being invited to extend his own capabilities. A case could be made for saying that type D solutions are what OR is all about, at least when such solutions are cost justified. It is by the implied cultural change that total organisational effectiveness improves, not by the occasional piece of OR work. It is the type D solution that gives the greatest chance of major benefits from an OR contribution, unless the problem is so potentially debilitating that time is of the essence and a solution of type A or B, and especially A, has to be pressed with all vigour. A potential worry to the OR worker about type D solutions is that, mishandled, they may limit the future contribution of OR. It is all very well equipping others to solve their own problems, but the fear is of creating a situation in which further OR work, which may be desirable as circumstances change, is denied simply because what may be a transient means of problem solving has been successfully handed over. However, a type D solution must be judged a failure unless it includes the planting of the skill, in the other people concerned, to recognise when they need more OR. Of course, an effective type D solution may be among the more expensive ones to effect.

THE CONTENT OF THE SOLUTION

The above discusses types of solution without addressing the question of the degree of detail into which the solution might go. This is clearly culture dependent. For example, the solution might be documented in a report, and the extent of the evidence expected in reports (as opposed to the results being taken for granted) observably varies between cultures.

A general issue of this kind which merits comment is how far the OR worker should go in offering direct, action-orientated solutions as opposed to more profuse solutions bearing on process. Take type A solutions, for example. The OR worker might offer to work towards a simple proposal ('buy a new crane', say) or towards one richer in detail ('buy a new crane, using this purchase tender procedure and this method of installation').

The choice of level of detail depends among other things on the OR worker's perception of where the value of this particular piece of OR work lies. At a simple level, it may be that no one can see how to evaluate the effects of buying a new crane. The OR work might best be devoted to generating and communicating the appropriate methodology for making that evaluation and, therefore, subsequent ones. Correspondingly, the solution emphasis would be on that evaluation, and the offered solution is simply whether or not to buy the crane. Alternatively, purchase or installation processes might be so ineffective that the obviously desirable purchase of a new crane is being inhibited through fear of the effects of purchase or installation inefficiencies. The question of whether to buy a new crane may be the one the client feels happiest to ask for help on, but hopes really for help on purchase and installation procedures. This discussion could go on almost indefinitely. The key point is that the kind of solution offered should relate to the resolution or alleviation of whatever problems are revealed as the work progresses. It follows that the solution aimed for will change as the work progresses.

However, there are possibly deeper considerations which might affect the type of solution offered. One is that the problem reveals itself as of such importance that a quick solution is of the essence. Here the thing to do will sometimes be to propose any solution which will improve things and leave any details to look after themselves. Priority might best be given to any action by the OR worker that generates action on the issue of concern. A second consideration, which relates to all types of solution but C, is the extent to which the OR worker's 'solution' is to offer his involvement in reaching a solution together with the client or his staff ('set up a team with me in it to tackle this problem—to decide whether we want a new crane and, if so, to buy and install it'). This may in any case be an excellent method of working. It could be particularly relevant if the issue is a recurrent one and the appropriate help is to improve responses to future instances as well as the present one, and even more relevant if the issue is one of those which offers scope for big improvement. It is sometimes a demonstration of ways of going about things, in this case the OR worker's ways, that teaches the more longstanding lessons. This kind of solution is more likely to induce cultural change than a more disengaged advisory one. It can also, incidentally, be a good way of securing continued involvement with that client group.

IMPLEMENTATION

So far the discussion of solutions and OR contributions to them, while acknowledging their setting within social processes, has not considered how a part in the solution process can be secured and put to good effect. To do so means considering relationships with others and the handling of the human side of doing effective OR.

There is, of course, an implicit assumption in addressing these issues at all. It is supposed that having been invited to work on a problem, the OR worker is motivated to do something about it and confident enough to think he has something to offer to its solution. The implied engagement in work on the problem and the associated social process can be undertaken more or less effectively. To be judged effective, the engagement would presumably have produced a solution accepted as good and appropriate by the problem owners, and the OR worker would have made a noticeable contribution to this. The management of that contribution, and in particular its successful management, can be called implementation of OR. Implementation of a particular solution, to which the OR worker might contribute but for which he is unlikely to be responsible, is causing the changes necessary to make the solution work. What follows is mainly about implementation of OR but, of course, that is subsidiary to implementing a good solution. Implementation of OR is, therefore, about the part the OR worker plays in finding and enacting good solutions.

Implementation, in this sense of someone managing for effectiveness his own contribution to a process, tends to be one of the major worries of any grouping which thinks it has a message to state or change to cause. It presents particular difficulties to the OR worker, who will almost always be trying to get people to look at things differently, indeed this may be his main motivation for working in OR. Generally speaking, he is involved (not necessarily alone) in trying to cause change in many directions at once—thus, in a particular case he may be trying to change people's behaviour, their approach to problem solving, their attitude to their job, their relationship with other people, as well as their beliefs and understanding. Moreover, the OR worker trying to cause change is usually doing so from a position of no or minimal power, using logical but often unfamiliar arguments together with whatever personal skills of communication and influence he can bring to bear. It would not be surprising if he often failed. A prudent attitude to implementation, except for a masochist, may well be to be grateful for comparatively small mercies.

APPROACHES TO IMPLEMENTATION

A facile view of implementation of OR, that the OR worker should offer his contribution on a take-it-or-leave-it basis, presumably falls short of the aspirations of most of those engaged in OR, who, it will be assumed, are motivated to see actual change as a result of their labours. If this view is taken, a possible approach to implementation would be to select only that work which the OR worker is sure will be valued and acted on. Thus, it might be said that at all key stages of an engagement the OR worker should discuss the work very thoroughly with the sponsor and ensure that he agrees and understands what the OR worker will do next and what he, the sponsor, should do at this stage. Generally speaking, there would be a number of lines of action acceptable to both the OR worker and the sponsor, but if none can be found that are acceptable to both, or more strongly if there are none acceptable to the OR worker that the sponsor will clearly support, then, the argument goes, no more work on this particular issue should be done.

This approach should not be regarded as a despicable one. Indeed, it is arguably the right approach for the majority of OR work. Given a sponsor, it is only where the OR worker feels he has perceived a deeper level of importance of the issue than has the sponsor—and it is this imbalance of perception which leads to the lack of agreement—that the approach might be objected to. Even then the fact that the OR worker cannot communicate his perception of the importance of the issue does not auger too well, although, of course, it is to be hoped that the OR worker would press his point of view.

What the above paragraphs say, in essence, is no more than a reiteration of the argument that effective OR links closely with the culture of its employing group. Implementation of OR is not a single dramatic act which changes the culture or (more likely) does not. Instead, it is the activity which links the OR worker to the culture at all stages of the OR engagement. It is the OR worker's management of his direct contribution to the problem solving. Importantly, it includes the management of the process by which the OR worker makes himself aware of the content of the problem, of its whole context—why it is an issue, something of the relevant history and so on—and of the social processes in which he will be engaging and to an extent intervening.

There is, however, another consideration, namely that OR might legitimately claim an evangelical role. The OR worker may perceive, or have drawn to his attention, ways of improving the capabilities of his parent group that are so far outside the present concepts embodied in the culture of that group that no one can be found with whom to agree or even to negotiate.

It is helpful to look at these questions as far as they affect certain extreme cases. (What follows are views about working in OR which are likely to be valid in most cultures. Nevertheless no objective validity can be claimed for the views. They are offered more as stimuli to thinking about working in OR than as recipes for success. Moreover, the OR worker will be one of a team, drawn perhaps from various sources, working on the issue. What immediately follows is cast as if he were working alone, but extends readily to the case where he is a member of a team. However, team working raises some specific issues which are discussed separately.)

THE CHOICE MAKER AS SPONSOR

One extreme case is that the sponsor is the choice maker, namely that he has asked for OR work on a problem about which he can make relevant choices without reference to anyone else. This is, it goes without saying, somewhat of an idealised abstraction. Only rarely would someone be an absolute choice maker, at least about matters on which he would engage OR advice. However, it is approximated often enough to be a helpful abstraction. (Of course, the choice maker in this context may actually be a group of people.)

The mere fact that the sponsor is the choice maker makes it likely that the problem to hand is reasonably clear-cut and, while it calls for technical know-how, it probably calls for little by way of engaging in a complex social process. Such OR work seems to present no difficulties of implementation except those which might arise from personal incompatibility between the OR worker and the sponsor—barring this it is merely a matter of working together in a sensible kind of way. Within this context, it is possible to offer advice with which many experienced practitioners would agree. There is much to be said for the OR worker seeking to maintain a continual discourse with the sponsor. (There is no need to be compliant in this discourse—argument is an essential part of it—but it is important to be sure that both parties, the OR worker and the sponsor, agree about what each is doing.) A consequence of this discourse, or if not a consequence then an aim, should be that the OR worker will not make major changes of direction without consulting the sponsor. It is helpful to agree quite early in the work at least a skeleton plan, including costs and timings of the intended work, step by step, including the general nature of the solution aimed for, and what that will ask of others, while recognising that the plan may change as the engagement develops. It is usually also helpful to let everyone else concerned (e.g. the relevant subordinates of the sponsor) know what is going on, why and how, either through the sponsor or at least with his agreement. Every effort should be made to meet deadlines. If it appears a deadline might be missed, the client must be forewarned. If at all possible, something should be delivered by the deadline: much better something, if not fully what was promised, than nothing at all. In relation to all this, a good rule is that nothing the OR worker does should ever come as a surprise. What he discovers might be a surprise but his mode of discovery should never be.

It is no more than common sense, but worth saying, that the OR worker should try always to act, and to cause the sponsor to act, in ways which help to solve or alleviate the relevant problem. Remember, this is what the OR worker is there for, not to try to sell a solution or to prove what a clever person he is. (He and the sponsor might sometimes disagree about what constitutes useful help to the point where confrontation is necessary, but this is a last resort and it is probably wisest for the OR worker to leave it to his boss.) Given this drive to tackle the problem the OR worker should not stand too much on his dignity. He should be prepared to 'muck in' to get a workable solution.

Finally, to repeat a point made earlier, it pays to be sensitive to when the solution has been reached. In this connection, the OR worker should not accept unquestioningly obvious diversions of his efforts unless to something plainly more urgent. If the sponsor attempts to divert the OR worker it is almost certainly because he has lost interest in what the OR worker is doing and does not feel inclined to say so. The OR worker should confront the sponsor and get the truth.

THE ADVISER AS SPONSOR

Consider now the case in which the sponsor will be choosing what he wants other people to do. Here the sponsor is in a rather similar position to the OR worker, namely that the kinds of choice he can make are that things ought to be done in a certain way by his subordinates, who are perhaps themselves fairly senior and expect to be allowed to exercise considerable judgement, or by his seniors, who expect him to make proposals to them. In some ways the sponsor in this role is asking the OR worker to advise him what advice he should give others, or perhaps he is asking in what direction he should try to influence them. The problem of working with such a sponsor is not really any different from the case in which he is an absolute choice maker, although there is one important additional aspect, namely that the OR worker will have to persuade the sponsor, or at least agree with him, that what the OR worker is doing is implementable by or through the others. This makes work on the problem intrinsically more difficult because the social process in which the problem is set cannot be ignored (it never can, but it is not always central). Again advice with which many experienced OR workers would agree is offered.

If the others are the sponsor's subordinates, the OR worker may have to help the sponsor to do the job by canvassing opinion among his subordinates and feeding back to him their attitudes to various proposals, their view about how to convince them (e.g. two or three of the subordinates might be found who are sold on an idea and who might advise about training for the others) and their views on such matters as what complexity of calculation can be tolerated, etc. It is sometimes helpful to think of the OR work being done hand-in-hand with the sponsor to try to cause change in the organisation. This puts a premium on knowing the organisation and its relevant culture pretty well—who in the relevant set of people wields the power, who are most influential among them, what media are available to propagate solutions, what coalitions of interests are necessary to allow what change, and whether and how these coalitions can be set up. As many of the subordinates as possible should be carried along with the work. It may be possible to organise the OR work to include some problem solving for individual subordinates—if this can be done without too much loss in efficiency, it should be. As well, wide contact may be possible by getting access to routine gatherings of the subordinates; or it may be worth organising, or getting organised, *ad hoc* gatherings to keep them informed at key stages of the work—this, as well as contact with individuals. Note that the most influential people in the sort of context here being discussed are not necessarily the most successful—sometimes the most receptive and influential of the subordinates will be respected for such qualities as intelligence, creativity, etc. but not necessarily be successful managers. (Because it is rather unlikely to be a totally unstructured problem being addressed in this context, this case will not be discussed here, but see below.)

If the others the sponsor has to influence are his seniors, the OR worker's scope is more limited. The OR worker will probably have to accept the sponsor's view of what can be 'got through', at least unless or until he has observed himself how the senior people act. Other members of the OR group might, of course, know or have worked directly for the senior people and be able to help; the OR worker will be able to form his own judgements of the senior people's response to his work as it develops and discuss this with the sponsor; and he should miss no opportunity to sit in (even as a silent observer) when the sponsor meets the senior people to discuss the problem.

THE ABSENT SPONSOR

Finally, consider the case where there is no sponsor in that there is no one who is empowered to act in the area in which the OR worker believes useful change can be made. Because there is no sponsor, it is likely that the problem which the OR worker would wish to address is somewhat unstructured. Suppose also, as again the chances are, that effective work on the problem requires its recognition by, and contribution from, someone other than the OR worker himself. How can the OR worker go about making the desired impacts? Again, advice of a kind many experienced OR workers would offer follows.

The problems are very different from the other cases discussed. Because of the likelihood that there is no readily structured problem but rather just a feeling of unease, eager responses cannot be expected to overtures made to busy men who, by and large, prefer to have clear-cut problems, with some idea of their solution, brought to them. Perhaps, therefore, the main problem for the OR worker is to get someone to take him seriously. Almost by definition he does not know at the start who this should be. He must, therefore, be prepared to talk a good deal to almost anyone who might be interested, taking and creating every opportunity for formal or informal communication until a sympathetic ear is found. It is sometimes helpful to try to identify those whom the powerful respect as men of ideas, even if not of judgement. They can be useful allies, particularly as they may be prepared to present a case much more extremely than it would be prudent for the OR worker to do himself without risking his reputation for judgement.

There are other ways of approaching this problem, which are also applicable to the somewhat related problem of getting OR recognised in a new field. One is by extension of present work—a work programme which is acceptable to the employing group might be constructed merely in order to create an opportunity to extend the work into problem areas which the employing group does not yet recognise. Another is to offer to generate knowledge—it is much more likely to encourage support if people can be persuaded that the OR worker wants to find out what is happening, rather than his implying that he is going to make everything better because of their ignorance. A further possibility is to seek to frighten the employing group, for example by pointing out that their rivals are one up on them in this field—this is probably inferior to other approaches except in situations where a natural ally can be found with some power who is looking for just this kind of argument to advance his own cause. Finally, OR help might be directly offered, with the implication that it will improve things—again, this is probably an inferior approach to the others unless there is a natural ally who is anxious to use OR help for his own causes and has the power or personality to carry his colleagues.

If, by whatever means, a sponsor is found, the general remarks under 'adviser as sponsor', amended in obvious ways, apply.

GENERAL REMARKS

Already some of this chapter might be thought to be platitudinous. The author's excuse, if one is needed, is that platitudes are not always acted upon. Some further platitudes which fall into this class follow. They relate to implementation generally. In import, they boil down to the fact that implementation is about working with people to help tackle problems or cause useful change. Thought, care, courtesy and consideration in establishing and maintaining productive relationships with those with whom one is to work are obviously desirable. Success in implementation is closely linked with success in managing working relationships.

An important and widely recognised factor in good relationships is the ability to see things from the other person's point of view. It will usually pay the OR worker, therefore, to try to look at the problem and his approach to it from the sponsor's point of view. He should balance this point of view with his own but never ignore it.

In order to get things done on time, or in order to exercise influence, it may be necessary to compromise or to cut corners. In doing so, the OR worker should make sure he is not fooling himself. It may be necessary for him to simplify his perception of the truth to stand any chance of causing change, but he can only do this confidently if he is fairly confident his own perception is somewhere near the 'real' truth.

One of the great dangers in any OR work is for the OR worker to get himself out on a limb so that no one knows what he is thinking and doing, and, equally, he does not know what others are thinking and doing. This is a recipe for failure. He should try never to let it happen. He should seek or create opportunities to talk. Useful communication, including in this many aspects of data collection, should absorb a fair amount of time, perhaps as much as a third or perhaps even a half of the time averaged over OR work as a whole. However, it is wise to ensure that those with whom the OR worker is communicating are able to differentiate what he is actually doing as opposed to what he is talking about.

Where the OR worker should spend his time is often an important consideration. An engagement in any social process, if it is to be successful, usually means developing an understanding of that process and gaining acceptance as a participant in it. Commitment may need to be exhibited in various ways—for example, by showing a willingness if necessary to work long hours, to accept some personal inconvenience and so on. Identification with the aims of those with whom the work is being undertaken also helps. An important factor in all this, and in much that has gone before, can be a willingness to work in close physical proximity to the clients. This is not always to be desired and sometimes, perhaps usually, a full commitment to working close to the clients has its dangers. But generally it is better to err on the side of being there than of being elsewhere.

TEAM WORKING

The above is cast in terms of the OR worker and the sponsor working together. The sponsor is viewed as one other person, or a coherent group acting much as if it were an individual. Commonly the OR worker will also not be an individual so much as a member of a coherent team, the OR team. There will be roles within that team such as that of leader. There will probably also be roles corresponding to division of labour: one person might be charged with research into one aspect of the issue in hand, another with model building; and so on. OR teams, to be effective, appear to need a rather unusual blend of team discipline and freedom for individual action. While the team leader will usefully discuss and stimulate the work of his team, as a general rule he will not find it productive to direct it in other than the most indicative way. This is because each team member will usually have at least some part of his task which requires cultural familiarity of a kind that is difficult to forecast or to communicate, and he will correspondingly need to engage with the sponsor or the sponsor's colleagues. Moreover, each team member will, unless there is over-rigid team leadership, have to make frequent methodological choices without reference to the team leader if the work is to proceed apace.

The team may be able to work as a team, in the sense of working together all the time, when the cultural learning and choice making can be done jointly, but this is not always possible. The wise OR team leader might try, however, to simulate this method of working. He might, for example, have the team meet daily or weekly, perhaps in some relatively informal setting, for experience sharing, joint discussion of choices made and the planning of the next stages of work. He will also have clear understandings about freedom of action with his team members, or at least of commitments into which they can enter, and of mechanisms for reporting to him. He will be wise to keep all the team informed about all the team's work, with errors in the direction of over-informing to be preferred to those in the opposite direction.

Sometimes, in practice fairly commonly, the OR worker will be a member of a team whose other members are not all OR workers. The above remarks apply here also if they can be put into effect. They almost certainly will be if roles in the team are reasonably well defined. The implied methods of team working may be unusual to some of the other team members, but experience suggests people respond to them. If the team leader is unfamiliar with them, however, some difficulty might be experienced. The OR worker might usefully act in this case as if the team leader were the sponsor and adopt some of the suggestions made above about relationships with sponsors.

Difficulties can arise if roles are not well defined. The leader of a team whose members are all amicably disposed towards him and towards each other will early on negotiate and agree roles for each of the team and, assuming these are kept under continuous review and renegotiated as necessary, few difficulties need arise. Sometimes, however, the team members will not be amicably disposed towards each other, nor all towards the leader. Two team members might, for example, be competing for roles, for good reasons or not. Such is often the case where there are team members from two activities, say IT and OR, who both feel that they can best occupy some particular role, in this case perhaps designing a decision support system. The competition would be given added bite if each party to it had quite different value systems. Such disputes are not easily resolved. Diktat by the team leader is possible but heavier guns, say the functional bosses of the competing team members, might then come forward. Negotiation, led by the team leader and involving the sponsor and the functional bosses, seems the best way out of non-trivial disputes of this kind. They are certainly better settled, even at the expense of time lost, before the relevant part of the work is started than their resolution left to time and chance. (Overt disagreement among the team members for, as it appears to him, no very good reason, is unlikely to raise the sponsor's confidence. He will usually be tolerant of disagreement which he can understand, and in whose resolution he can assist. He will indeed usually see it as part of the problem-tackling process.)

CAUSING CHANGE

There has already been frequent allusion to causing change and the OR worker's frequent desire to do so. Usually he will not expect to cause major physical change himself, although he may be asked to participate in doing so. However, he will hope and expect to cause changed perceptions in other people and, therefore, to influence their behaviour. Much of the immediately preceding material can be viewed as comments on causing change but the topic deserves further comment. In particular it might be asked whether there are generally useful strategies for causing change.

A few moments thought is enough to suggest, if not prove, that there is no sure-fire way of causing change. The world is full of people who wish to change it but plainly fail to do so. Those who succeed often do so because, by luck or judgement, their timing is right. They act when there is a 'climate for change' of the kind they wish to make, that is there is a widespread sense among the relevant people that change is necessary and perhaps what broad direction it should take. The would-be change maker places himself in a position to take advantage of this, perhaps by exercise of his social or political skills, and causes the change. In such circumstance getting into the right place may be decidedly more difficult than causing the change. However, it can be argued that, interesting as who occupies what positions may be to the individuals concerned, the change will come whoever they are.

The more interesting question is how a would-be change maker creates the right climate, how he generates the political desire and will for the change he wishes to make. The method usually adopted is to exercise persuasion in every way possible. Power helps, of course, in extreme cases in the form of the physical exercise of power by armed force, revolution and so on. At a less dramatic level, power may be used to command media access. Without power or money (which amounts to much the same thing as power), talking, rallies, demonstrations, strikes, and so on are common strategies. The OR worker is likely to have little power, and many of the strategies of the powerless are unavailable to him or would usually be counterproductive. He will usually have to persuade, either orally or in writing, one or two people who have some power, in order to acquire through them the means of exercising his persuasive powers more widely. (His understanding of the culture, of the power networks in it, of who can cause change and who can prevent it, are supposed adequate to the task.) This is a common tactic in OR in practice. The OR worker persuades someone to sponsor work and then, perhaps with his endorsement, uses the results of that work to persuade others, thus hoping to set up a climate for more work of that kind. (The work, of course, is of a kind that will create the climate for the required change. Thus, suppose the OR worker felt that his employing group were continually managing their capital projects in ways which could be markedly improved by the use of some technique he has read about. He would, following this strategy, try to get into the management team of one project and so on from there.) Various other devices for causing a climate for change have been referred to indirectly on pages 186–188. Yet another might be getting in on appropriate training programmes. In this connection, well-built management exercises or games can sometimes be a powerful way of causing people to face the need for change. People on training courses are often, in any case, in a mood for reflection. If the course is a residential one, the people on it can be accessed informally in ways seldom otherwise available. The OR worker might usefully seek to set up opportunities to attend courses himself or to assist on them, so as to take advantage of what may be an excellent environment in which to exercise his persuasive skills.

The OR worker will sometimes find himself asked to help someone who knows what changes he wants to make but whose problem is how to make them. This would-be change maker will also have to create a climate for change by some means or other but, if he has power, there are means other than simple persuasion he might adopt. He may in an extreme, for example, be able to resolve conflict among his colleagues by sacking those opposed to change. He will probably be able to take actions that communicate very clearly that he means to make change and to make it stick. Here, of course, is someone wishing to make a choice from the various change strategies available to him and asking the OR worker to help him choose, a subject covered at length earlier. Common difficulties in choosing the right strategy for change are whether to pick off the constituent changes one at a time or all at once, and whether to consult widely and bring in the change by consent, or to change by edict and pick up the pieces afterwards. These are decisions that plainly depend on context. They depend also, in any context, on questions like how quickly must the change be made, and whether it is intended to be durable. The OR worker must help as he can on these matters. His skill in structuring may be the most useful contribution he can make, including in this simple modelling.

The time taken to bring about change, unless the climate is right and change is 'in the air', can be surprisingly lengthy. The OR worker engaged in or assisting change making must expect to require patience.

APPENDIX: A COMMENTARY ON THE SERVICE PROVIDER'S PROBLEM

by Emma's father

Objectives

The general position of the firm is that it is profitable. Making a generous allowance for the cost of some presumed headquarters it seems quite likely that Mr Avery is making at least £250 000 a year. However, the profitability level is not remarkable (except insofar as it flows into the pocket of one man) and it is unlikely that the firm would be exposed to an undercutting operation of its own kind.

Against this background it is a little unclear what Mr Avery's objectives might be. I suggest there are three possible broad kinds of objectives consistent with the picture painted of Mr Avery.

(1) He may wish to maximise profits.
(2) He might be mainly interested in growth of activity subject to some such constraint as continuing profitability.
(3) He might be morbidly anxious to stop the practice he is complaining of, again subject to some constraint like profits not being too badly affected.

Data Analysis: General

The statistical information available tells us, via the market research data, that demand provides no limit to growth.

The table on job duration suggests that the Southampton and Brighton schemes have been equally effective in reducing the malpractice. The Southamptom scheme does not seem, as might be feared, to inhibit one-day jobs, for otherwise we would expect the proportion of one-day jobs at Brighton to be decidedly higher than at Southampton. The average duration of jobs at Southampton is 2.35 days, 2.37 at Brighton, 2.13 at Portsmouth and 2.11 at Hastings.

On its own the table of costs indicates little more than that the operation is profitable. However, I will return to an analysis of the costs shortly.

The table of results over the last four years is capable of much analysis. Superficial examination reveals a clear seasonal pattern, and an upward trend at Southampton.

Data Analysis: Southampton

The effect of the Southampton scheme is not easy to decide. It appears to have had no effect during the second half of year (n-1) (i.e. when it was first introduced) but the very high growth of business at Southampton in year n strongly suggests a large delayed effect. If we assume that the Southampton scheme has done nothing more than lengthen jobs, we can estimate the number of job days for year n at Southampton had the scheme not been introduced by estimating the number of jobs ($221/2.35$) and multiplying by the average duration at Portsmouth and Hastings, which it seems likely would have been the duration at Southampton in the absence of the scheme. This gives 199 as the estimated job days (in thousands) at Southampton in year n if the scheme has had no effect other than lengthening jobs. It seems doubtful whether on trend alone the figure would have reached 199. I think we can safely conclude that the Southampton scheme genuinely increases business in terms of jobs and job days.

On the other hand, the Southampton scheme greatly reduces revenue per job day. Allowing for the seasonal effect I estimate that Southampton could have got the same revenue under the old scheme as it did with the new from 172000 job days in year n. On trend alone it is quite likely such a target would have been reached. It is therefore reasonable to conclude that the Southampton scheme does not increase total revenue.

However, it almost certainly does increase costs. The table of direct costs shows, if nothing else, that costs rise with the number of jobs undertaken or with the number of jobs or both. The Southampton scheme has increased the number of job days well over that necessary to obtain its current revenue and has also increased by about 13000 (221/2.35 versus 172/2.12) the number of jobs. The Southampton scheme is therefore almost certainly losing money. Crude analysis of the direct cost figures suggests this loss is around £60000 per year. The only reservation to this statement is that Southampton may not need the same amount of advertising, owing to its favourable terms, as the other branches. It is difficult to infer anything from the table of indirect costs. Possibly Southampton is doing more advertising, the other three branches having roughly equal indirect costs with Southampton's well above; on the other hand, Southampton is plainly the biggest branch and may be expected to have the highest indirect costs in any case, possibly even higher than those shown if it were advertising in the same relative proportion as the others. The possibility of higher advertising at Southampton might, of course, explain the upward trend in business there.

Data Analysis: Brighton

The Brighton scheme, assuming it has lengthened the duration of jobs, has actually led to a reduction in the number of jobs since the number of job days has remained roughly the same over the whole period. This is not necessarily a bad thing. Profit may actually have increased if the saving in setting up jobs is sufficiently high compared with the cost of the chauffeurs. This is a question which can only be resolved by estimating both the cost of setting up a job and the cost of the chauffeurs. If we assume that the direct costs are made up of a fixed element plus a set-up cost per job this would give us an upper bound on the cost per job. Doing this for Southampton, Portsmouth and Hastings gives a cost per job of about £4.80. This means Brighton is saving at most just over £27000 per year, compared with the number of jobs at the average Portsmouth and Hastings length necessary to achieve the number of job days achieved by Brighton. However, on wages alone the chauffeurs cost £22500 a year and the hire of cars etc. would almost certainly take the total cost over the saving.

Longer-term Effects

Taking a longer-run view there seem to me to be objections both to the Southampton and Brighton schemes. Although difficult to make any inferences from the given figures it seems quite likely that the £1.50 commission for the second and subsequent days of the job at Southampton fails to cover marginal costs. If this is the case it only needs some clever customer to hire enough staff for very long periods greatly to reduce Southampton's present profit. It is perhaps surprising that this has not already happened, although presumably any such customer would hire his labour direct or would at least attempt to do so in the first instance. (I am not sure about the strength of this objection. I have little idea what the cost of recruiting casual labour is. If it is sufficiently low this point is no worry, but it might be high enough to make quite long jobs cheaper through Service Providers than by recruitment. But Service Providers could, of course, easily act to prevent abuse.)

The Brighton scheme would, I would have thought, inevitably reduce business in the long run, and the reduction in number of jobs supports this view. I would have thought also that its effectiveness in inhibiting the malpractice would diminish, although here there is no evidence to support this.

Southampton, Brighton or Do Nothing

Let us restrict our attention to the alternatives: Southampton, Brighton, do nothing. If Mr Avery wants more and more jobs and more and more job days he can get this by using the Southampton scheme, but almost certainly at the expense of profit. The reduction in profit at Southampton does not produce a loss there, but a similar scheme at some branches might put them into the red.

If Mr Avery is interested in maximising profits he is almost certainly best advised to introduce neither scheme.

If Mr Avery is adamant that he wants the practice stamped out at a reasonable cost he would probably do best to go for the Brighton scheme. However, it is to some extent a guess whether the Brighton or Southampton scheme is the cheaper. On common-sense assumptions about car-hire costs etc. it seems likely that the Brighton scheme is costing at the very most £36 000 per year (assuming all direct costs are relatable to job days and not to jobs). Against this the Southampton scheme is almost certainly costing at least £60 000 per year on direct costs with some questionable saving in advertising.

Other Alternative Schemes

Are there any worthwhile further alternatives? All obvious variants of the Brighton scheme are subject to the same criticism as the scheme itself unless the same effects can be achieved by employing fewer chauffeurs. Four chauffeurs (versus six at the moment) might just about break it even, if they get the same effect (which I guess they probably would).

Variants of the Southampton scheme might work. For the scheme not to lose money about £60 000 a year extra revenue is needed. The most straightforward ways to get this are (i) an initial charge of £9.60 or (ii) a run-on charge of about £1.95 per day. If neither alters the pattern of job length (a matter of judgement, but I would have thought not) this is the scheme to go for. It would still no doubt have the other advantages accruing at Southampton and the only reservation is that £1.95 or £1.50, as the case might be, might not cover marginal costs. (But see comment in brackets above on 'longer-term effects'.)

The only more radical alternative I can think of is to introduce some method for estimating the duration of jobs and making a once-for-all charge for each job on the basis of these estimates. The arguments for and against such a scheme cannot be resolved from the given information.

Finally, an obvious bit of gratuitous advice is that Mr Avery should find out how Southampton have managed to increase business so effectively over the years to see whether the implied managerial skill is transferrable to the other branches.

Conclusions

Obviously there is no right answer to this problem. However, there are a number of key points of which that both at Southampton and Brighton the present schemes lose money is perhaps the main one, followed by the realisation that most plausible objectives could probably be met by some simple variant of the Southampton scheme.

EXERCISES

(1) Look again at the Profitable PAM case (pages 108–109). Set out what problems you think the Marketing Director thought he had at various stages of the events described and when he thought he had solutions. Are there any differences in thinking about the whole process described as a continuing engagement, as opposed to a sequence of problems and their respective solutions? Consider various major public issues (e.g. some aspect of education policy, some particular facet of taxation policy, etc.) which sporadically attract much media interest. Taking 5- or 10-year views, answer the same questions for these topics as you did for Profitable PAM.

(2) Sketch out kinds of solution that might be appropriately offered to Mr Bird (pages 1–3 and 10–12) and the Cox family (pages 167–170). If you were an OR worker engaged by Mr Bird or the Cox family what kinds of considerations would lead you to offer what kinds of solutions? In each case, list the key questions (if any) to which you would want to know the answer in order to decide on the type of solution. Having proposed working towards a particular type of solution, what kinds of development in each case might lead you to revise your proposal?

(3) Consider some problem-solving process in which you have recently engaged yourself, preferably as a member of some group. Try to recall all the solution-proposal activities that took place. Examine and reflect on the reasons why those solution proposals were accepted or rejected at the time they were made, and why all but presumably one were eventually rejected. Are there problem-solving processes in which proposing a solution is the dominant activity (as opposed to gathering and analysing data, modelling, and structuring choice making)?

(4) Reflect on some situation in which you have been invited to give advice. (If you cannot think of one, ask a friend to use you as an adviser on some choice, however trivial, he or she is facing.) What factors, with the benefit of hindsight, were most influential in generating your success or failure as an adviser? How, without the benefit of the

hindsight, could you have acted more effectively on the particular issue which determined your success or failure? Could you have managed the process of advising better? How? Is your answer to this question valid for any situation in which you might give advice and, if so, is it advisable to cast your answer in a more general way that covers more situations? Did the person or group whom you were advising act as responsible sponsors? Is it possible to say anything about managing adviser/client relationships which are context-free? If you were the editor of the next edition of this book what would you do with the relevant part of this chapter? (You are allowed options from deletion to expanding it into a book into its own right.)

(5) List significant changes which you have witnessed or to which you have been party. Try to include in the list changes of a physical nature, changes in the goals and aspirations of a group, and changes in an individual's or group's perception of some relevant feature of the world. For each example, decide whether you think the change has been for the good and why. Again, for each example, analyse how you think the change was effected. Is there some identifiable individual or group who might be described as the agents of change? Was there exploitation of power? Was the individual or group ripe for change or, if so, was there any prolonged period of establishing a climate for change? Might any of the changes have been made significantly more quickly? If not, what means might have been adopted to achieve this?

(6) Together with a few friends, form yourselves into a team to carry out some more or less meaningful task. Keep a brief diary or record of events as the team goes about this task. Include your perceptions of the thoughts and motivations of yourself and the others, and your perceptions of your and their contributions to the task. Try to persuade your friends to do likewise. At the end of the exercise compare your different perceptions of what was going on.

Did you as a group read the situation well as far as your respective perceptions of the value of different people's contribution to the task is concerned? Is there any systematic tendency for each individual to over-estimate his own contribution? Is there any systematic tendency for one individual's contribution to be consistently valued more highly than that of the others, or to be discounted more than others, by the rest? If so, what qualities of his contribution led to this assessment? Was his ownership or lack of social skills more or less important than the intellectual quality of his contribution? Was there competition for roles? Was this competition helpful or did it hinder the completion of the task? Did it lead, or might it have led, to the abortion of the task? If there had been a clearly designated manager for the team's work, what might this person have done to improve the execution of the task? Would the task have actually been better done? Are there any key qualities that the manager as a person would have needed, or which management as an activity would have needed, for it to have been helpful?

(7) List some of the occasions when you have asked for, and been given, help. For each occasion, decide whether and how much you actually were helped. What distinguished the good from the bad helpers? Is it usually wrong for the helper to take responsibility for solving the problem, as opposed to helping the person with the problem to solve it himself? In what circumstances would it be right?

(8) Think of something you are aiming to accomplish over a period of weeks. Set out your plan for doing so, listing your aims, key activities and intended timings. Look at this plan a week hence. Is it still valid? If not, amend it. Repeat the process weekly. Does the amount of emendation surprise you? What caused it? Which of your changes of mind, your forecasting, or other people's actions, was most important? What general lessons do you draw?

(9) Consider again the Service Providers case (pages 59–62). Emma's father used to work in OR. In the evening of the day Emma got the problem, she told her father about it. He spent a couple of hours on it and wrote the above Appendix (pages 193–196).
   (a) How many marks out of 10 would you give Emma's father if his commentary were the answer to a question posed in an OR examination?
   (b) Would it be sensible for Emma to give her father's commentary as it stands to Messrs Fell and Robertson? Look carefully for
       (i)   Points they might misunderstand or simply not understand,
       (ii) Ideas or views they might find unacceptable,
       (iii) Assumptions they might feel are so derisory that they would reject the whole thing.
       If you were Emma, what would you give Messrs Fell and Robertson? Anything written at all? If so, how long would it be and how much graphical material would you include? Or would you prefer an oral presentation? With or without slides? What should Emma be aiming to do? (Candidate answers are to help Messrs Fell and Robertson understand what is going on, to propose a solution, to keep Mrs Avery quiet, etc.) Should Emma be concerned about how change can be made? Is it possible to answer these questions without knowing, or at least having met, Messrs Fell and Robertson? Or without relevant knowledge about the way things are done in Service Providers?

(c) Various of Emma's student friends comment on the case, having seen her father's commentary.

(i) An economist points out that the increased price of one-day jobs at Southampton should have depressed demand for one-day jobs, other things being equal. It has not done so. Therefore, other things are not equal, and demand has increased for reasons other than pricing policy.

(ii) A statistician points out that a suitable statistical test shows that the distribution of job lengths at Southampton and Brighton are not the same. Nor are those at Portsmouth and Hastings. He believes this undermines the whole analysis.

(iii) A social scientist thinks the various stakeholders, including the registered workers, merit more attention. All Mr Avery wants, she says, is to earn enough money to enjoy his yachting.

(iv) An OR student says that the key questions are about objectives. Emma should say and do nothing until these are clarified.

(v) An engineer says the only thing of interest is: what is going on at Southampton? Emma should insist on going there, gathering all the information she can, and only then offering any advice.

Discuss these viewpoints. Are any of importance? Now answer (a) again.

(d) How do you think the Service Providers problem will be solved?

Chapter 11

——— Some Organisational Aspects of OR

This chapter raises some of the considerations relevant to thinking about the organisation of OR as an in-house activity (i.e. OR for the organised group that employs the OR workers), though topics are covered which probably have a relevance also to OR as a consultancy activity (i.e. OR for organised groups different from the one that employs the OR workers). It is, of course, difficult if not impossible to offer culture-free recommendations about the organisation of OR. The questions discussed below seem to be relatively culture-free and the answers may have some relevance to most cultures in which OR has a part. However, the aim of the chapter is to stimulate ideas rather than to give pat solutions.

WHY HAVE AN OR GROUP?

This chapter supposes (as where relevant, do all preceding chapters) that an organisation (i.e. an organised group) employing an entity called an OR group is doing so because the organisation recognises the possibility of a positive OR contribution to its problem-solving activities. (This supposition might well apply to some group which does not have the phrase OR in its title. Here, and throughout the book, the phrase OR group, OR and OR worker are meant to cover the group doing OR, the activity OR and someone working in it according to the definition of OR given and discussed in Chapter 5, whatever these things might be called in any particular context.)

There are other possible reasons why organisations might employ an OR group, or rather a group called an OR group, and brief discussion of some of these follows. Someone called an OR worker will do well to think why his OR group exists. While it is to be hoped that the supposition of this chapter is the most common reason, it may not be the only one. This chapter, and other parts of the book, may need to be read from a different perspective where the reason is different, and even ignored in some extreme cases.

One reason to have an OR group is as a means of recruiting able people to the organisation who might not otherwise join it. As soon as appropriate, people are moved from the OR group into suitable managerial posts. The organisation might well regard the time in the OR group as valuable training or a useful period of familiarisation. Some people will stay in the OR group, including some who will manage it. On the whole, this chapter is not invalidated if this is the reason for having the OR group.

There are other possible reasons which do not fit so easily with the broad stance of this chapter. Among these are:

- The OR group's primary purpose is to contribute to the organisation's image for efficiency.
- The OR group exists to further the aims and interests of a select few in the organisation.
- The OR group is a transit camp for those who have failed elsewhere and are waiting for another job to come up.
- The OR group has an executive role (e.g. it is the sales forecasting branch or the market research department under another name).
- The work of the OR group is restricted to the use of specified methods (e.g. it is the simulation shop) or to specified problems (e.g. it is the body which advises on staff rostering).

These reasons are not necessarily good or bad, but they are decidedly different from that assumed here. (The reader might find it of interest to look back to pages 71–72, where various definitions of OR were discussed. These various reasons include ones which are not consistent with any of these definitions.)

CONDITIONS FOR EFFECTIVENESS

If it is accepted that OR is concerned with helping to solve problems using a broadly scientific approach, then at least two things are implied for OR to be effective and/or efficient.

A   The OR group must have access to relevant problems or the ability to obtain it.
B   It must have the capability to help solve them 'scientifically' and to implement the solutions.

A can be thought of as access to the market place and B as the product for sale. OR's sphere of influence in an organisation is, of course, the product of A and B. Each equally determines effectiveness, but neither is any use without the other. Each requires appreciation of the organisation's culture.

A and B in turn imply their own requirements. Thus, A implies that the OR group should be in a good position to know what is going on in the organisation, either by being in a position to find out directly or by having good access to whatever grapevines are relevant; it must have knowledge of the alternative specialist skills available so as to judge the relevance of its skills to the particular problems that come along; it is desirable that it should be capable of creativity so that it can recognise the application of problem-solving concepts from one field in apparently unrelated fields; and it should have the social and political skills to effect entry to the problem-solving processes. It must also seek to ensure that its client base is aware of the kind of contribution it can make, so that clients come to it when appropriate.

B reveals something about the kind of technical skills needed in an OR group and, therefore, something about recruitment and training. It also implies that the OR group needs the opportunity to collect and analyse any relevant data, the freedom to communicate to any relevant people, at least some measure of objectivity, and a reasonable opportunity to implement. The social and political skills to do the relevant things effectively are again necessary. Again, the OR group must also seek to ensure that the client base is aware of the general capability of the group.

Taken together, the requirements for A and B indicate much about the mix of personal skills desirable for a successful OR group. In some ideal world, this mix of skills might be found in each member of the group, but more realistically it might be hoped to find the mix available in the group as a whole.

PLACE WITHIN THE ORGANISATION

Some of the above points clearly relate to the place of OR in the organisation. It is assumed here and below, unless specified otherwise, that the in-house OR group is intended to be a continuing activity, and not, for example, set up simply to undertake some finite task. If the OR group is big enough to justify independence then this independence, perhaps reporting to a member of the main board, overcomes any organisational impediments; it is then up to the OR group to satisfy its own needs and secure A and B above.

If the OR group is not big enough automatically to justify independence, then its place in the organisation can be a severe restraint on its effectiveness. On the whole the dangers are pretty obvious, especially in a bureaucratic kind of organisation. Given its place in an organisation under anyone, it matters very much who that anyone is, and there are cases where a lack of understanding of the needs for effective OR by the (non-OR) person in charge of it have killed OR in an organisation.

For the small group there seem to be three major alternative placements in the organisation:

(a) Attempted independence—this is probably viable in the medium term only if the OR group is patronised by a very senior and powerful person or persons;

(b) Selective OR from any base—for example, splitting up the group so that individuals in it work for specific clients and their work is co-ordinated. This approach is obviously limiting in that OR is deployed on the problems of the few people to whom the OR workers are attached, but within these limits it often works well, particularly if the clients to whom attachments are made can be hand-picked. The closeness of the relationship which the individual OR worker can attain with his client satisfies most of the organisational needs, unless the client's influence (and interest) is not powerful enough to meet them;

(c) Linkage with some other activity or activities, in the sense that the OR group, while remaining a distinct entity, becomes organisationally part of a larger unit.

Option (c) is the one most commonly chosen. The question is, linkage with whom? There are two important considerations in answering this question.

The first point is that the linkage should not impede the attainment of points A and B above. This is perhaps best negotiated, in that the OR group seeks agreement with those with whom it is linking that it will be allowed to do whatever is necessary to secure A and B. If linkage with others who themselves work in similar ways to the OR group is possible, so much the better. An important point of similarity could well be that the others are charged to help, as opposed to their being charged to impose. (To take an example, the IT activity in an organisation could be simply providing a service and reliant for its success on helping those managing the organisation. In another organisation, the senior management might have decided that IT is of such potential benefit that aspects of it must be imposed whether those more junior want it or not, and the IT activity has been empowered to do the imposing. OR would probably link happily with the first IT activity, less so with the second.)

The second consideration is whether the broad aim of the OR group is to be one of enhancing the organisation's efficiency or of helping to cause organisational change. In most organisations there are some activities whose principal task is to ensure efficiency assuming the status quo continues. Often those engaged in these activities, subconsciously or otherwise, become keen to preserve the status quo. There are usually also activities intent on making change, and those engaged in these become keen on change almost for its own sake. (Which of all these activities are currently powerful depends, of course, on general organisational wishes.) The OR group might link, according to its aims, with a relevant activity on one side or other of this divide.

It is impossible to generalise but, among the contending activities with which OR might link, are other 'management services' (O&M, systems engineering, work study) and corporate or strategic planning. These activities are usually, but not invariably, intent on change making. They also commonly work in ways similar to the OR group. Other candidate activities, which may work like the OR group, include IT and management accounting, which may be change making or not; and financial accounting, which often seeks to underpin the status quo. In some organisations a possible linkage might be with management training. Sometimes this activity will be charged to impose 'the company line'. However, it often has a helping orientation. In addition, it often has a foot in both the change-making and status quo camps, extensive access to the organisation and much contact with managers, often in congenial circumstances. Science has many of the virtues which OR finds desirable, and linkage with R&D is superficially an attractive possibility, particularly if the R&D activity includes a help-based service. Unfortunately, R&D is not often seen by managers as a natural activity to which to turn for comparatively short-term problem solving.

To be entirely on one side or the other of the change making/supporting the status quo divide potentially dangerous; change makers tend to get sacked and those supporting the status quo tend to be stifling of innovation. Perhaps the healthy OR group might almost offer to split itself, attaching some of its number on the change-making side and some on the other, particularly if it can find groups on either side who work in ways like its own.

CHARGING AND MEASURES OF EFFECTIVENESS

An OR group does not usually have a life of its own, or power in its own right, but is given life by the value placed on it by powerful members of the group it is serving. Different cultures have different outward expressions of this kind of patronage. For example, in some cultures the OR group would simply be given resources and told to do what it liked. The risk here is clear: the resources could be withdrawn as power shifts in the employing group.

It would seem prudent for the OR group to have some more durable way of securing its resources and one which draws on a widely spread power base. One way of doing this, whether the OR group is assimilated with someone else or not, is to have a programme of work endorsed ahead by a cross-section of the currently powerful. A good position, if it can be achieved, is to have this cross-section supporting the OR group against cuts or predators to the point that the OR group does not need to do it itself.

This support might find an expression by charging clients for the OR work. Often there is no choice for the OR group: it must charge or not according to the general cultural norms. If there is a choice, considerations include that charging could easily affect the work balance—perhaps less speculative work, more work for the already powerful, etc. The work programme will tend to reflect the short-term interests of the powerful. There is merit in levying charges so as to generate a surplus for discretionary work of a speculative and similar nature. (Of course, the charges must be such as to allow for training and keeping up with new developments by the OR group.) Another consideration is that charging may alter the manner in which the work is carried out, as indeed may the method of charging. On the whole, the changes that charging induces in work practices are widely felt to be for the good (as opposed to the changes in work balance, which generate more controversy).

Note that there are many different bases for charging—by subscription, by project, by person-time, etc. Some will be more or less appropriate to different kinds of work. Care in choosing the charging base is recommended, but the issues are left for the reader to think about. Many more detailed arguments could be developed, although most would be culture dependent. The main virtue of charging is that it demonstrates the strength or otherwise of support for the OR group. It will usually do so provided the OR group is responsive enough to merit that support. In the long run, responsiveness to client demand and the capacity to change to new fields as issues are worked out and absorbed into the culture (or simply as the world changes), are the crucial things for survival of the OR group—or, making due changes, for anything at all. Charging—if the culture allows it—may be a suitable mechanism for forcing these things. (No implication is here intended that the capacity to respond and change measures the relative effectiveness of OR groups. This is plainly not so, as two groups may each respond and change sufficiently to survive but one be greatly more effective than the other. The less effective group has simply passed some threshold of effectiveness for which its clients are willing to pay. However, the incapacity to respond and change certainly threatens survival.)

It is well to be clear, however, that any absolute measure of effectiveness, such as the financial contribution made by the OR group, is likely to be difficult to find. If the OR group has some narrow specialist role it is just conceivable that a simple comparison of the parent group's performance with and without it could be made and its effectiveness thereby evaluated. More likely, however, the impact of the OR group will be impossible to disentangle. Much of its work will have been joint with others and even if the value of that work could be measured its apportionment between the OR group and others would be controversial. In any case, its effect, let alone its value, would be hard to measure. The argument might also be advanced that the OR group often achieves nothing in its own right. It simply helps others who have the actual responsibility for solving problems and, therefore, deserve the credit. Many measures of specific aspects of effectiveness or efficiency can, of course, be made—proportion of work done to time, cost versus the cost of engaging consultants, etc.—but total effectiveness seems elusive to measure.

INTERNAL ORGANISATION: RECRUITMENT AND TRAINING

Some of the points made earlier must be met by policies which either the OR group controls for itself or in which it has a large say. Two of these are recruitment and training. It goes without saying that these are highly important matters for an OR group. The OR group's only productive resource is its people.

The main things to look for in recruitment are, following the arguments given earlier, the ability to study problems analytically and to think creatively (in other words, a particular kind of intelligence), the abilities to assimilate problem context, to communicate and to negotiate (and hence to work effectively with others), and (closely related) the likelihood of fitting into the organisational culture in some useful way. There are reasonably objective measures of some of these qualities but by no means all, so that recruitment can be a chancy business. Many OR groups respond to the mixture of importance and chanciness of recruitment by investing considerable resources in it. They take pains to stimulate many applicants. Desirable applicants are usually sought by many employers, and advertising, in some general sense, is required. OR groups usually take pains also to select effectively among applicants. It is not uncommon for a one- or two-day process of interviewing, personality and aptitude testing, group discussion of set problems, talks with recent recruits to the group, and so on, to be used. While, no doubt, in some measure stimulated by a quest for more certainty than can reasonably be achieved in staff selection, such extensive processes seem worth while. They also probably meet the candidates' expectations of fair treatment as well as giving them a chance to inform themselves about the group. This last is an important point: recruitment can fail as much from the person recruited having made a mistake in joining the group as from the group having recruited the wrong person.

The ability to communicate effectively includes the skill to communicate across two gaps. There is nearly always some kind of generation gap—OR people being predominantly younger than those they seek to help—and what might be called an attitude gap—OR people being on the whole interested in abstract and general views of problems, their clients being on the whole more pragmatic. These gaps have their strong points as well as their bad points and, indeed, the second gap is one of the reasons why OR exists at all. The first gap has the advantage that OR does not often go unnoticed, and it is some guarantee of a freshness of thinking and approach being injected through the OR activity. There are ways of retaining these good

points while alleviating the bad ones. One obvious possibility is to introduce a few older people with management experience into the OR group to
give it 'respectability' and, as occasion demands, a mouthpiece to bridge
the generation gap.

Training has three aspects. First, there is that training which is concerned
to give the OR person every opportunity to get to know the organisation in
which he is working and to understand its culture—induction courses, visits
to various work places, contriving for him to meet a range of management,
asking him to help plan work, etc. fall into this category. Second, there is
the type of training which is designed to extend the person's competence
in a technical sense by introducing him to methods and concepts which
others have found useful. In the main these are the methods of model
building (statistics, linear programming, simulation etc.) and appropriate
computer training. They also include the more general concepts of the
social sciences, including economics. Third, and perhaps more controver-
sially, there is training in what might be called social skills, such as communicating, presenting, chairing, or effectively participating in meetings.

The main points about these kinds of training are that they should be
done in some form or another. (For the typical recruit to an OR group some
will, of course, already have been done.) Forms of training vary and will be
appropriately different in different cases. The value of on-the-job training
is unusually high in OR. The encouragement by those managing the OR
group of a climate in which the group members exchange experiences,
expose their mistakes and expect constructive criticism from their peers
and superiors, without fear or a sense of loss of face, can greatly help self-
learning. The healthy OR group will enjoy such a climate and the subject
matter of the implied discussions will be both technical and cultural or
social. The learning will, therefore, cover learning about effective participa-
tion in the relevant social processes. The process of learning about the
employing group can often be facilitated by frequent changes of work,
although carried to extremes this might reduce effectiveness.

INTERNAL ORGANISATION: LEVELS OF HIERARCHY

Internal organisation of the OR group in the sense of whether there is a
hierarchy, and how many levels there are in it, is often controversial. There
appears to be merit in three levels of hierarchy, at least two of which
should be in the OR group itself—the third may be the person, not himself
an OR person, to whom the OR group reports. The first level is obviously
the worker. He will usually be either under a project manager or himself a
project manager, a project being simply a defined piece of work. The second
level, call him the section leader, is there for a variety of reasons. He will

normally have oversight of several (probably linked) projects and himself be a worker, probably the manager of one of the projects. One of the main reasons he is there is because the worker needs a section leader in order to have someone with whom frequently to discuss the progress of the work in a comparatively objective, but nevertheless informed, way. The section leader has the responsibility to see the work through its ups and downs, questioning excessive enthusiasm for the work, as well as keeping morale high when things appear to be going badly. Perhaps most important of all he has, or should have, the means of seeing the study in its cultural perspective which makes him more likely to see when to cut corners, when to compromise with clients, how to present the results and, indeed, what the important aspects of the solution are. He it is who keeps the role of the OR worker and his contribution under review, seeking to negotiate new roles and shifts in the work as circumstances change, or stimulating the worker to do this. All this is part of the important on-the-job training referred to earlier, and the section leader has much of the responsibility for making this effective.

The third level, call him the group head, is likewise necessary for a number of reasons. For a start there has to be someone deciding how the resources—the section leaders and the workers—should be deployed. The group head should be able to talk to the relevant client base more or less as an equal and in a completely dispassionate way, and be able to kill or inject whole projects as the needs of the organisation change. He is the monitor of relevant cultural changes, including the employing group's attitude to and expectations of OR, and the person responsible for actions necessary to meet those changes. It is he who would be expected to gain entry, or to manage the process of doing so, to new fields for OR in the employing group. He should also be able to act in a fatherly kind of relationship with both the workers and the section leader, not so much telling them what to do as ensuring that they are learning from their experience all the time.

INTERNAL ORGANISATION: ACCOUNT MANAGEMENT

If the organisation which the OR group is serving is large and complex, with sub-organisations within it, and if the OR group itself is large, several of the tasks suggested for the group head would be impossibly demanding for one person to carry out effectively. It may be necessary to spread the work among a set of people. Where this is done it is common for the work to be split by giving each of the set responsibility for all of the OR work for a particular sub-organisation and for the OR workers and project managers engaged in that work. Each member of the set will thus have responsibilities of his own, but some of the group head responsibilities (for example, that of resource allocation) will be exercised by the set as a whole. On all matters, the set are likely to keep each other well informed about their respective activities.

The role outlined above, the member of the OR group assigned to attend to the interface between the OR group and part of the organisation, is often referred to as account manager. The account manager may easily, perhaps desirably, wear two hats, that of the group head as previously defined and that of the section leader. There is a good argument, at the least, for the account manager involving himself in some project work, if only because that is often an effective way of monitoring the culture of the sub-organisation. However, to wear two hats calls for nice judgement and managerial skill, for otherwise the wearer himself and more particularly those with whom he is dealing can become confused or uncertain about which hat he is wearing at any particular time.

The difficulties appear in practice to be surmountable by some people, and to good effect. Where complexity makes it desirable there seems much to be said for the OR group organising itself around the account manager concept. Experience suggests that the advantages outweigh the sometimes messy disadvantages of the possible uncertainties of role.

The successful account manager, or group head in a group not organised by account management, will desirably be adept at gaining an understanding of the concerns, aims and values of his client group. To these ends he might usefully engage in their essentially social activities—for example, joining them for lunch, attending their office parties and so on. His full effectiveness may depend on his being accepted as part of the social network that his client group forms. Reciprocally, he and they will naturally communicate with each other when they need help or when they have helpful pieces of information.

INTERNAL ORGANISATION: WHAT WORK TO DO AND HOW TO DO IT

A further area which more often than not comes at least partly within the OR group's own control is how it goes about its work and how, if at all, it chooses to balance its work load. In earlier chapters the view has been expressed that successful OR is a co-operative venture with clients and others and, by implication, is not a passive, dispassionate, backroom activity but one which is committed to causing change of a broadly desirable kind. The OR group must seek to keep its activities in line with the changing concerns of the employing group. In other words, it should be responsive to the concerns of the employing group, as indeed to all facets of the employing group's culture. (These points apply, of course, not just to what work is being done but to how it is being done and to what ends.) It will normally be the group head's duty to ensure this for the group as a whole, but for project leaders and workers also to do so within their sphere. If this view is accepted, then it important that OR should be managed so as to allow its expression. There are implications here for the encouragement of initiative and action, for the OR managers to allow the OR workers unchaperoned access to clients or their representatives and, in turn, for recruitment and reward policies. Undue bureaucracy could be damaging.

The view that OR should be organised to take advantage of the probably infrequent opportunities for large improvements has also been earlier expressed. Its realisation implies trying to get a balance of work across the entire range of the parent organisation's activities, in type and level, in long- and short-term issues, in strategic and tactical problems, etc. The balance has other virtues. Particular pieces of work are more clearly seen in their perspective, and 'systems effects' (i.e. interactions between different problems and their solutions) are more easily spotted by an OR group whose work is wide ranging. Equally, the OR group should not constrain itself. There should be a balance of methods of attack (if OR in an organisation becomes identified with simulation, say, or more seriously with applied mathematics, its effectiveness is naturally reduced); and a balance between short-term assistance and longer-term research (the former provides the 'cash flow' and the latter is the 'investment', to provide the framework and concept development for cashing-in at the right time—how much of an OR group's work should be speculative or anticipatory of problems yet to be more widely perceived?).

It might be argued that the previous paragraph offers a recipe for a somewhat dilettante approach, lacking the depth and effectiveness which only specialisation can produce. Another argument concerns risk. Should an OR group aim to become indispensable specialists or highly dispensable dilettantes? Certainly there is a balance to be struck here and perhaps it is that a fair degree of specialisation, in type of work and client base, is appropriate for the individual, while the OR group as a whole should seek the wider-ranging aims. Nevertheless, it is by no means clear that the individual, within his specialisation, is different from the OR group as a whole.

INTRODUCING OR INTO AN ORGANISATION

Hitherto the problem of introducing OR into an organisation has not been specifically discussed, though some of the points already made obviously bear on it. There is much evidence to suggest that most new OR groups go through (or fail to get through and die) a series of identifiable crises.

If the group is set up to do a specific task it is off to a flying start. The first crisis (unless the task disappears for one reason or another) occurs when the task is complete. Unless a new role is quickly available the group will very likely collapse.

If, on the other hand, the group is set up just to do OR, the first crisis is immediate: short-term returns (via easily obtained savings) seem to be a nearly essential for survival. This crisis met, the next one may arise through failure in the next natural phase, the expansion to more strategic problems: over-ambition and/or too high client expectation can lead to frustration, disillusionment, etc. on one or many sides. The final crisis is the 'living death' risk. The group becomes accepted as a team of valued experts but in a narrow field.

Avoidance of these crises is a matter for managerial skill. Most of what might be said about this is explicit or implicit in earlier remarks.

Much of what is said above applies equally to introducing OR to a new part of the organisation or to a new client.

COMPETITION WITH OTHER ACTIVITIES

Whether part of some larger grouping or standing alone, an OR group is likely to find itself competing with other groups for the right to help particular clients on particular classes of problem. Such competition can arise for many reasons. In some organisations there may be competition to survive, or the competition might reflect the ambitions of the members of competing groups. In other cases, the competition may arise because each party genuinely thinks it can be helpful, possibly more helpful than the other and even more helpful if the other is not involved. The client, the natural arbiter, may be uncertain if not positively ignorant of the issues. Among possible competitors are external consultants, parts of the IT activity, other 'management services', and do-it-yourself OR by the client or his staff.

The first thing to be sure about is what constitutes competition. Others than the OR group might be asked to do OR work for reasons other than simple client belief in their greater competence. External consultants are commonly employed for political reasons, such as the need to persuade people that the work is objective, or because it is thought they may be more aggressive in causing change because they will not have to live with those affected.

A second reason to get others to do OR is that they are cheaper than the OR group, and, although conceivably less effective, they have a more favourable cost/benefit ratio. This reason is continually at work. Its most obvious manifestation is via the regularisation of what was innovative work by the OR group, that is, the absorption of such work into normal management processes. For example, the OR group may have built planning models which have been found useful. The client's staff have become familiar with them and their use, and all concerned are confident that these staff can use the models, and even keep them up-dated, to high benefit. Moreover, the models are frequently enough used to justify continuing attention. It would, in such circumstances, be likely that the planning activity would gain by running the models themselves. Usually this a sign of success for the OR group. Most OR groups will desire it. Generally it is a process that the OR group will do well to encourage and facilitate, including proposing it and, where appropriate, helping to train those intended to do the work. The OR group should also offer, and in some cases press, to keep an eye on the absorbed activity. It might otherwise become unresponsive to changing need or cease if those doing it leave and cannot be replaced—the OR group is likely to be better equipped to ensure continuity.

Sometimes, however, the competition will be simple, literal competition. Assuming the OR group wishes to respond to this competition, some political activity seems necessary. The role of the account manager, whether so-called or not, is of clear importance to the political aspect of this issue.

There are considerations, however, other than political. The OR group should almost certainly take steps, by whatever means seem appropriate, to ensure that its skills, its achievements and the type of work suitable to it are all known about and understood by the population of actual and potential clients. The appropriate means of disseminating this information will be culture dependent. Means that might be considered include all the opportunities organisational life offers for the formal and informal chat; the propagation of written material, either general or specific accounts of successful work; and formal talks to conferences and courses. In all these things, emphasis will be placed on what the OR group can do that the client is likely to value. Examples of what the OR group has done, at what cost and to what effect, might helpfully be developed.

The projection of this information, including preparation where appropriate, can usefully engage much of the time of the managers of the OR group. However, it is an activity to which all the group members might be encouraged to contribute as opportunity presents itself.

In many cultures, it is worth adding, belittling others is poorly regarded. As a general rule, it is what the OR group can do, not what the competitors cannot do, that should be broadcast by the OR group. Indeed, the members of the OR group will often gain by understanding what the competitors can do and acknowledging this. The OR group might well be valued as a source of informed advice about which of the helping groups can most usefully be engaged in the particular case.

A clear understanding of the kind of help he can expect should help the client decide to which helping group he should turn, and the above paragraphs suggest how the OR group might inform clients.

Another response to competition is to co-operate with it. Co-operation also might take several forms. One is for the competitors to promulgate jointly their agreed spheres of interest and competence. This is often to OR's disadvantage, because of the difficulty of offering precise enough statements about the range and applicability of OR. Another form of co-operation is to pool all or some class of requests for help which either competitor receives, and to have some mechanism for deciding who should respond. This is natural perhaps only where each competing group feels secure. Even then it will tend to degenerate into a fair-shares-for-all mode of operation. If either group feels threatened the whole approach is liable to break down.

Co-operation usually occurs when each party sees some advantage from it, indeed some might argue this is the only time it occurs. This thought has led to examples of successful co-operation between OR groups and competing groups. One reason is that sometimes a client will prefer no help at all to inadequate help. There may, for example, be a choice for the OR group between doing nothing or doing something jointly with an external consultant whose special skills the client values highly, but whose associates he would not wish to employ. In the same vein, the client will sometimes want a larger effort if, in his judgement, it is suitably staffed. He expects returns from the mixed team sufficiently higher than from the unmixed team to justify the extra effort. The OR group, invited to help with a problem, will do well to reflect on these possibilities and to propose accordingly. In some cases, the invitation may not come because the client does not expect the mixed team response. A willingness to work with others can usefully, therefore, be advertised.

MONITORING AN OR GROUP

Although measures of effectiveness are difficult to define, there do appear to be some indicators of whether an OR group is healthy, that is, whether it is in a state robust enough to survive the buffetings of organisational life. These buffetings include such things as periodic reviews of non-core activities, cost-cutting exercises in response to some perceived crisis, the exercise of political power by would-be empire builders, and aggressive predatory activity by competing groups.

Points already made bear on this topic—for example, the capacity to change, the pursuit of a broadly based clientele and so on. Indeed, the whole chapter might be said to be about this topic. Some of these points can be given formal expression, and the OR group might be wise to keep records that indicate, for its own benefit, the way its activities are going. Some of these are discussed, together with the reasons for them.

First, a record of the effort devoted to different clients and different organisational activities might be kept. This obviously bears on the breadth of the client base. It also provides a check on whether the group's activities bear on the expressed organisational priorities. For example, an OR group in a retailing organisation might be concerned if none of its activities related to sales, the likely core activity of the parent organisation. The management of such an organisation might, for various reasons, suddenly decide to stop everything that did not bear directly on sales. Equally, the OR group would usually not wish to have all its work related to one activity, however important that activity, for this would make the group vulnerable to absorption into the regular management of that activity.

Records of how the OR group's work is initiated might also prove useful. For example, the work might be categorised into repeat business (second or subsequent work for the same client), duplicate business (repeating successful work for one client for another), follow-up business (work extending already successful work), new business (issues not previously worked on) and self-started (work for which no client can readily be found). Such records can provide many insights into client perceptions of the OR group and its general effectiveness. The desirable balance, in most cases, would include some in all categories, but more in some than others. An excess of self-started work is clearly dangerous. An excess of duplicate business might suggest a narrowing of aim and interest in the OR group, bringing a risk of ossification or absorption. It might also be suggestive of a failure to get ideas across in a simply exploited form. The reader is invited to continue these arguments.

Statistical information about staff can be useful. Records noting in which kinds of work people have been engaged, and their performance in them, monitor not just the people but the skill with which they are being managed. A healthy group might aspire to a purposeful career development of its staff, by ensuring suitable experience is obtained in a sensible manner. The suitability of an individual for a particular piece of work, perhaps because he will be able to draw on earlier experience in doing it, or perhaps, conversely, because it will enrich or round his experience, can probably more easily be judged with suitable records. The records might include, therefore, some appraisal of an individual's development needs as well as his already acquired and demonstrated experience and skills. A record of why people leave the group, and for where, might also be instructive. Again, the reader is invited to reflect on such matters.

Simple monitoring that individual engagements are going to plan, and that the work is of an adequate quality in the sense of its technical soundness, is obviously desirable. The group head will probably find it helpful to review work with the account managers regularly—say, quarterly. Progress against project plans and the quality of the work might then be reviewed, as well as more general topics like continued responsiveness. The group head will probably find it useful also to review the work with the clients, at more or less the same time and in more or less the same spirit.

More generally, the OR group will wish to be sure that it has satisfied customers. Opportunities to obtain feedback should be taken as well as created. In this same connection, the group head will wish to check whether and why work apparently suitable for the OR group is being placed elsewhere or not commissioned at all. Should he hear this of some major piece of work on an important issue, he will not wait for some routine meeting, of course, but will want to know why very quickly. (He will probably be wise not to ask too aggressively though. Perhaps an informal call to a friendly member of the potential client's staff is best.) He would ideally like to be forewarned and given the chance to comment, if not compete where relevant. If this is not happening, he should be concerned enough to think why and what he might do about it.

Finally, and perhaps too obviously, the OR group should keep some account of expenditure, income (where relevant) and resource utilisation, including staff as a resource. Sometimes it will be only by such records that gross imbalances of cost and value of the OR work can be detected, or charges of imbalances refuted. The amount of resource spent on non-essential, but important, activities like training, preparation of publicity material and so on is best known. It might equally, of course, be too low as too high. With all these things, it will probably also be wise to maintain forward projections, so that anticipatory action can be taken to prevent foreseeable difficulties.

With all these things in place, and all the advice of this chapter taken to heart, an OR group can still fail. The most enthusiastic health seeker can be the victim of accidental death, but his statistical expectation of life probably exceeds that of the dissolute. In the same way, the well-managed OR group has the better chance of survival, but cannot immunise itself against accidental death.

EXERCISES

(1) Is it wasteful to deploy people likely to make good OR workers to practising OR (as opposed, say, to being managers or accountants)? Some organisations deliberately recruit to their OR groups people who, it is expected, will be good managers. The people are encouraged to move on after, say, three years in OR. Discuss this practice. What are the benefits and drawbacks (a) for the people and (b) for the employing organisation?

(2) In this chapter (page 202) A and B imply simple definitions of the market and of the product for OR in an organisation. Expand these definitions giving particular attention to relevance and value. (The expansion is likely to be culture dependent and the reader is invited to relate his expansion to a culture with which he is familiar. Thus, the class of relevant problems would be those relevant to the culture, per-

haps along the lines discussed in Chapter 5, and different kinds of solution activities will enjoy values which vary between cultures.) Do the expanded definitions render any of what is said in this chapter inappropriate? If so, try to write those parts of the chapter in ways appropriate to the expanded definitions.

(3) Reflect on some of the reasons why an organisation might choose to employ external consultants when, in terms of technical content, the work the consultants are given could readily and effectively be carried out by the organisation's own internal OR group. What responsibilities does the internal OR group have in relation to such work? In particular, what kinds of relationships might it usefully establish with the external consultants? A possible broad stance for the internal group is to offer to collaborate, perhaps forming a joint team with the external consultants. An alternative for the internal group is to seek the role of criticising (here intended in a wholly constructive sense) the work of the external consultants. Are there any special sets of circumstances in which either relationship is greatly to be preferred to the other?

(4) List some of the various balances of an OR group's workload suggested in this chapter. How far is the attainability of this balance a function of the place of the OR group in the organisation? (The answer to this question seems obviously culture dependent, and the reader is invited to answer it in relation to a culture with which he is familiar.)

(5) What measures of effectiveness of an OR group might the chief executive of an organisation usefully require? Reflect on how the particular management style of the chief executive might affect the measures he asks for. Draw up lists of measures which three different kinds of chief executive (e.g. one who manages through consensus, one who is driven by short-term profitability, and one who is intent on causing drastic change) might use. What might be the effects of these three different lists on the behaviour of the OR group? How far should the management of the OR group go in challenging any lists which it finds particularly unfavourable? Or should the OR group be prepared to adapt to any list?

(6) Consider the following six questions. Is any of them capable of a relatively culture-free answer?
    (i)   Which of the three levels of worker, section leader and group head should plan projects, monitor project progress (and how frequently) and script/write/approve communications, including final presentations/reports, to clients? If there is an account manager, what should his role be in relation to these matters?
    (ii) Are basically different personal qualities required in each of

the worker, the section leader, the account manager and the group head? As a corollary, what promotion policy should be adopted?

(iii)   How important is it to agree formal terms of reference with clients?

(iv)   How far should the group head go in discussing his individual staff with their contacts in the organisation but outside the OR group (i.e. clients and their staff)? And how should he use the information he gains?

(v)   What special features does managing OR (as group head, account manager or section leader) have, as opposed to, say, managing a supermarket or an accounts office?

(vi)   How long should an account manager stay in the same job?

Answer the questions for a culture with which you are familiar. Are the issues addressed by the questions of equal importance? Suppose you were appointed manager of an existing OR group working within that culture and you found it was managed inconsistently in every respect with your answers to the six questions. What changes would you seek to make, in what order, and to what timescale? What factors might influence your choices?

(7)   Discuss the purposes and means of an OR group publicising itself to its employing group.

(8)   This chapter has tended towards advice about what an OR group should do. Are there golden rules about what an OR group should not do? Are they culture-free?

(9)   Asked to carry out a 'health check' on an OR group of, say, 5 to 10 people in a week or two, how would you go about it? In particular, what relative emphasis would you place on matters internal to the group (including data gatherable inside the group) and matters external, such as gathering clients' opinions? Would it depend upon who had asked you to do the work?

(10)   Set out in general terms your ideal training programme for *any* OR worker, that is, that programme which would be useful whenever and on whatever issues the worker was to be subsequently engaged. How much of it is specific to OR? Draw inferences about possibilities for joint training with those engaged in other activities. Are there any strong advantages or disadvantages to such joint training?

Postscript

This postscript summarises the main points that the book tries to make.

(1) OR is helping groups to solve their problems by methods which would enjoy the consensus support of scientists.

(2) Groups are collections of individuals, with cultures—rules and beliefs, power patterns and goals, conflict and coalitions—which it is necessary to understand and be responsive to if the OR worker is to be as helpful as possible to the group.

(3) Problems arise from dissatisfaction or surprise, to which the problem owner(s) thinks he (they) should respond but he is (they are) uncertain how. Problems, and hence solutions, are subjective. Solutions usually alleviate, as opposed to remove, problems, and may themselves cause other problems.

(4) Scientists generally support the methods of logic, the basing of belief on fact and/or observation, and debate and criticism of beliefs.

(5) OR's role in relation to a group is likely to be concerned with those issues to which the group sees scientific method as applicable, but for which there is no established scientific expertise.

(6) OR works as in 5, but might also work to extend the group's perception of where scientific method might help.

(7) Defining a problem is essentially deciding on some line of activity which will alleviate the problem. The definition should be kept under review.

(8) Data collection includes not just gathering the numerical facts but also gaining an understanding of the context of the problem and the culture within which it is set. The OR worker's client/sponsor should be able to help interpret the culture.

(9) Models are devices for developing understanding and for making predictions. They gather together beliefs about an issue. Model building structures research and beliefs.

(10) There are many types of model. It pays to think which will be most effective in any given context.

(11) Defining the problem, data collection and analysis, model building and other parts of the OR process are continuous, concurrent activities and not just sequential stages in carrying out a project.

(12) It is not always the case that choice is made by a single choice maker using a relatively simple criterion. When it is the case, OR has much by way of developed technique to offer in preparing for choice and in making it. These techniques can also help individuals engaged in debate about who and how to decide.

(13) When there is a disagreement about who should decide and how to decide, OR might have to take sides (i.e. help one of the disagreeing parties) or work on the common ground.

(14) Some of the big gains from OR are when it generates cultural change. OR should be managed to this end.

(15) Implementation is about working with people and establishing and managing the working relationships. It pervades the whole OR process, and is not a single step in it.

(16) An OR group needs exposure to its market place (clients and problems) and to be competent in meeting its market. It needs to keep in touch with the culture in which it is operating and to ensure its continued effectiveness and viability within the culture. Different cultures will value different facets of their OR groups. The OR group should be staffed, managed and organised with these things in mind.

Bibliography

The purpose of these final pages is to provide a bibliography which lists various kinds of work—for example, those which either justify or somewhat elaborate material covered in this book, or those which extend the material or present a different viewpoint. It is hoped that the commentary which precedes the detailed listing will clarify the reason for a work's inclusion in the list.

The bibliography is not intended to be exhaustive. The works listed are, of course, intended to be relevant and of quality. However, these two criteria alone would generate an overly long list. Some effort has been made, therefore, to include works whose own bibliographies will take the interested reader further or deeper if he so wishes. Some attention has also been paid to the accessibility of a work when choice has been exercised among several contending references.

The commentary that follows relates references to the previous chapters. Works are referenced by the author only, except where the author is referenced twice or more, when the date of publication is used to distinguish different works.

CHAPTER 1

Most books on OR, and many papers, implicitly treat the question of help. Two books that place particular emphasis on help are those by Bryant (1989) and Eden, Jones and Sims (1983), indeed the latter book uses the word 'helper' more or less throughout to indicate what this book has called 'the OR worker'.

Many textbooks are concerned to structure a subject, or perhaps more accurately to depict a structure. This is commonly done by setting out certain principles with or without justification, and developing other principles from them by means of logical deduction, again with or without introducing extra data. Mathematics and the hard sciences provide numerous examples but so do more everyday subject matters. A few examples from somewhat disparate fields, which discuss the structuring as opposed to postulating it, are books by Dirac, Jeffreys and Jeffreys, de Finetti, Lindley, Lipsey and von Neumann and Morgenstern. (There is no thought of urging the reader to study all or any of these books, but a browsing of one or more, according to the reader's prior knowledge, will illustrate the notion of structuring.) Good reference books provide an everyday example of the power of structuring. The material is presented consistently with a few simple rules, although successful use of a particular book may require hard-won familiarity with the rules. Dictionaries provide obvious examples. *Chambers* is a well-regarded dictionary: by exploiting structuring beyond the merely alphabetical listing, it includes many more words than its size might suggest. Another example is the celebrated *Gray's Anatomy*.

CHAPTER 2

Popper has been an influential philosopher of science. His work is described, and a bibliography given, in an easily read book by Magee. Hawking, Watson, Ne'eman and Kirsh, and Dawkins (1986, 1989) have written books which give good readable accounts of science as well as their direct subject matter. Biographies of scientists, for example Pais's of Einsten, also provide relevant reading. Kuhn famously introduced the ideas of normal science and paradigm shift. Checkland (1981) writes interestingly about science and about systems science as well as his own soft systems methodology. Wolstenholme describes system dynamics. Checkland (1992) critically reviews the state of systems science.

A book by Stewart gives a more technical account of chaos than one by Gleick, but the latter is highly readable. The anthropic principle and its implications are discussed in a fascinating book by Barrow and Tipler and catastrophe theory by Zeeman and by Woodcock and Davis. The proceedings of a conference on OR and the Social Sciences, edited by M.C. Jackson, Keys and Cropper (1989), contain several relevant papers.

CHAPTER 3

Among numerous books on organisations some of particular interest are those by Handy, Morgan and Pettigrew. Keys (1991a) and Walsham have related Morgan's work to OR and information systems respectively. Simon's work (1960, 1961) is also relevant. Ulrich examines the relation of science and its cultural context. Eilon (1979) includes much interesting material.

Much excellent fiction is about culture in the sense the word has been used in this book (including, in British literature, the cultures of the various social classes), and much is about activities set within some organised group with a strong culture of its own. To mention two well-known examples, Jane Austen's *Mansfield Park* can be viewed as a description of value systems in conflict, while Anthony Trollope's Barsetshire novels, e.g. *The Warden* and *Barchester Towers*, are classic works about the organisational life, the organised group in the cited cases being the nineteenth-century Anglican Church. More recently, Lodge has described a culture clash of particular relevance to OR.

Non-fictional works, of history in particular, also frequently illustrate the power of culture to shape or influence action. Two illustrative books of this kind are one by Annan, who describes the culture of his generation and (broadly) social class, and its effect on the development of the UK, and one by Kennedy, who writes, among other things, about the difficulties cultures can encounter in adapting to changed circumstances.

CHAPTER 4

Libraries are full of books about particular classes of problems and the means of tackling them. Many if not most people have some hobby which presents them with problems—they may have the hobby just for that reason. Presumably it is such people who buy books with titles like *Improve your Golf*, *How to be Your Own Car Mechanic*, and so on. Reflection on the generality behind the subject matter of such books may prove helpful in thinking about problems more widely. Among treatments at a more general level are parts of books by Simon (1960, 1961), Checkland (1981), and Eden, Jones and Sims (1983).

CHAPTER 5

Many books on OR are written around paradigms markedly different from that adopted in this book. The introduction by Rosenhead in a book edited by him (1989) gives relevant references as well as his own view of the nature of OR. Books which adopt approaches similar to the present work, but different enough to make stimulating companion reading, include those by Boothroyd and by Eden, Sims and Jones (1983), and a book of distinctive style by Bryant (1989). Interesting essay collections have been edited by M.C. Jackson and Keys (1987) and by Tomlinson and Kiss (1984). Eilon (1973, 1975, 1979, 1980, 1987—the first two references are included in the third) writes stimulatingly about OR. See also Bowen's remarks on Eilon (1975). A report on the future practice of OR, which was commissioned by the OR Society, may be found of interest. (It is listed by its title,

Report of the Commission on the Future Practice of Operational Research.)
Bennett and Macfarlane (1992) update some of the report's findings. Tobin,
Rapley and Teather discuss the changing nature of OR from a practitioner
viewpoint. Keys (1989), in discussing whether OR is a technology, affords
useful insights. Flood and M.C. Jackson (1991a) have interesting points to
make.

CHAPTER 6

Some of the books already referred to, including those by Bryant (1989),
Checkland (1981), Eden, Jones and Sims (1983), and Rosenhead (1989),
have much to say about problem definition. Two papers by Pidd and
Woolley (1980 and, listed under Woolley and Pidd, 1981) are of interest and
one by Pidd (1988b) alone. Methods appropriate to specific kinds of problems are covered by Kepner and Tregoe, and M.C. Jackson (1987) suggests
a relevant classification of problem contexts. Huxham writes comprehen-
sively about facilitation: although her emphasis is on voluntary collaboration, much of the material has a wider relevance. A book edited by Miser
and Quade discusses problem formulation along with other topics. Flood
and M.C. Jackson (1991b) cover relevant material.

CHAPTER 7

There are many books at various levels on the relevant mathematical statistics. One appropriate to those who are numerate but without extensive
mathematical knowledge is that by Connacutt and Connacutt. Chatfield
and Collins and Everitt deal with multivariate analysis, and Cox with
designing experiments.

Eden, Jones and Sims (1983) discuss data collection via interview and,
more generally, the capture of subjective data, and its useful representation
by means of cognitive mapping. Survey design, and in particular questionnaire design, is thoroughly covered by Moser and Kalton. The book edited
by Miser and Quade also covers relevant material.

CHAPTER 8

The actual mechanics of building and manipulating models are treated in
numerous textbooks. Models commonly found useful in OR are treated at a
level accessible to those without advanced mathematics by Chapman, Cooper
and Page. The mechanics of somewhat more specialised but widely used
modelling methods are discussed by M. Jackson (1988, 1989), Pidd (1988a),

Williams and Wolstenholme. Reflections on the use and misuse of models feature extensively in the OR literature. Some example references include papers by Bryant (1988), Turner and Dyson, the latter two being case-study based. Ward discusses the merits of models of varying complexity and their likely effectiveness.

CHAPTER 9

Many books, including fiction, biography and autobiography, and works in other media, are about making choice. Much fiction deals, for example, with choices about personal relationships, such as who to marry. Political, military and managerial biographies and autobiographies often deal with multi-criteria choice, describing how the subject and his colleagues responded at the time. Such books can be instructive about the limitations of rationality and the power of emotions and, more positively, about the handling of the social and political processes. The most obvious examples from fiction are perhaps the plays of Shakespeare, especially the tragedies. The classic novelists already instanced, Austen and Trollope, also deal with these matters in, for example, *Persuasion* and *Sense and Sensibility* by Austen, and the books already mentioned by Trollope. Political biographies, of which Jenkins on Asquith and Manchester on Churchill are examples, serve to remind about constraints on choice as well as how choice is made. Autobiographies are, of course, commonly self-serving, but those that rise above this provide many insights. Those by Healey and Galbraith are examples which many feel belong to the latter category.

Simon (1960, 1961) was a seminal writer on choice making in an organisational setting. Some of the methods alluded to in this chapter are reviewed in papers by Eilon (1972) (multi-criteria) and by Howard (the various gaming methods). (The Eilon paper is reproduced in a book by Eilon, 1979, which includes other relevant material.) Roy and Vinke treat the multi-criteria question somewhat more abstractly, and Lindley treats decision theory. Huxham discusses some of the difficulties of choice-making for a group, and gives useful references, which in turn, give further references. Rosenhead (1980a, b) discusses robustness as a criterion, and the case for it. Among interesting case studies are those by Allett, Bennett and Dando (1979a, b), Tadisina, Troutt and Bhasin, Dessent and Hume, Jones, Hope and Hughes, and those in an entire issue of the *Journal of the Operational Research Society* (listed under *The Practice of Decision Analysis*), whilst Dawkins (1989) describes a fascinating application of game theory in the life sciences. Again, the book edited by Miser and Quade includes relevant material.

The rules about choosing between gambles given in this book are a simplified paraphrasing of the famous rules published by von Neumann and Morgenstern. The stated conclusion is proved in the referenced work.

There are other ways of looking at choice making, in particular from the psychological viewpoint. See, for example, the book by Hogarth.

CHAPTER 10

The nature of solutions has been treated on a number of occasions by Eden, for example in Eden (1987). Successful practitioners who have written reflectively about implementation and project management include Tomlinson (1980 and references given there), Whiteman and Wise, Houlden, Mercer and Taylor. (Some writers place great emphasis on implementation, in the sense of the management of the OR contribution, implying, probably correctly, that it is the essence of effective OR.) Among papers describing case studies which illustrate aspects of solutions and implementation are those by Lyness, Beech and Fitzsimons, O'Keefe, Saunders and Kirk, and Stainton.

CHAPTER 11

Tomlinson (1980 and references given there) has written authoritatively about managing OR, and other references already given in relation to Chapter 10 are also of relevance (Whiteman and Wise, Houlden, Mercer and Taylor). Conway reports interesting research on the development through time of OR groups. His work suggests diagnostics for determining future developments. He proposes almost a health check.

REFERENCES

Allett, E.J. (1986). 'Environmental impact assessment and decision analysis', *Journal of the Operational Research Society*, **37**, 901–910.
Annan, N. (1990). *Our Age*, Wiedenfeld & Nicolson, and Fontana, London.
Austen, J. (1814). *Mansfield Park*, (1818) *Persuasion*, and (1811) *Sense and Sensibility*, available in numerous editions (e.g. Penguin Classics, Penguin Books, London).
Barrow, J.D. and Tipler, F.J. (1986). *The Anthropic Cosmological Principle*, Oxford University Press, Oxford.
Beech, R. and Fitzsimons, B.A. (1990). 'The application of a decision-support system for planning services within hospitals', *Journal of the Operational Research Society*, **41**, 1089–1094.
Bennett, P.G., Dando, M.R. and Sharp, R.G. (1980). 'Using hypergames to model difficult social issues: an approach to the case of soccer hooliganism', *European Journal of the Operational Research Society*, **31**, 621–636.
Bennett, P.G. and Dando, M.R. (1979a). 'Complex strategic analysis: a hypergame study of the fall of France', *Journal of the Operational Research Society*, **30**, 23–32.
Bennett, P.G. and Dando, M.R. (1979b). 'The Ardennes revisited', *Journal of the*

Operational Research Society, **30**, 670–671.

Bennett, P.G. and Macfarlane, J. (1992). 'Sampling the OR world: the Strathclyde "Apprenticeship Scheme"', *Journal of the Operational Research Society*, **43**, 933–944.

Boothroyd, H. (1978). *Articulate Intervention: the interface of science, mathematics and administration*, Taylor and Francis, London.

Bowen, K. (1989). 'An Eighth Face of Research', *Omega*, **18**, 215–216.

Bryant J. (1988). 'Frameworks of inquiry: OR practice across the hard-soft divide', *Journal of the Operational Research Society*, **39**, 423–436.

Bryant, J. (1989). *Problem Management: A Guide for Producers and Players*, Wiley, Chichester.

Chambers English Dictionary (1988). Chambers, Cambridge.

Chapman, C.B., Cooper, D.F. and Page, M.J. (1987). *Management for Engineers*, Wiley, Chichester.

Chatfield, C. and Collins, A.J. (1980). *Introduction to Multivariate Analysis*, Chapman and Hall, London.

Checkland, P. (1981). *Systems Thinking, Systems Practice*, Wiley, Chichester.

Checkland, P. (1992). 'Systems and scholarship: the need to do better', *Journal of the Operational Research Society*, **43**, 1023–1030.

Checkland, P. and Scholes, J. (1990). *Soft Systems Methodology in Action*, Wiley, Chichester.

Conrad, S. (1989). *Assignments in Applied Statistics*, Wiley, Chichester.

Conway, D. (1987) 'Planning the project mix: a practical application of methodology', presented at EURO VI Conference, Vienna, July 1983 (revised July 1987).

Cox, D.R. (1958). *The Planning of Experiments*, Wiley, Chichester.

Dawkins, R. (1986). *The Blind Watchmaker*, Longman, and Penguin Books, Harlow, London.

Dawkins, R. (1989). *The Selfish Gene*, Oxford University Press, Oxford.

De Finetti, B. (1974). *Theory of Probability: A critical introductory treatment*, Volume 1, Wiley, Chichester.

Dessent, G. and Hume, B. (1990). 'Value for money and prison perimeters—goal-programming for gaols', *Journal of the Operational Research Society*, **41**, 583–590.

Dirac, P.A.M. (1958). *Quantum Mechanics*, Oxford University Press, Oxford.

Dyson, R.G. (1983). 'Operational Research on the peat bog: a case for qualitative modelling', *Journal of the Operational Research Society*, **34**, 127–136.

Eden, C., Jones, S. and Sims, D. (1983). *Messing about in Problems: An Informal Structured Approach to their Identification and Management*, Pergamon Press, Oxford.

Eden, C. (1987). 'Problem-solving or problem-finishing'. In *New Directions in Management Science* (Eds M.C. Jackson and P. Keys), Gower, Aldershot.

Eilon, S. (1972). 'Goals and constraints in decision-making', *Operational Research Quarterly*, **23**, 3–16. See also correspondence in *Operational Research Quarterly*, **23**, 223–224, and 580–581 and **24**, 134–136.

Eilon, S. (1973). 'How Scientific is OR?' *Omega*, **3**.

Eilon, S. (1975). 'Seven faces of research', *Operational Research Quarterly*, **26**, 359–367.

Eilon, S. (1979). *Aspects of Management* , 2nd edn, Pergamon Press, Oxford.

Eilon, S. (1980). 'The role of management science', *Journal of the Operational Research Society*, **31**, 17–28.

Eilon, S. (1987). 'OR is not mathematics', *Omega* , **15**, 87–92.

Everitt, B. (1978). *Graphical Analysis for Multivariate Data*, Heinemann, London.

Fitzgerald, J. (1987). *Fundamentals of Systems Analysis: Using Structured Analysis and*

Design Techniques, Wiley, Chichester.

Flood, R.L. and Jackson, M.C. (Eds) (1991a). *Critical Systems Thinking: Directed Readings*, Wiley, Chichester.

Flood, R.L. and Jackson, M.C. (1991b). *Creative Problem Solving: Total Systems Intervention*, Wiley, Chichester.

Galbraith, J.K. (1986). *A Life in Our Times*, Corgi Books and André Deutsch, London.

Gleick, J. (1987). *Chaos: Making a New Science*, Viking Press, New York.

Gray, H. (1989). *Gray's Anatomy*, 37th Edition (Ed. P.L Williams *et al.*), Churchill Livingstone, Edinburgh.

Handy, C.B. (1985). *Understanding Organizations*, Penguin Books, London.

Hawking, S.W. (1988). *A Brief History of Time*, Bantam Press, London.

Healey, D. (1989). *The Time of My Life*, Michael Joseph and Penguin Books, London.

Hogarth, R.M. (1987). *Judgement and Choice: The Psychology of Decision*, 2nd edn, Wiley, Chichester.

Houlden, B. (1979). 'Some aspects of managing O.R. projects', *Journal of the Operational Research Society*, **30**, 681–690.

Howard, N. (1987). 'Invited Review: The present and future of metagame analysis', *European Journal of Operational Research*, **32**, 1–25.

Huxham, C. (1991). 'Facilitating collaboration: issues in multi-organizational group decision support in voluntary, informal collaborative settings', *Journal of the Operational Research Society*, **42**, 1047–1060.

Jackson, M.C. (1987). 'New directions in Management Science'. In *New Directions in Management Science* (Eds M.C. Jackson and P. Keys), Gower, Aldershot.

Jackson, M.C. and Keys, P. (Eds) (1987). *New Directions in Management Science*, Gower, Aldershot.

Jackson, M.C., Keys, P. and Cropper, S.A. (Eds) (1989). *Operational Research and the Social Sciences*, Plenum Press, New York.

Jackson, M. (1989). *Creative Modelling with Lotus 1-2-3*, 2nd edn, Wiley, Chichester.

Jackson, M. (1988). *Advanced Spreadsheet Modelling with Lotus 1-2-3*, Wiley, Chichester.

Jeffreys, H. and B.S. (1956). *Methods of Mathematical Physics*, Cambridge University Press, Cambridge.

Jenkins, R. (1978). *Asquith*, Collins, London.

Johnston, F.R. (1980). 'An interactive stock control system with a strategic management role', *Journal of the Operational Research Society*, **31**, 1069–1084.

Kennedy, P. (1988). *The Rise and Fall of the Great Powers*, Unwin Hyman and Fontana Press, London.

Kepner, C.H. and Tregoe, B.B. (1965). *The Rational Manager: A Systematic Approach to Problem Solving and Decision Making*, McGraw-Hill, New York.

Keys, P. (1989). 'OR as technology: some issues and implications', *Journal of the Operational Research Society*, **40**, 753–761.

Keys, P. (1991a). 'Operational research in organizations: a metaphorical analysis', *Journal of the Operational Research Society*, **42**, 435–446.

Keys, P. (1991b). *Operational Research and Systems: The Systemic Nature of Operational Research*, Plenum Press, New York.

Kuhn, T. (1962). *The Structure of Scientific Resolutions*, University of Chicago Press, Chicago.

Lindley, D.V. (1985). *Making Decisions*, 2nd edn, Wiley, Chichester.

Lipsey, R.G. (1983). *An Introduction to Positive Economics*, Weidenfeld & Nicolson, London.

Lodge, D. (1988). *Nice Work*, Secker & Warburg and Penguin Books, London.

Lyness, F.K. (1981). 'Consistent forecasting of severe winter gas demand', *Journal of the Operational Research Society*, **32**, 347–360.

Magee, B. (1985). *Popper*, Collins, London.

Manchester, W. (1988). *The Caged Lion, Winston Spencer Churchill, 1932–1940*, Michael Joseph, London.

Mercer, A. (1981). 'A consultant's reflections on client management', *Journal of the Operational Research Society*, **32**, 105–112.

Miser, H.J. and Quade, E.S. (Eds) (1988). *Handbook of Systems Analysis: Craft Issues and Procedural Choices*, Wiley, Chichester.

Morgan, G. (1986). *Images of Organization*, Sage Publications, Beverly Hills, California.

Moser, C.A. and Kalton, G. (1971). *Survey Methods in Social Investigation*, Heinemann Educational Books, London.

Ne'emom, Y. and Kirsh, G. (1986). *The Particle Hunters*, Cambridge University Press, Cambridge.

O'Keefe, R.M. (1985). 'Investigating outpatient departments: implementable policies and qualitative approaches', *Journal of the Operational Research Society*, **36**, 705–712.

Pais, A. (1982). *'Subtle is the Lord ......' The Science and the Life of Albert Einstein*, Oxford University Press, Oxford.

Pidd, M. (1988a). *Computer Simulation in Management Science*, 2nd edn, Wiley, Chichester.

Pidd, M. (1988b). 'From problem-structuring to implementation', *Journal of the Operational Research Society*, **39**, 115–122.

Pidd, M. and Woolley, R.N. (1980). 'A pilot study of problem structuring', *Journal of the Operational Research Society*, **31**, 1063–1068.

Polding, E. and Lockett, G. (1982). 'Attitudes and perceptions relating to implementation and success in Operational Research', *Journal of the Operational Research Society*, **33**, 733–744.

Popper, K.R. (1959). *The Logic of Scientific Discovery*, Hutchinson, London.

'Report of the Commission on the Future Practice of Operational Research' (1986). *Journal of the Operational Research Society*, **37**, 829–888.

Rosenhead, J. (1980a). 'Planning under uncertainty: I: The inflexibility of methodologies', *Journal of the Operational Research Society*, **31**, 209–216.

Rosenhead, J. (1980b). 'Planning under uncertainty: II: A methodology for robustness analysis', *Journal of the Operational Research Society*, **31**, 331–342.

Rosenhead, J. (Ed.) (1989). *Rational Analysis for a Problematic World*, Wiley, Chichester.

Roy, B. (1990). 'Decision-aid and decision-making', *European Journal of Operational Research*, **45**, 324–331

Said, A.K. and Hartley, D.A. (1982). 'A hypergame approach to crisis decision-making: the 1973 Middle East war', *Journal of the Operational Research Society*, **33**, 937–948.

Saunders, C.J. and Kirk, J. (1985). 'O.R. in the company car fleet: when simple is efficient', *Journal of the Operational Research Society* , **36**, 713–730.

Shakespeare, W. (Various dates between 1590 and 1613). *The Complete Works of William Shakespeare*, available in numerous editions (e.g. Oxford University Press, Oxford).

Simon, H.A. (1960). *The New Science of Management Decision*, Harper & Row, New York.

Simon, H.A. (1961). *Administrative Behaviour*, Macmillan, New York.

Stainton, R.S. (1979). 'Modelling and reality', *Journal of the Operational Research Society*, **30**, 1031–1036.

Stewart, I. (1989). *Does God Play Dice? A new mathematics of chaos*, Penguin Books, London.

Tadisina, S.K., Troutt, M.D. and Bhasin, V. (1991). 'Selecting a doctoral programme using the analytic hierarchy process—the importance of perspective', *Journal of the Operational Research Society*, **42**, 631–638.

Taylor, A.J. (1982). 'Some experiences in planning a distribution system', *Journal of the Operational Research Society*, **33**, 891–898.

The Practice of Decision Analysis (1982). Special issue, *Journal of the Operational Research Society*, **33**, 297–387.

Tobin, N.R., Rapley, K. and Teather, W. (1980). 'The changing role of OR', *Journal of the Operational Research Society*, **31**, 279–288.

Tomlinson, R. (1980). 'Doing something about the future', *Journal of the Operational Research Society*, **31**, 467–476.

Tomlinson, R. and Kiss, I. (Eds) (1984). *Rethinking the Process of Operational Research and Systems Analysis*, Pergamon Press, Oxford.

Trollope, A. (1985). *The Warden*, and *Barchester Towers*, available in numerous editions (e.g. Penguin Classics, Penguin Books, London).

Turner, I. (1988). 'An independent system for the evaluation of contract tenders', *Journal of the Operational Research Society*, **39**, 551–562.

Ulrich, W. (1987). 'Critical heuristics of social systems design', *European Journal of Operational Research*, **31**, 276–283.

Vincke, P. (1992). *Multicriteria Decision-aid*, Wiley, Chichester.

von Neumann, J. and Morgenstern, O. (1944). *Theory of Games and Economic Behaviour*, Princeton University Press, Princeton, New Jersey.

Walsham, G. (1991). 'Organizational metaphors and information systems research', *European Journal of Information Systems*, **1**, 83–94.

Ward, S.C. (1989). 'Arguments for constructively simple models', *Journal of the Operational Research Society*, **40**, 141–154.

Watson, J.D. (1968). *The Double Helix*, Weidenfeld & Nicolson, London.

Whiteman, R.P. and Wise, P.J.S. (1981). 'Lessons for OR from the world of banking', *European Journal of the Operational Research Society*, **32**, 519–534.

Williams, H.P. (1990). *Model Building in Mathematical Programming*, 3rd edn, Wiley, Chichester.

Wolstenholme, E.F. (1990). *System Enquiry: A System Dynamics Approach*, Wiley, Chichester.

Wonnacott, T.H. and Wonnacott, R.J. (1984). *Introductory Statistics for Business and Economics*, 3rd edn, Wiley, New York.

Woodcock, A. and Davis, M. (1980). *Catastrophe Theory*, Penguin Books, London.

Woolley, R.N. and Pidd, M. (1981). 'Problem structuring: a literature review', *Journal of the Operational Research Society*, **32**, 197–206.

Zeeman, E.C. (1977). *Catastrophe Theory—Selected Papers, 1972–1977*, Addison-Wesley, Reading, Mass.

Index

of model builder, 118–119
of OR worker, 72–73, 74, 80, 209
playing, 40
Rules, 39, 44, 46, 66, 69, 100, 101, 136, 138, 177, 219
  data about, 94, 100, 101

Sample(s), 95–96
Sampling, 95–96
  quota, 95
  random, 95
  stratified, 95
Satisficing, 152–159
Science(s), xiv, 6, 15–34, 47, 64, 67, 205, 221, 222
  and society, 23–24
  methods of, xiii, xiv, 47, 65, 66, 73
  nature of, 17–19
  scientific beliefs, 37, 39, 131
    knowledge, 34
    method(s), 7, 15, 32, 37, 67, 219
    process, 19
  social, see Social sciences
Scientific, see Science
Scientist(s), xiv, 17, 18, 22, 23, 65, 67, 74, 131, 219, 222
  methods supported by, 32, 219
  methods used by, 6
Simulation, xi, 71, 103, 120, 123, 128, 208, 211
Social
  context, 10, 67
  process(es), 70, 176, 182, 189, 208, 225
  sciences, 24–26, 208, 222
  setting, 8, 57
  skills, 197, 203, 208
Solution(s), 49–54, 68, 70, 175–182, 185, 196, 219, 226
  contingent, 81
  proposal, 196
  subjectivity of, 50
  types of, 178–181
Sponsor, 183–191, 197, 219
  absent, 187–188
  adviser as, 186–187
  as source of data, 95

choice maker as, 184–186
role of, 104–105
see also Client
Stability, 164
Stake-holder(s), 63
States of nature, 155, 155–158
  uncertain, 155–157
Statistical, see Statistics; Theory(ies)
Statistics, 105–107, 208
  mathematical, xi, 224
  statistical test(s), 21, 106
Stock control, 124, 125
Strategy, 171
Structure, 6, 8, 10, 29, 67, 140, 142, 154, 219, 221
Structuring, 5, 6, 8, 29, 32, 140, 192, 222
  mathematical, 31
Survey design, 224
System(s), 26–27, 82, 126–127
  approach, 28, 71, 127
  dynamics, 222
  effects, 211
  movement, 26–27
  science, 222
  theory, 45

Team(s), 184, 189–191, 197, 217
  leader, 189–191
  member, 76, 189–191
Technical context, 10
Technology, 18, 68, 178, 223
  technologist(s), 67
Theory(ies), 15–19, 22
  scientific, 16, 17, 18, 19, 21, 33
  statistical, 25
  test of, 22
Travelling salesman problem, 146

Uncertainty, 157
Utility, 156, 160–162
  theory, 151

Value(s), xii, 9, 35, 65, 68, 75, 92, 94, 101, 130, 143, 147, 180, 205, 210, 216, 220

'What if' questions, 115, 133